Praise for *Dummy: A Memoir*

"Your book is fascinating. I read it with the greatest interest. Your story is a real epic of triumph over adversities of every sort, but also a loving portrait of many interesting people… Your book is genuinely inspiring because it isn't written as a self-help manual, though it could have been. Your modesty is more striking in some respects than your very genuine reasons to boast, which is also admirable. I felt better about myself after reading it, though I had none of your problems, and all the luck some people take for granted. Your insight that one is in effect a spectator to an Awareness that goes on with or without one is valuable and applies equally to all us human beans… Anyway, thank you, congratulations, and all the best with the publication. I hope that your story will be read widely and distributed to many. There are all sorts of reasons to delight in it."

— ANDREI CODRESCU
NPR commentator; author, *Whatever Gets You through the Night*

"*Dummy* is well written, compelling and humanising. David Patten has succeeded in producing a gritty, unapologetic addition to autobiographies about triumph over adversity, particularly those of one's own inner demons." —DONNA WILLIAMS
best selling author, artist, and consultant-presenter in the field of autism

"This is a very moving book, uniquely told with great heart."
—ANDREW HARVEY
author of *The Hope: A Guide to Sacred Activism*

"*Dummy* is a classic page turner! The twists and turns of David Patten's journey are particularly compelling because of his open hearted self-reflections and insatiable thirst for freedom. An important book. A well-written book. And an inspirational read for anyone who feels isolated or hopeless about their circumstances."
—SUNNY MASSAD, PH.D.,

Au~~thor of Ho'o~~ ~~ponopono~~ *logy for Enlightened Living*
Hawaii Wellness Institute

Dummy

Dummy

a memoir

David Patten

Joslyn Press

KAILUA, HAWAII

NOTE: This work is a memoir. It reflects the author's present recollection
of his experiences over a period of years. Certain names, locations,
and identifying characteristics have been changed, and certain persons
described are composites. Dialogue and events have been recreated
from memory, and, in some cases, have been compressed to convey the
substance of what was said or what occurred.

Joslyn Press

Published by Joslyn Press
http://dummyamemoir.com
email: service@dummyamemoir.com

International Standard Book Number: 978-0-9857466-0-5
Library of Congress Control Number: 2012911168

1 2 3 4 5 6 7 8 9 0

To my wife, Maria

I am not bound to win,
but I am bound to be true.
I am not bound to succeed,
but I am bound to live up to what light I have.

—Abraham Lincoln

Only to the extent that we expose ourselves
over and over to annihilation can that which is
indestructible be found in us.

—Pema Chödrön

Contents

Acknowledgments

Books have always represented something bigger than life and entirely inaccessible to me. Because of my learning disabilities, I couldn't have written this book without the dedicated, in-depth support of friends and professionals. For some of them, it was an arduous and time-consuming commitment. To all, I extend my deepest gratitude. Their support, and some electronic assistance, made something I had thought impossible possible. The story of my life clawed at me to get out. Now it's a book—ironically, one I can't read without electronic assistance.

First, I want to thank my wife. She has been a deep source of profound and loving support for me for nearly thirty years. During the writing of this book she was my most important editor, the most honest and critical. I valued her opinion and her judgment above all others.

I also thank my son and daughter for their loving support. They've learned more about their father's life than any kids should ever have to know. My daughter, the first to encourage me to write, helped me organize a beginning storyboard.

Along the way I worked with many editors, but two stood out: Doug Childers, a brilliant and talented published author and book doctor who came in as the book was floundering and gave it structure and new life. He became one of my dearest friends and dedicated himself far beyond anything I could have ever asked for. Also, David Smith, a talented writer and dear friend of more than thirty-five years, whose patience and perseverance helped me bring the manuscript to fruition.

I offer my gratitude to others who helped with the manuscript in various ways. Many friends and acquaintances read early drafts and provided valuable comments. In particular, I thank my two brothers, Emerson and Neil, as well as Laurie Rotecki; Margo Siegenthalar; Marcia Fields; Hannah Eckersley; Janet Voss; Jesse King; Sema Arslan; Dan Millman; Paul, Marilyn, and Ben Hughes; Angelina and Suzanne Saunders; Holly Thurlow; Cara Patten; and Jodi and Dan Dresel. Also, my thanks to Jacqui Schiff and to Adi Da, for invaluable lessons learned along the way, and to Adyashanti, whose teaching, which I listened to almost constantly, illumined a path through some of the darkest places, and led to final clarity in the end. Many thanks to all. I apologize if I have inadvertently omitted anyone.

How this book was written

A well-written memoir by a man with autism spectrum disorder, dyslexia, and other learning disabilities naturally raises the question, How did he write this book? As the primary developmental editor who helped David Patten bring his memoir, *Dummy*, to its present form and polish, he has asked me to answer this question.

After multiple attempts with other writers to begin putting his story on paper, David approached me to work with him. He had written hundreds of pages of narrative containing all the dyslexic spelling quirks and grammatical flaws one would expect. Yet the material, written in David's inimitable style, was compelling and put the reader inside his perceptions and thought processes. We began working together. I initially recorded over twenty hours of interviews in which David told me his story in great detail. I then outlined a structural map for the book. The interviews, transcribed into text, and scenes already written, were distilled, edited, and developed into initial chapters of the present book. Each chapter underwent a series of revisions. David would listen to each draft of each chapter on a transcribing machine that translates written text into spoken words. Then he and I would go through each chapter together in great depth and detail. In these lengthy, often exhaustive conversations, David would articulate the nuances of the experiences, perspectives, and insights that occurred in each key moment and phase of his early life.

In my lengthy conversations with him, I frequently typed detailed notes, writing down David's words as he spoke and then integrating these new elements into the text in the next revision. In this way, the vivid detail of incidents, the emotions they evoked in David at the time, and the insights that emerged in him as a result were woven through the fabric of his memoir.

The 200-plus hours we spent in these exhaustive conversations alone, as well as David's thousands of hours of deep reflection and writing outside of these sessions to record the raw version of his memories, reflect David's fierce commitment to articulating every detail and nuance of his inner and outer experiences as precisely and accurately as possible. As a result, this book is truly David's book and reflects his experiences, insights, and perspectives. The same determination that allowed David to survive and evolve through the difficult, at times strange events recorded in his memoir is what allowed David to persist through the long and difficult process of writing his story. This remarkable book you now hold in your hands is the result.

Doug Childers
May 2012

A brother's testimony

As a young boy growing up, I admired and even worshipped my older brother, David. I followed him around whenever I could. I knew he had problems, but at the time, I didn't know exactly what they were. I knew his life was a struggle. I clearly remember the drugs and the attempted suicide, but for me, it was "normal" because it was what I was familiar with at the time and I only had a child's perspective. Reading about these past events now conjures up a lot of memories and emotions. The combination of seeing these events through David's eyes and the wisdom I have gained through my own life experience has given me a new set of lenses to understand him. It has also helped me to see my own life and our family dynamics in a more complete and objective light.

Many people, family and friends, knew many of the outer details of David's struggle, while never really understanding the inner struggles he tells of in his memoir. He was so busy getting through his life he rarely talked about what was going on inside. For example, I knew of his reading and writing problems, but I never knew of his fear that he might end up in a mental institution—though of course he did spend time in one when he was fourteen. I worried a great deal about what might happen to him at times. But I always thought he was so intelligent and resourceful and such a goodhearted person that he would manage to succeed somehow.

It was painful to read parts of the book, but it helped that I knew how things came out in the end. Knowing that David can't properly read or write, and the fact that he wrote a book I would recommend to anyone, is remarkable to me. And seeing how he experienced his life from the inside and the philosophy of life he came to along the way made this a very rich read for me. In a way, it feels cleansing. I also think the challenges he survived, got through, and became stronger from as a result will be helpful to others, not just those with learning disabilities. Knowing David as I do, hearing his story in hindsight, seeing what it took for him to overcome the significant obstacles life placed in his path, and the success he has achieved, amazes me yet doesn't surprise me. Somehow, even if I worried about him at various points and even if he doubted himself along the way, I always believed he would make it through.

Neil Patten
May 2012

Prologue

It's 2005. I can't read. I can't write. But I'm great at what I do.

I poke one key on my keyboard, then another. With my mouse, I find some old emails saved in a special folder labeled "Pieces of Boss's Emails." I'm looking for an email, or a piece of one, my boss sent me about the cable company he wants me to use for a job. I'm not supposed to, but I have a personal program on my company computer. It reads aloud to me in my headset when I move the cursor through a document. I try to hide how I work from my coworkers. It's better if they just see the results. I open one email after another, looking for the word *cable*. I scan, looking for the letter *c*. Finding *c*, I look for *c-a*. *There it is.* I copy and paste it into the email I'm piecing together for this project.

My office phone rings. "Hello. IT support; this is David Patten."

It's my boss, Kenji. "David, come to the main conference room."

I've been dreading this call ever since my coworker, Kenji, got promoted and became one of my bosses. Things are changing in the company and in the telecom industry. My specialty is troubleshooting mainframe computers for large telephone systems.

Now the technology is changing. Systems are becoming Internet-based and no longer driven by room-sized onsite computers. In previous jobs, I took my paperwork home. There I had special software to read to me, and my wife's help on reports. I always got by. I'd been very successful in the telecom business for twenty-seven years; now I was working in the head office of a major phone provider. I've known this moment was coming. I thought I'd feel more prepared.

"I'll be right there," I say.

Kenji abruptly hangs up. I save my work and slowly head for the conference room. I enter the room and glance around at all the faces.

The head of Human Resources and her assistant both give me kind but cautious smiles. Kenji isn't here, but his boss, Nancy, her manager, Rod, and his boss, Tony, the director of operations for the western region, are all seated around the conference table. Tony greets me with a somber look and waves me to my seat. I look around; no one makes eye contact with me. Tony announces that the head of HR for the western region is on the speakerphone and she'll lead the meeting. I'm handed my yearly review and told that we'll be reviewing it item by item, to make sure I'm clear about my new job description and performance expectations.

The woman on the speakerphone reads out each item. Suddenly I'm on probation, and I'll need to meet the following requirements: I can no longer take work home; all my communications to management and other employees will have to be through email or written documentation; I'm not allowed to get assistance from other people, software, or devices not supplied directly by my manager. I can no longer quote other people's emails, and all my communications must be error-free. There's also a list of new responsibilities, each one requiring reports and documentation, with the same restrictions.

I'm stunned. Suddenly I'm seven years old again, being told I'll have to repeat second grade. Other memories wash over me: being trapped in a snow cave by my brother, being institutionalized in a mental hospital at fourteen after attempting suicide, and more. I can't believe this is happening. Once again I'm confronted by an irrefutable fact about myself: I'm functionally illiterate. I can barely read or write.

I listen and hold my tongue. Being defensive never did me any good. I think about my newly promoted boss who used to be a coworker and how I've never gotten one complaint about my work, only about how I do it. All my reviews have been excellent. I've always given them clean, quality work. They never knew I wrote my emails by patching together pieces of other people's emails until Kenji read the handicap statement in my file that says I'm functionally illiterate and asked me, "If you have trouble reading, how do you write all your emails?" I had to tell him.

I feel the floor shifting under my feet as the woman on the speakerphone asks if I have any questions. I begin, "You all knew about my disabilities when I was hired as a handicapped person. I was told my skills and certifications were invaluable, that the company would work with me to accommodate my liabilities, and I'd be given the necessary equipment to help me with my reading and writing."

Tony responds, "Your work was excellent for the position you were in, but the job has changed. It's now primarily IT, not telecom; it's no longer about servicing equipment. Now we need a traceable path of accountability."

It's clear. If they want to get rid of me, they have an excuse. They can find someone "better qualified" to be on their team, someone who can read and write. The new job description gives them a loophole to evade the handicap discrimination issue when they replace me.

"This all seems disingenuous," I say. "You've written this specifically so that I won't be able to do the job. You could at least allow me to use the equipment necessary to do what's required."

The speaker on the phone breaks in. "No, we want you to be able to meet all the expectations laid out for you here, and we'll do all we can to support you in that."

When they first hired me, they provided a cheap software program that read aloud to me, but it didn't work. When I asked if I could bring my own program to the office or take the work home, they said no. So I did it anyway and hid it from them.

I look right at Tony. "Tony, can you look me in the eye and tell me you want me to meet these expectations?"

He looks at me and says, "No, I don't."

The HR person on the speakerphone screams, "Yes, we do!"

I say to Tony, "Thank you for your honesty."

Then I turn to the phone as if it were a person in the room. "How can you say you want me to succeed when you won't allow me to use the tools I need?"

"Speaking for the company, we want you to succeed," she replies.

"But without the tools?"

"Yes."

I'm desperate. I turn to the group. "I can't do what you're requiring. Can anyone help me find a way to get the job done or let me do part of it from home? I promise I'll get it done right, as I always have, without putting anyone out."

Tony jumps in. "No, it's been decided."

I face Tony again. "I know if you want to get rid of me, you'll find a way. So just tell me you want to get rid of me one way or the other, and I'll quit now."

Tony says, "Yes, one way or the other."

My thoughts swirl, looking for answers or an argument to make them understand. But they're the same old thoughts that have never worked before. I've never been able to make someone else understand my situation. I say nothing. Everyone looks at me, wondering what I'll do or say next. I feel immense pressure. I'm disoriented, in full-blown panic. My perceptions are distorted. My field of vision becomes fragmented, as if it's breaking apart.

What am I going to do? What's going to happen to me? What good am I?

The woman on the speakerphone breaks the terrible silence. "David, what do you say?"

My throat chokes, and my eyes tear up. I can't speak. The ground of my existence opens up. I'm falling with no net and no idea where to or how far. *What's happening to me? Shit, I'm falling apart in front of everybody. I can't let them see this.*

Finally, I say, "What can I do?" Then I hear the words—with an unexpected crack in my voice—come from my mouth, "What's going to happen to me?"

Realizing what I've said, I look around the room. The HR woman's and Nancy's eyes are filled with tears. This only makes it worse. I'm losing it. I can't think. Struggling to come back strong, I say, "Then I quit."

At age fifty-two, the life I've fought so hard to put together is falling apart. I've owned my own business. I've traveled all over the United States as a technical consultant in the telecommunications field. Corporations have flown me in as a highly paid specialist to fix their phone systems when they crashed. I've made top money by taking over computer systems in crisis and handing them back in perfect shape, saving customers millions of dollars in lost revenue—and winning my company millions in new contracts. Earning an excellent reputation by helping people out in critical situations, being the coolest head in the room when everybody was freaking out, gave me immense satisfaction.

But I wasn't the coolest head in the room now. I was the kid who couldn't meet the world's expectations, who couldn't keep up with his peers, who couldn't learn to read. I was the kid who got left behind. Old ghosts swept over me like a tsunami. I thought I had outrun that boy long ago.

I left the room in shock, unaware that a slide into deep depression had begun. The solid ground I'd stood on so surefootedly all my adult life crumbled. The world seemed to have no place for me, all because I couldn't read and write. All the old questions, even the suicidal thoughts, that tormented me when I was growing up returned with a vengeance: *Why is this happening to me? What am I going to do? What value do I have? How will I ever be happy? Why should I keep on living?*

In the following weeks I turned these questions over and over in my mind, tormenting myself. In time, I noticed that these repetitive thoughts never led to anything new. They pointed to an unconscious pattern—a story—I'd been living out, over and over, unaware.

I didn't set out to write a memoir. I just thought if I wrote down my thoughts, I might discover these repetitive patterns and uncover the meaning underneath—the real me. I soon realized that these thoughts were inseparable from the actions of my life. And I found myself beginning to write the story of my life. Ironically, it seemed my only hope of pulling out of my depression was doing the thing that seemed the most impossible for me—writing a book.

Aided by my specialized software programs, I began typing one letter at a time, trying my best to sound out the words. Spelling and grammar programs helped convert my often-unintelligible spelling into words and sentences. With the speech program reading it back to me, I was able to work with what I'd written.

As I struggled to tell my experiences as truthfully as possible, I realized that no matter how deeply I dug into my past or how good a job I did on the book, I could never capture who or what I truly am. The more I examined my patterns of thought, the more I saw them as just patterns. It seemed there was no "real me" at the bottom of it all—no objective entity that was truly "me."

What was there, in every moment of my experience, was conscious Awareness, observing it all while being completely untouched by the experience. I couldn't find myself in my story. I was the witness to my story. This witness, this Awareness, didn't care if I could read or not; it was unaffected.

This awareness of Awareness changed me. I began to think this book might be useful to others. This isn't the conventional story of a hero who triumphs over all obstacles. It's the story of someone faced with constant rejection and failure who discovers his true self. My disabilities were extreme. And I know many people suffering similar problems are struggling to find their way in life. "Normal" people don't understand that conventional solutions don't work for nonconventional people. I was forced to find a radical solution. I hope my story will offer inspiration to those facing extreme hardships in their lives and serve to let them know that the strength they're looking for is already there—if they just know where to look for it.

1

The Plan

What is it? Something's on the back of my neck. It's driving me crazy. I can't stand it another second!

Squirming in my seat, I reach back, pull the collar of my shirt around, and tilt my head to peer inside it.

Oh, it's the tag.

Glaring at the offending tag, I grab it between my thumb and forefinger and rip it off with a tearing sound. A thundering crash startles me out of my inner world.

"David!"

I whirl around to find the rubber tip of a crutch a foot away from my face. My second-grade teacher has slammed it on my desktop.

"Pay attention when I'm talking to the class!" she shrieks. "Next time I'll hit *you* instead of your desk!"

My body vibrates with the freight-train energy of rushing adrenaline short-circuiting my brain. I try to force myself to look up at her but can't move my gaze from the dirty rubber tip of her crutch.

"You're the laziest student I've ever tried to teach! You won't look at me, and you never pay attention! I've had it with you! If you don't care enough to try to learn, I can't teach you!"

Her anger overwhelms me, filling me with hopelessness and shame.

"Take your desk and chair," she says sharply, "and slide them to the back of the class between the toys and the windows. Then you can stare into space to your little heart's content. That will be your permanent place from now on." She returns to the wheelchair by her desk and sits down with a sigh, as if I'd worn her out.

The room is silent. I feel a shiver and a sense of release; now I can move. Shaking, I drag my desk to my new location, apologizing to the students who have to move out of my way.

This wasn't the first time Miss Terry had raged at me in front of the class. I thought she was right: I was lazy, stupid, and slow. I tried to pay attention, but I couldn't focus long enough to learn and to memorize facts and information. I wasn't a daydreamer. Things inside and outside just distracted me and absorbed my attention. Well into second grade, I still hadn't mastered page one of my first-grade reading book. I'd learn a new word one day, and the next day it was forgotten. No matter how hard I tried, nothing seemed to stick.

Yet in some ways, I seemed to know more than my classmates. My mother took me to some experts who gave me a series of intelligence tests. I performed in the genius range in abstract thought. But the tests and the experts couldn't tell me how to focus my mind and use my intelligence to succeed in school. Sometimes, I even had trouble controlling my body. At times, my eyes locked in a stare for a few seconds or even minutes, and I couldn't focus or respond, even when my name was called. This infuriated Miss Terry, who thought I was daydreaming or being disrespectful and rebellious.

It was 1961. Hardly anyone knew about learning disabilities. Kids were smart, average, stupid, or lazy underachievers. Corporal punishment was the norm at school and at home. The common assumption that laziness could be spanked or whipped out of you, that you could be demeaned and humiliated into academic improvement, hadn't worked with me.

I truly wanted to learn. I was curious about life and even the subjects in class. But I was separated by a mysterious, impenetrable barrier, a weakness of attention it seemed I couldn't overcome. Often, when I tried to find a word or a name, it didn't come. It was as if the word was an object behind a crystal-clear waterfall. I could clearly see it through the water, but when I reached for it, my hand disappeared into the water. The word remained visible on the other side. I knew what I wanted to say. But though I'd try with all my strength, I had no hand to grasp the right words. Instead, I experienced profound frustration, followed by anger.

I was told I was just lazy, so I saw my inability to grasp right words as laziness. Was there some way to learn I hadn't yet discovered? Pain always got my attention, so maybe I *needed* to be spanked and yelled at to help me learn. But it never worked. I never paid better attention the next time, and my difficulties remained.

All Miss Terry's yelling, demeaning, and paddling never produced a positive result, but her lack of success didn't discourage her tactics. She was convinced that I was lazy, stupid, and disruptive.

My new location at the back-right corner of the classroom, behind the shelves of toys, was exile. I wasn't facing Miss Terry anymore, only the back row of students. At first, I was excited to be out of her direct view, with toys and blocks close by. I wasn't sure if I was allowed to play with them or not, and I didn't want to get into more trouble.

As the days passed, I began feeling separate from the class, realizing how alone I was. Now Miss Terry only yelled at me when I made too much noise or moved around too much in my seat.

One morning, weeks later, I arrived at school to find that Miss Terry had given me an alternate location, out in the hall. I now had two desks. At first, she only sent me to the hallway occasionally for brief periods. Then she began sending me there more frequently, for longer periods, until the hallway became my primary location. I spent most of the rest of that year there.

Alone in the hall, I'd play with my erasers as if they were cars, and my pencils as if they were people. I'd sharpen my pencils shorter and shorter, obsessed with the pencil sharpener, with the gears inside, the sound it made, how the shavings uncurled as I slowly twisted the pencils down to nubs. I brought little toys and electrical wire from home to play with. I wound the wire around the leg of my desk in the shape of a gearshift and pretended to race up and down the halls. Often, I'd get up from my desk and peek into the classroom through the small window in the door, straining to hear whatever I could. On bad days, when I was sure no one was looking, I'd cry.

I wasn't smart enough to keep up with the other kids, but I was desperate to know what I was missing. They were learning all the important things they'd need to know to live on their own someday.

Things they did with relative ease—reading books, memorizing multiplication tables, passing tests—seemed like magic to me. Sometimes I'd find a way to sneak into Miss Terry's trash can and pull out my classmates' discarded worksheets to see what they were learning. Later, when I was alone, I'd study these, trying desperately to make sense of them. But I never could. I carried these wrinkled trash-can worksheets around in my pocket, hoping they'd help me, that somehow I'd understand them in time, with the help of someone, maybe a friend. But understanding never came.

It hurt that I couldn't understand things my friends grasped so easily. It was a deeply disturbing emotional, even physical pain. I was an outcast in school. There was nothing I was measurably good at. Yet my neighborhood friends all liked and respected me. We'd start a club, and they'd often want me to be the leader. When we played war games, they'd follow me into battle. Outside of class, I was their equal. They appreciated me. Many even told me I was their best friend.

✳ ✳ ✳

That year, my older brother, Emerson, took me to see a science-fiction movie about three astronauts who land on Mars. While exploring the planet, they encounter hostile aliens and are separated from their spaceship. At the end, the Martians chase the astronauts back to their spaceship. But only two astronauts board the ship. The third astronaut falls behind and arrives after the doors have closed and the ship is taking off. Knowing the Martians are coming for him, the abandoned astronaut cries out to his departing comrades, who sadly watch him as the ship slowly rises from the surface of the hostile planet: "Don't leave me! Please don't leave me alone!"

As the movie ends, he stands heroically on the desolate landscape, waiting for the Martians coming to kill him. Instead of running back to hide in a cave and live in fear, he chooses to face his enemies and die.

The movie made a deep, haunting impression on me. For weeks afterward, I had nightmares about the man left behind. I started daydreaming that I was stranded on Earth from another planet—like Superman. Superman must have felt out of place, alone, and misunderstood. Then he found a way to excel. Maybe I could too. Superman knew he was stronger and smarter than the others. I knew I wasn't Superman, but maybe I had some special powers I didn't yet know about. Maybe one day I'd figure out what they were, and then I could live a happy, normal life like everyone else. But for now, I was abandoned in a long, dark, empty hallway, day after day, alone.

Looking through the little window separating me from the class and my friends, I recalled the astronauts in the movie looking through the portal at the friend they were leaving behind to die. But my classmates weren't looking through the portal at me; I was looking at them. They didn't seem to remember I was there. They had moved on without me to learn everything I couldn't learn.

Sometimes I thought, *I'm the guy in the movie being left behind. I'm going to be stuck on Mars the rest of my life.* I loved my friends. I knew they loved me. But they were moving on in their lives without me. I was being left behind, alone in a hostile world, where I wouldn't survive. I realized then I hated this world that would let someone fall behind and not reach back for him, that wouldn't even look to see the fear in his eyes. I swore to myself if I ever saw that kind of fear in someone else's eyes, I'd do whatever I could to help. I'd never leave someone else behind, especially someone I loved.

The last day of school was warm and sunny. Miss Terry wasn't teaching the regular curriculum that day and let me stay in the classroom to participate in the activities. We were doing fun stuff. It felt like a celebration. I was so happy to be with everyone I could hardly contain myself.

Before the first bell rang, a group of my closest friends gathered around my desk. We talked excitedly about how we'd spend the summer. We'd build a fort, maybe even a tree house. We'd go swimming together in our community pool. My best friend, Roger, and I talked about how my parents would buy us baby ducks we'd keep in his backyard pen. We'd take care of them together. I told my friends Debbie, Laurie, Jessie, Beverly, Don, John, Mary, and Allen how my dad was going to install a rope swing in the giant cottonwood tree in our front yard. I was so excited about our plans and about being included again now that school was over and summer was here. I hugged them all, a rare gesture for me.

Miss Terry was on her best behavior. I did my best not to make her mad. She barely yelled at me the whole day. Finally, she handed out our report cards. Then the final bell rang. I was surprised how quickly the day had passed and how nothing bad had happened. I quickly opened my report card and saw a row of incompletes. There was a note in red at the bottom of the page. I asked Roger, who was standing next to me, to read it to me.

"Not advancing to third grade," he read.

I was stunned. Devastated. My nightmare fantasy was coming true. I *was* being left behind. In disbelief, I asked several students around me what the notes on their report cards said. Only mine said, "Not advancing." Everyone else was moving forward. My mother had warned me I might not go on to the third grade, but I didn't know exactly, or perhaps couldn't believe, what that meant.

I ran all the way home to ask her. She was at work, so I turned on the TV to watch Bugs Bunny. I couldn't focus. Anxiety coursed through my body. I pressed myself into the couch, alternately holding my ears and closing my eyes, trying to shut down all my senses. Everything was too much, too intense, too disturbing.

In that last month of school, my mother took me out of class every Tuesday and Thursday to see a psychiatrist. And she stopped coming into my room at night to comfort me and stopped telling me everything was going to be all right. I didn't know the psychiatrist had told her not to coddle me or give me false expectations. Now it seemed like nothing would ever be all right again.

That night before bed, she took me into her bedroom so we could talk in private. I knew this was serious. My brothers and I rarely went into my parents' bedroom. My father stayed in the living room. He had great faith in my mother and always relied on her to handle the difficult moments with us. He'd never known his father and didn't trust himself to deal with such things.

My father was a very loving man. We all respected him. When he said something, we listened, and when he whistled for us, we dropped everything and went to him immediately. But he was detached from most family matters. He handled the physical discipline, when necessary, but otherwise took refuge in his 1950s role as chief breadwinner. I loved my dad and felt his humor and warmth. But he left my extreme problems for my mother to handle.

Mom turned on the small light on her dresser. The room was dim. The walls, covered with bookshelves, were in shadows. Through the open sliding door of my father's closet I saw his shoes lined up on the floor and his familiar flannel shirts, suits, and starched white dress shirts on hangers. I wished he was in here with us now. He always seemed to make things brighter and funnier.

Mom and I sat on my parents' huge bed, and she explained to me that I wouldn't be going on to third grade with the rest of my class. I'd be staying back in second grade for another year. The thought of repeating Miss Terry's class was too much for me. I started crying and yelling, thinking my mother could change things.

"No! No! I have to go to third grade! All of my friends are going!" I cry while she sits there with me. She seems sad.

"I'm sorry, honey. I did the best I could to change Miss Terry's mind. There's nothing else I can do."

I finally calm down.

"Why am I the only one flunking?"

She is crying now. I can see she wants to comfort me, but there is nothing she can say. She gives a little, artificial smile. "I don't know, David. You're just having trouble learning in school."

"Why am I so stupid? Why can't I be smart like the other kids?"

"You're not stupid. Don't think that. You're very smart. You just have more trouble learning than the other kids."

"Why? What's wrong with me?"

"I don't know. Nothing's wrong with you. You're just having trouble learning."

My questions went on, even after she ran out of answers. Finally, I lay on the bed, exhausted. I wished I had a secret power that could stop the world, make time go backward, and make myself normal like everyone else.

At one point, I looked up at her and saw a flash of fear in her eyes. That was all it took. In that moment, I saw that she was afraid for me, afraid of who I might become, afraid of who I *was*. She thought I'd never be able to function like a normal person. At that moment, I felt she had completely separated from me emotionally. In an instant, I felt the fear move from her body into mine. This fear was now alive in me. I didn't want her to ever be that far away from me again, so I willingly took her burden in, as deep as I could. I took on my mother's fear about me as my own. If she was afraid for me, then I was afraid too. Only now, I felt afraid of who I was. I felt afraid of *myself*. That moment became a set point for the level of fear I had to maintain in my approach to life. The fear became my inheritance.

Later, alone in my own bed, I stared into the darkness, unable to sleep or stop my mind. Worst-case scenarios ran through my head. I imagined being in class with younger kids, watching *them* learn things I couldn't learn. I imagined flunking second grade again, being with even younger kids after that. I imagined Miss Terry being my teacher over and over. Maybe I'd never pass second grade. Thoughts of failure, humiliation, and ever-increasing isolation paralyzed me.

Why me? What did I do? What's wrong with me? What's going to happen to me?

Finally, tormented by my thoughts and unable to sleep, I get out of bed. I know my mother doesn't want to talk about this anymore, but I can't stop myself. I open my bedroom door and look through the family room. I can see her standing at the kitchen sink washing the dishes. I call out to her, "Mom!" but get no response. So I call louder. "Mom!"

Her body freezes. Then she turns off the water, and I hear her low sharp voice. "What?"

I can tell she is upset. I try to hold back my tears. "What's going to happen to me?" my voice quavers.

She still doesn't turn around. "I don't know," she says.

"What am I going to do when I'm grown up?"

"I don't know."

"Will I be able to have a job?"

"I don't know," she says, a little louder.

"Can I ever have kids and a family?"

"*I don't know!*" Her voice is sharp and irritated now.

"Can I ever get married?"

"I—don't—know!" She drops the pot she's been scrubbing into the sink with a loud clatter, grabs the front of the sink with both hands, and stands staring down, her body quivering. She is crying, but she still doesn't turn around. Then she speaks in a firm, measured voice, pausing for emphasis throughout, "David, I'm going to say this just *once*. And don't *ever—ask—me—about—this—again!* You may have to be institutionalized when you're eighteen."

I lay awake all that night, churning in anxiety over my future. My family was smart and successful. My dad managed a medical clinic. My mom was a school psychologist. My grandfather, aunts, and uncles were doctors, pharmacists, lawyers, and accountants. But I was different from them. I would never learn the things they'd learned. I'd never have a job or a family. Who would marry me? I was going to end up in a mental hospital. That was how it was. My mother said so, and my whole family probably believed it.

I lay there imagining my dismal, lonely future life in a mental institution. Back then, the autistic and "retarded" were put into mental institutions with the insane. I didn't know about autism but knew my mother didn't think I was insane, so she must think I was retarded. I'd seen mental institutions in movies and TV shows. They were dark, dirty places where crazy and retarded people sat silently all day, or walked around mumbling to themselves, or screamed and acted out until men in white coats came and dragged them away. There was nothing to do there but play checkers and walk up and down the halls. And once you were sent there, you never got out.

My mother told us stories about her psychology training at a teaching hospital. One story was about a small, unusual-looking child she'd done developmental testing on. After passing the low results on to her instructor, she was given the child's records. The child was older than she was! It wasn't a child at all! From the way she told the story I knew it had profoundly affected her. This story came back to me now as I lay in bed. I wondered if she thought I was more like that strange adult child than like a normal person.

I wondered if I could somehow change my fate. Maybe if I worked harder, I could get my school lessons through my thick skull. I lay there, repeating over and over: *I've got to learn to read. I've got to learn to read. I've got to learn to read!*

The world seemed a horrible place. I had no control over my life. If my mother was right—that I'd be put into a mental institution—then I couldn't trust the people who were taking care of me and controlling my life. I couldn't even trust my mother, who was now preparing me for a life I wasn't willing to live. I couldn't believe this was happening to me. I had to find a way out.

I often thought of the abandoned astronaut in the movie and the decision he'd made when his ship took off and left him behind. Abandoned and alone, without resources in a hostile world, he turned to face the Martians coming to kill him. He chose to die rather than hide. By choosing death, he took control of his life and kept his self-respect. The movie portrayed him and his decision in a heroic light. It inspired me. Now his courageous decision seemed to offer a solution to my dilemma. I also wanted to take control of my life. If I was going to end up in a mental institution with no way out, I had nothing to lose. If I had any hope of changing my fate, I'd have to start living as if my life was at stake. I'd have to be willing to do anything and try anything. And if everything failed, I could kill myself. But would I be willing to die? To take my own life? The thought of suicide had never occurred to me before.

One night as I lay in bed, it came to me in a flash, the perfect plan. I knew exactly how I'd do it. It was simple and guaranteed to work. Months earlier I'd attended a father-son program called Indian Guides. Each father gave a presentation to the group. My dad gave a talk about liquid mercury and brought a test tube of the magical silver liquid from his medical clinic. He rolled it around in a bowl. We all thought it was so cool. Then he told us mercury was a deadly poison.

It could make you very sick if you even touched it. If you swallowed it, you'd die a painful, violent, certain death. No one could save you. Now I imagined swallowing mercury from my father's test tube and dying. In that moment, I felt incredible relief. I felt more powerful than I'd ever felt before. I felt free! I had no concern for the future. That's when I knew I could commit suicide. Not right away—I'd still try to learn and succeed. But now I had another option. I could end my life anytime I chose. I wouldn't have to go to a mental institution. This gave me a super strength. It felt like my secret superpower.

I wasn't afraid of disappearing or dying, maybe because I couldn't really imagine what death was. What terrified me was living a left-behind, lonely, powerless life. The possibility of suicide seemed a magical solution. I suddenly wasn't worried about my future in the same way. Everything had changed.

Still, I had to secure my plan. My bedroom was behind the garage. The rest of the family slept upstairs on the other side of the house. It was after midnight. Everyone had gone to sleep. I got up and snuck from my room into my father's workshop in the basement and stole the test tube of liquid mercury from the cabinet near his workbench. The tube contained about a half of a mouthful, enough to do the job.

I snuck back to my room and hid the test tube in my sock drawer, within easy reach from my bed. When I finally lay down again, I felt calmer. Eventually I fell asleep. When I awoke, I felt fundamentally different. Death was now within arm's reach. I had ultimate control over my life. From now on, my life would be a fight to the death, but I'd have the final choice. I could now live with more natural abandon in my relations with the other kids, not smothered by fear of my future, which remained a dark cloud. These weren't just thoughts in my head, but feelings, mysterious certainties that gave me relief.

The mercury would wait, hidden in various locations, giving me another choice besides the inevitable isolation in my future, possibly in a mental institution. Over time I improved the plan. I realized I'd also need sleeping pills. My mother always had some in her medicine cabinet. I'd find a way to steal some when she was out. I could take them first, wait a bit, and when I began to get drowsy, take the mercury before I fell asleep. That way, death might not be as painful.

I'd never stolen anything before my dad's mercury. But this was life-and-death. From now on, I had to be willing to do anything. With the mercury safe in my hiding place, I possessed the power and the means to end my own life. This knowledge proved to be an immense comfort in the hard times to come.

2

The Co-op

In the mid-1950s, my parents, both progressive idealists, moved into the York Center Community Co-op, a progressive alternative community located on a hundred-acre cornfield in an unincorporated area near Lombard, Illinois, eighteen miles west of Chicago's Loop. Founded by members of the Brethren Church, one of three American "peace churches" along with the Quakers and the Mennonites (best known for the Amish), the Community Co-op invited people of all races and religions to live together as a witness for peace and brotherhood. The earliest families to move in built their own homes with their own hands in pioneer barn-raising spirit, joining together to help one another pour concrete foundations, "raise roofs," and even build a community water and sewer system. The community eventually grew to more than seventy families. We moved there when I was three years old, and my older brother, Emerson, was six. My younger brother, Neil, was born in the co-op the following year.

In addition to members of the Brethren congregation, people from varied backgrounds came to the co-op. This motley, controversial group included conscientious objectors who'd spent World War II in prison; Japanese who'd been confined to internment camps; educated "negroes," as African Americans were then called; labor organizers, civil-rights activists, mixed-marriage couples, and even theologians. All gathered together to live their various faiths and creeds and create a community of tolerance in very practical ways.

Each family had building rights for one lot (usually about an acre), but the co-op jointly owned the entire property. Each family lived in its own separate household, often with its own garden, but all the families did things together as a community. They held work bees to maintain the community park, the shelterbelt, and the water system. They planted trees for seclusion around the co-op's perimeter. They built the main roads and the water system. Road rights were ceded to the local government, which maintained them as public streets, but everything else, including the water system, remained privately owned by the co-op. Everyone was independent financially, but people tried to help each other however they could. Some families shopped in bulk together to cut costs. The children attended the nearby public schools. And there were endless committee meetings.

The prevailing spirit of neighborly goodwill and innocence in the early years of our community had a great impact on me. No one locked their doors because we all trusted one another. If we got thirsty playing outside or got hurt and needed a wound washed and a Band-Aid, we could go into almost any home and be taken care of. The usual social boundaries didn't apply in our hundred acres. I could visit the homes of my friends anytime, walk in without knocking, and feel completely welcome. If no one was there, I could turn on the TV and wait for them to return. The community was my whole world and life, the people were my family, the other children were my brothers and sisters. We went through everything together and formed deep bonds.

The very conservative community outside regarded our co-op with suspicion, fear, and mistrust. The main issue was our racial integration. We were the classic "there goes the neighborhood" real-estate nightmare multiplied by seventy families. The year before my family moved there, someone burned a cross on our neighbor's front yard and fired a gunshot into another house. The co-op's racial diversity lowered its property value, so our homes were assessed at values less than those in the surrounding communities.

The racial tension and the animosity toward our co-op were relatively passive until the mid-1960s, when it intensified during the Civil Rights Movement, the Vietnam War, and the hippie phenomenon. Many co-op kids were multiracial and a visible target in the local community. Outsiders started coming into the co-op at night to make trouble. Once they threw a Molotov cocktail at a house. On other occasions, they painted swastikas on cars and homes. It was a frightening time for our community.

One night when I was eight, during my father's turn as co-op president, I was awakened by angry voices in the entryway. I peeked out my bedroom door and saw several strange men who had pushed their way into the house shouting at my parents, calling them communists. I recognized one man. My parents weren't communists or socialists, just liberals. My father raised his fists, roared back at them, then waded directly into their group and forced them back out the door. It was the only time I ever saw him raise a fist to anyone.

The man I recognized that night had joined the co-op as an extreme left-wing fanatic but later converted to the far-right John Birch Society and plastered his house with signs demanding the impeachment of Justice Earl Warren for his antisegregation rulings. He and several other local John Birch members from outside our community later sued the co-op to try to break it up. The lawsuit went before the U.S. Supreme Court, and our co-op's victory became a key ruling establishing the legal basis for the housing co-ops and condominiums that later proliferated.

✳ ✳ ✳

My mother was born in 1916 in Lynn, Massachusetts, into an old New England family who'd come to America in the 1600s. Raised in an intellectual environment by two well-educated parents, she excelled academically. After graduating from a renowned boarding school in Europe, she enrolled in the University of Illinois, studied developmental psychology, and became a child psychologist.

After a devastating miscarriage in her late thirties, doctors warned her that another pregnancy could jeopardize her life. But she decided to take her chances. My parents lived on the South Side of Chicago when my older brother and I were born. Emerson was born in April 1951. I came three years later, on May 17, 1954, at Cook County Hospital, after a grueling thirty-six-hour labor. I was a perfectly healthy, handsome, eight-pound, brown-eyed baby, with a full head of jet-black, wavy hair. My birthday was also the date of the *Brown v. Board of Education* victory, when Chief Justice Warren led the Supreme Court to rule unanimously that segregation in public schools was unconstitutional. This coincidence was very important to my mother. She mentioned it every year on my birthday, or whenever my birthday was mentioned.

Back then, hospitals kept mothers and newborns for several days after birth. Mothers were given sleeping medications, and newborns slept in the nursery at night. A nurse brought me from the nursery to my mother's room every few hours, waking her from her medicated sleep to nurse me. On the second night, the nurse left me with my mother for a feeding but neglected to raise the safety bar on her bed. My heavily medicated mother fell asleep, relaxed her grip on me, and I fell headfirst three feet to the linoleum-covered cement floor. My cries woke her, and the nurse rushed in and whisked me away to be examined by doctors. X-rays showed a skull injury. My mother wasn't allowed to see me until the next day.

Early on I became a distressed, colicky infant, who needed nearly constant attention. My first two years, I barely slept: my nervous system on high alert, my senses raw and fragile. Sudden lights, sounds, or uninvited touch overwhelmed me, causing me great anxiety and pain. When touched, my body stiffened, and I withdrew into myself. I'd cry hours on end with terrible stomach cramps and couldn't fall asleep even when exhausted. I had no regular feeding or sleeping schedule. In my second year, doctors prescribed me Seconal. This powerful barbiturate allowed me, and my mother, a few hours sleep at night.

I was a solemn, gentle baby, who seemed to have no inner drive to explore or to learn. My mother said I'd lie immobile, sometimes for hours, staring passively into space. Occasionally I'd smile at her, but I hardly ever laughed.

I was also very sick those first two years, plagued by severe and mysterious ailments that turned out to be a result of severe allergies to grains, eggs, and dairy products. This may have significantly contributed to my problems. My first allergic reactions were to my mother's milk after she ate any of those foods. When I was weaned from breast milk to cow's milk, my allergic reactions increased. When the doctors finally discovered the cause of my symptoms, I was weaned from milk onto soy formula, which relieved my worst agonies.

My mother's degree in developmental psychology was of tremendous value. It equipped her to discern my condition and to care for me with all my complex, baffling problems. She could observe, understand, and respond effectively to behaviors that would have overwhelmed most mothers. As her round-the-clock case study, I tested her capacity as a developmental psychologist and as a mother. She observed me tirelessly, determinedly maintaining eye contact with me, whether I was shrieking in pain or withdrawing into myself. Of all the experts I went to throughout my childhood, she was the most astute. No doctor came as close as she to discerning the subtle patterns and changing dynamics of my troubling condition. She continually sought ways to help me develop and become healthy, always believing she could make a difference.

She faced immense challenges with me in those first few years. Increasingly, I wouldn't look at anyone or anything, and it became harder for her to reach me. She saw me drifting toward autism, disconnecting from the outer world of stimuli, sensations, and human connections. She was determined not to let this happen.

She observed that after being held for a long period of time, being touched didn't seem like such a shock to me. I could tolerate more eye contact and was less likely to withdraw into myself. She began holding me for longer periods, often twenty hours or more, only putting me down briefly to change me. I became her constant companion. She carried me on her shoulder so often she called me her "little lapel pin." Because I was virtually a full-time job, my parents hired a practical nurse to take care of Emerson.

Had my mother not engaged me with such persistent, loving determination, I might have drifted deeper into autism and disappeared forever within myself. But I endured the pain of my hypersensitivity to maintain a sensory connection with her. This hyperconnected awareness was the antithesis of the natural tendencies I shared with most autism spectrum children.* Instead of shutting out awareness of the outside world, I maintained external awareness through this constant connection to my mother. I still had autism spectrum hypersensitivities and was easily overwhelmed, but I learned to modulate my nervous system by synchronizing with my mother's. Later, television began to replace my mother as an anchor for my attention and as a way to synchronize with the outside world.

My hypersensitivity subjected me to a degree of pain and stress most children never experience. Looking at a face on TV was safe, but looking into the face of an actual person could overwhelm me and provoke extreme anxiety. Feeling emotions through the eyes of others could trigger an avalanche of emotions that overloaded my nervous system. It was similar to looking directly into a bright light. Simple sensory input, especially something sudden, could also be overwhelming. Certain sights and sounds, unexpected or unwelcome touch, taste, smell, and emotions typically set me off, sending intensely painful sensations flooding through me. My body stiffened and felt like it was screaming.

In the depths of my inner isolation, feeling somewhat safe, I'd crave some limited contact or distraction, as long as it didn't pull me "out there," where I was vulnerable and afraid. At such times, I was willing to cautiously peek out at the world. It was like opening a thin crack in either my sense of vision or hearing. I'd look for a sparkle of light, or listen for a safe sound, something I could trust that wouldn't invade me. I craved touch but only on my terms, when I was ready and able to receive it. The more trust I felt, the more I could open to touch, bit by bit, more and more.

---

*All children with autism spectrum disorders (ASDs) demonstrate deficits in social interaction, verbal and nonverbal communication, and repetitive behaviors or interests. In addition, they often have unusual responses to sensory experiences, to certain sounds, sights or sensations. Symptoms can run the gamut from mild to severe and vary in each child. For example, a child may have little trouble learning to read but exhibit extremely poor social interaction. Each child on the autistic spectrum will display unique communication, social, and behavioral patterns that fit into the overall ASD diagnosis. National Institute of Mental Health, www.nimh.nih.gov

Looking to professionals for help, my mother was told many times that my problems were her fault. Back then, it was commonly believed that indifferent or cold-hearted mothers caused autism spectrum symptoms and developmental problems like mine. The root of such symptoms was believed to be psychological. But my mother was convinced mine were neurological and triggered, or at least intensified, by allergies. Eventually, she realized science didn't have the answers.

Describing my mother as warm and caring would be a vast understatement. She expressed the full spectrum of her warm and caring nature during my early childhood. Years later, the challenges became too much for her. In her desperation and self-doubt, she came to ignore her intuition and accepted the advice of a prestigious psychiatrist—which would prove to be a serious mistake.

Meanwhile, I developed unusual coping strategies. I found that by concentrating very hard on something, I could deaden physical pain and the simmering emotional anxiety that could erupt at any moment. I'd obsessively run the lobe of my mother's ear between my first and second fingers as she fed me or repeatedly wrap my fist tightly around her thumb and pull until I lost my grip. Sometimes, I repeatedly struck my head with the palm of my hand or bumped my head against a wall. Self-inflicted and controlled pain were preferable to pain inflicted from outside.

When too much input sent me into a panic, my senses began to shut down—usually sight first, then hearing, then touch. I'd instinctively compartmentalize my senses. This dissociative process felt as though I was retreating into a hole where pain couldn't reach me. These coping strategies distracted me from the overwhelming environmental input I couldn't otherwise control. This compartmentalizing of my sensory experience may have inhibited the sensory integration necessary for later multisensory learning, such as speech, aggravating my learning disabilities.

When I was older and got upset with my mother, I'd go into my room, squeeze myself between my mattress and the wall, and disappear inside myself. Squeezing myself this way put a consistent pressure on my nerves and helped calm them without irritating demands for attention and emotional connection. It was like squeezing an injured finger to relieve the pain. I could stay there all day, all night, and into the next day, with no sense of time passing, if my mother had let me. But she always stayed with me, maintaining contact, not letting me withdraw too deeply. She'd talk soothingly to me and run her hand gently through my hair, maintaining that essential thread of physical and emotional connection. But the urge in me to dissociate was overwhelming. Her opposition to this impulse and her insistent pull on my attention became immensely irritating to me. While her presence and touch made me want to crawl out of my skin, her fierce attention and monitoring of my states kept me from withdrawing into myself and slipping deeper into autism.

At first, I peeked out at the world through the filter of my mother's experience and emotions. As I got older, I began to open to my own perceptions in vision and hearing. Many believe that people are more inclined to one primary form of sensory input, which feels more comfortable. Whether their primary mode is visual, auditory, sensory, or emotional, they tend to perceive and learn more through that faculty. Research shows that most people on the autistic spectrum are more visually oriented and think in pictures. But, being so connected to my mother, I became more emotionally oriented, and that faculty became preferable. So I think in narrations of emotions. This is highly unusual; the opposite response of most autistic children, for whom even the existence of other people, let alone the impact of their emotions, can be overwhelming. I suspect that accounts for my exceptional emotional memory. As a child, I experienced and remembered events as florid, emotionally narrated stories, only remembering faces, names, times, or places if they played a part in the emotional context of the event.

I didn't begin using recognizable words until I was four. No one could understand my babbling. I seemed to be speaking a private language. My mother finally cracked the code of my weird jabber when she realized I was only pronouncing the last parts of words, omitting the beginning sounds.

Many people, including some experts, suspected I might be "retarded." The mother of one of my friends thought I might be deaf. At times, it seemed I might be partially deaf. My mother noticed how I'd watch people's faces intently, trying to figure out what they were saying. When I was five, doctors thought I might be severely hearing impaired; this defect would account for my slow learning and delayed speech. To improve my hearing, they removed my adenoids. I seemed to experience some improvement after six months. I've since learned that false deafness is another symptom associated with autism spectrum disorders.

Whether or not my fall from the hospital bed caused my learning disabilities is unknown. My learning disabilities were not typical of a traumatic brain injury. Still, my mother always felt profoundly guilty about the accident.

As I grew older, the symptoms of my disabilities increased. My instinctive tendency to shut down to control my sensory input caused problems with sensory integration—with learning. Conventionally, *sensory integration dysfunction* is defined as a neurological disorder that causes difficulties in processing information from the five senses. It might be more true to say of me that because of my neurological disorder, I consciously and unconsciously compartmentalized sensory input, causing difficulties with processing and integrating sensory information.

As an infant and a young child, feeling it necessary to separate and compartmentalize my sensory experiences, I chose what to let into my field of perception to guard against the shock of each sensory input. Too many sounds or sights were very difficult and confusing for me. When someone spoke to me, I couldn't accurately choose what to pay attention to. I couldn't put the sounds or words together to understand the relationship between them and whatever I was looking at. Later, it proved nearly impossible for me to comprehend the subtleties of unspoken social rules, because this required me to recognize people's facial expressions and coordinate those expressions with voice tone and words. This was especially difficult because I was cutting out or ignoring what was most intense. Unfortunately, what was often most intense, like emotions in faces, was also most important in understanding social interactions.*

A turning point came one day when I was four. I'd retreated to my safe place between the mattress and the wall, disappearing into that hole where I no longer felt, saw, or heard the outside world. I'd been there all morning and into the afternoon. My mother sat in her usual place on the edge of my bed for most of that day, talking to me, stroking my head, keeping me aware of her presence, preventing me from disappearing completely. Yet disappearing was my all-consuming need.

I remember hating her with my whole body for not leaving me alone, not letting me go. I began hitting my head against the wall harder than usual. I had to override the outside input with stronger and stronger responses. My mother tried to stop me, which sent me into panic and hysteria. When she finally let me go, I calmed down. She stayed with me, not touching me or talking to me, knowing that was what I wanted. When I finally "came out," it was dark outside. I hadn't eaten all day, and it was way past dinnertime. My mother was still sitting there on the bed. I became angry again when I saw her and yelled, "I hate you! Why can't you just leave me alone?"

She grabbed my shoulders. Tears filled her eyes as she spoke to me, "David! All your life I've known that look in your eyes. When you start to go away, I'm afraid you'll stay wherever it is you go. Maybe I'll never get you back. That's why I can't leave you alone. Do you think you would come back if I didn't fight for you?"

She told me her secret fear. Then I told her my secret. Her honesty pulled the words out of me, "I don't want to be here, but you won't leave me alone."

---

* This is a critical point, because body language, facial expressions, and tone of voice, rather than words, are the major elements in most interpersonal communication. I believe a better understanding in this area will create greater success in helping people with autism spectrum symptoms. I plan to explain this in more detail and cover ways to work with this in a later book.

With tears in her eyes, she leaned toward me and hugged me tightly. I cringed; my whole body tensed in overload reaction. I'd thought she already knew, but she hadn't known my secret at all. I was immediately sorry I'd told her. Somehow in that exchange, in that connection, the escape door inside me closed. From that day, I was aware of the passage of time and never able to disappear into myself in quite the same way.

3

Faith

At age four I began attending the local nursery school with all my best co-op friends, including two children of our teacher, Anna Hasegawa. At that point, because of my mother's heroic ministrations and my daily interactions with a group of kids my own age, I began coming out of myself in a significant way. I hadn't yet begun to speak coherently, but I was functioning mentally and socially far beyond the predictions of the doctors and other experts who had examined me.

I still had autism spectrum tendencies. When I was afraid, angry, or upset, my nerves felt as if they were on fire, my skin got hot, and I'd break into a sweat. If anyone touched me in this state, I'd instinctively strike out in self-defense. But I was now emotionally present, able to connect to others in meaningful ways, and available for relationships.

My keen sense of empathy allowed me to connect deeply with friends and schoolmates and gave me a strong protective instinct for the weak, vulnerable, and helpless, as well as a love for animals and babies. I befriended one little girl in my class who was too frightened to speak. I often took her by the hand, led her into the group, and encouraged her to participate. I also visited her at her house. Her father, an angry and abusive man, was the John Birch convert who later sued the co-op. Whenever he yelled at her during my visits, I'd go stand between them. After a while, I rushed to her side to protect her whenever he came around.

Nursery school connected me with my peers and made me feel like an integral part of our little community. The love and connection of my family and playmates, and my baby brother, who arrived when

I was four, absorbed my attention and nurtured me. I barely noticed my learning disabilities, since they didn't interfere with these primary relationships.

Because of my learning disabilities and autism spectrum symptoms, normal expectations were rarely placed on me at home. I looked normal, and other than not being able to speak coherently, I didn't seem different from other kids. I was a fully participating member of our group, making my unique contribution. Throughout nursery school, kindergarten, and grade school, my parents never pushed me to function at the level of my peers. They didn't know what to demand or expect of me and responded to my various difficulties and poor academic performance with compassionate support. My mother's prolonged struggle to draw me out of my autistic shell had already pressed me far beyond my natural limits.

In those early years, my life in the co-op and with my family was idyllic in many ways, with two major exceptions: my learning disabilities, and my older brother, Emerson. Emerson hated me almost from the day I came home from the hospital, when he was three years old. With my arrival, he essentially lost his mother. He went from being the center of her attention to a kind of exile, which must have been excruciating for him. For the next two years, I was rarely out of my mother's arms, and Emerson was rarely in them. Suddenly handed off to a live-in nurse and deprived of virtually all our mother's attention and physical contact, he suffered the anguish of abandonment and the torment of jealousy. I think he was too young to recognize that I was human, which enabled him to take it out on me with a vengeance. His behavior persisted into his young adolescence. I saw a coldness in his eyes when he looked at me and he was capable of doing anything to me.

Many times my parents found him at my crib, covering my face with a blanket or a pillow. I have memories of waking up suddenly, unable to breathe, kicking and thrashing in a panic, and finding Emerson standing above me. He'd also try to pull me off the changing table by tugging at the feet of my pajamas. He'd step on my hands as I crawled on the floor. Fear and panic of Emerson pervaded my childhood. He acted out to get my mother's attention and to express his pain. He had poor impulse control and broke things. Once, he flushed some of our mom's jewelry down the toilet. Today he might be called hyperactive.

My relationship with my younger brother, Neil, was a loving counterbalance to my troubled relationship with Emerson. Neil completely fascinated me from the moment he came home from the hospital. I'd watch him in his crib and learned to gently rock him to sleep. When my mother held him, I followed her around just to be near him. When Neil stopped breast-feeding, I fed him bottles. We grew very attached to each other.

I found Neil easy to be with. Physical contact, emotional contact, and eye contact with him weren't the stressful demand on me that they were with others. From the time he could walk, Neil was my little shadow, following me around the house. When he was old enough to go outside, I took him everywhere with me. He hated for me to leave him; sometimes, he'd rush out the door after me in his pajamas. My relationship with Neil drew me farther out of my shell and enabled me to love without being ambivalent or needy.

Emerson hardly seemed to notice Neil, who now enjoyed the lion's share of our mother's attention. I appreciated Neil for this too, since being the center of our mother's attention had made me the object of Emerson's wrath. Emerson picked on Neil just to rile me. I was Neil's protector. If I caught Emerson bothering him, I flew into a rage. I kept a watchful eye on both of them, always ready to intervene in an instant. I protected Neil more fiercely than I protected myself.

Our family life revolved around the dining-room table, where we gathered for dinner every night. My mother sat next to Emerson to control him. Neil and I sat together on the opposite side of the table. Emerson and I always got into some kind of fight, throwing things at each other or kicking each other under the table. I felt bad for Neil, who watched our battles in helpless fear, at times screaming and crying for us to stop.

As Emerson and I got older, our relationship degenerated into ongoing warfare. He taunted and teased me, jabbed and poked me with things, threw rocks at me, and once threatened me with a broken milk bottle. He often overpowered me physically and held me down, spitting on me or tickling me until I went into a claustrophobic panic. Though smaller and weaker, I fought back with all my strength, using my fists or whatever object was handy. Sometimes we fought with sticks and even boards with rusty nails.

At times, Emerson's abuse was dangerous. Once he was chopping wood while I watched from the side—safely I thought. But he swung the axe wildly in my direction and hit me in the head, slicing my forehead to the bone just above my eyebrow. Another time, he followed me onto the roof of our house, trapped me near the edge, and tried to push me off. Terrified of being pushed and of jumping but knowing being pushed would be worse, I jumped to the ground fifteen feet below. I landed hard, bruising both feet but fortunately not breaking any bones.

Emerson finally broke me. Bigger, stronger, and older, when he did get hold of me, he could overpower me and do whatever he pleased. I felt deep shame about this. But through Emerson, I learned the secret of dealing with pain and fear. I discovered this secret while being held down and tickled, one of Emerson's favorite ways of tormenting me. The tickling and the feelings of helplessness, panic, and rage were unbearable. On one occasion, these feelings became so intense that something shifted; instead of struggling and resisting, I relaxed into the discomfort and panic and moved through to the other side of them, into a remarkable state of calm.

After that, I was able to make this shift consistently, often immediately, relaxing, taking slow, deep breaths, and focusing intently on the feelings of panic or pain. Then I could remain physically relaxed and aware while Emerson tickled or hurt me. Some might call this a state of dissociation, but I experienced being distinctly present to reality, detached from any suffering while filled with a calm, surreal clarity. In this state, things seemed to unfold in slow motion, and everything appeared brighter than normal, as if someone had turned on a light. Sometimes I also heard a loud rushing noise in my ears. Finding this calm, clear place inside—on the other side of fear, pain, and rage—proved itself an invaluable skill. On more than one occasion, this ability to relax in high-pressure or dangerous situations and to respond with unusual clarity saved my life.

After a record-breaking snowstorm when I was ten, I dug a long, narrow tunnel into a ten-foot-tall snowdrift that ran the length of our house. When Emerson found me in it, he collapsed the tunnel behind me, trapping me in pitch-black darkness with my body jammed in tightly packed snow. I couldn't move, let alone turn around. At first, I panicked. A couple of feet of thickly packed snow separated me from daylight. I didn't know if I could dig through it or how much oxygen I had in the confined space. In that moment, I experienced the terror of being buried alive. I pushed against the wall with all my strength, moving the snow an inch or two, until realized I was only packing it harder and tighter. My thoughts raced; my fear escalated. So I began my well-practiced routine, consciously relaxing into the panic and slowing down my breathing. Within moments, I passed through the fear into the familiar calm and clear place. Then, literally buried alive, I assessed my situation, got my sense of direction, and figured out a strategy to dig my way out. In that tightly confined space, I was able to wriggle my body, creating just enough space to distribute and pack handfuls of snow around me. Slowly, I managed to dig my way through two feet of snow to daylight.

As long as I can remember, the mere sight or presence of Emerson triggered anxiety and fear in me. I was living with an enemy, who I believed wanted me dead. I felt as threatened watching TV in the same room as if he were chasing me through the house or physically overpowering me. I believed he might really kill me, either in an impulsive act or out of gross carelessness at an opportune moment. Whether his motives were conscious or unconscious, he was the source and symbol of terror throughout my childhood.

My parents remained in denial about this side of Emerson. Most of what went on between us happened out of their sight. He'd tell them, "It was a mistake. I didn't mean to hurt him." Though unwilling to consider that he wanted me to disappear or to die, they were painfully aware that ours was no garden-variety sibling rivalry. Our conflict had such a reputation in the neighborhood that they couldn't find babysitters. It reached a point where they began locking Emerson in his room for hours a day. When they let him out, they tried to reassure me that he wouldn't kill me. Still, I felt they didn't take my fears of Emerson seriously or recognize the threat he posed to me in my own home.

My conflict with Emerson also taught me that it was a short jump from terror to rage. I learned to make that shift too, like flipping a switch. When Emerson was around, I'd feel a rush of fear. If he came near me, I'd flip the switch to anger and hit him in the face. Once, he came after me, and I pushed him backward down the stairs. Sometimes, my own anger frightened me. I didn't know if I had control of it anymore. But Emerson continued to push me to that point. This culminated in an incident when I was ten: I tried to kill him with a screwdriver.

I'd been practicing throwing knives and screwdrivers for a couple of years and had gotten very good at it. I had excellent aim, power, and control. By visualizing each throw in my mind and following through with full force, I could hit my target almost every time and bury the blade deep. I could usually tell by the feel of the throw, as it left my hand, if it would find its mark. On that day, Emerson and I had one of our usual fights. I fended him off with my fists. To get back at me, Emerson went up to Neil and pushed him down on the floor. Neil hit his head very hard on the stone entry and began to wail. I went berserk and ran after Emerson. He took off, running up the stairs. When I reached the bookshelf near the bottom of the stairs, I stopped to grab a large screwdriver I kept there on top of some books. I'd hidden screwdrivers in various places around the house as ready weapons exactly for an occasion like this. Now it was time.

I stood at the bottom of the stairs in a throwing stance. With tunnel vision, I saw Emerson as he ran up the stairs and already I visualized the throw, seeing the screwdriver hit its target—Emerson's right temple. As he reached the landing, I took a deep breath, whipped my arm back, and threw the screwdriver with deadly force. A thrill of anticipation ran through me as the screwdriver left my hand. Mesmerized, I watched it fly, blade first like an arrow, and with my mind helped it to hit and penetrate Emerson's temple. Emerson glanced back and ducked his head. My heart sank as the screwdriver flew past him, missing his head by a fraction of an inch. The screwdriver stuck in the wall behind him with a thud. Emerson ran down the hall into his room, shutting and locking the door. I went upstairs and pulled out the screwdriver embedded in the wall. Holding it in my hand, I relived the thrill I felt when I thought I had him. And I was stunned by the realization: I had tried to kill my brother and almost succeeded! If he hadn't ducked, the blade would have punctured his skull. I had crossed a line I'd never crossed before. I realized something about myself I hadn't known until that moment: I had it in me to deliberately kill someone. This scared the hell out of me—and I hated Emerson for pushing me to this point.

Emerson also knew a line had been crossed that changed things between us. When he told my mother what I'd done, how he'd felt the screwdriver fly past his head, the look in her eyes again brought home the severity of the act. Emerson was afraid of me after that. I still hid my screwdrivers in new locations, but Emerson never picked on me in quite the same way again. He later admitted to me that until that incident he hadn't considered me human.

First grade marked the onset of my academic troubles. My co-op classmates and I now attended the local Lombard public school. Mrs. Brent, my first-grade teacher, began to single me out, criticizing me for not paying attention, sometimes slapping my hand with a ruler. I had no idea what I was doing wrong. I wasn't misbehaving. I was doing my best. But so much was going on inside me it was hard to pay attention to classroom instruction. Any physical discomfort or sensation, any noise or movement around me, drew my attention.

I slipped in and out of my inner world without noticing. Unaware, I'd start one of my self-soothing activities, softly tapping or clicking my fingers, scratching myself, or wiggling in my seat. I was often literally uncomfortable in my own skin. I don't think I disturbed the class, but my teacher perceived my odd behavior as a problem and distraction to her class. Mrs. Brent punished me for things I could not control. I didn't understand and felt unfairly picked on. I began to feel different from the other kids, inadequate and excluded—something I'd never felt before.

None of this seemed to change the way my co-op friends viewed me, but it strongly influenced the other kids' perceptions, who took their cue from Mrs. Brent that something was wrong with me. Most of them began excluding me from their activities; some ignored me when I tried to talk to them. I started feeling bad about myself and wondered what was wrong with me. My co-op friends mixed easily with these Lombard kids, but it was much harder for me. I lacked the social and communication skills most kids my age possessed. I was behind developmentally and academically. I missed many key developmental stepping-stones because of chronic illnesses.

Everything seemed disjointed and random to me. I had terrible difficulty sequencing and organizing my thoughts and remembering the days of the week and people's names, even my brothers' names, and my home address and phone number. I had difficulty with hand-eye coordination, knowing my right side from my left. I also had trouble understanding directions—north, south, east, and west—and sensing my location in space, which made me terrible at sports. I couldn't pay attention to anything for very long, and only the irritated reactions of others told me this was a problem. All this increased my feelings of frustration and isolation.

That year my developmental state and learning problems became significant issues. My parents began taking me to experts, who administered a variety of tests. After extensive testing, noting the discrepancy between my exceptionally high IQ test results and my exceptionally low practical abilities, the experts decided I wasn't "retarded." They concluded that my problems must be psychological. Although my parents thought I had neurological and perceptual problems, they accepted the prevailing psychological view, hoping it would provide a solution. They sent me to see a psychiatrist and got me a private tutor.

From the end of my first year in second grade all the way through sixth grade, I saw my private tutor daily and a psychiatrist twice weekly for traditional talk therapy. The era of prescribing psychotropic drugs to children with learning or behavioral problems hadn't begun. My parents and teachers scheduled my sessions during class subjects I was unable to learn. It was embarrassing. The psychiatrist gave my parents an ultimatum: he'd meet with me only if they did everything he said, even if it went against their instincts. The ground rule was that they couldn't "lie" to me anymore to protect me from painful truths. Ruthless honesty was essential. I had to understand the consequences of being unable or unwilling to learn.

On a family vacation when I was eight or nine, my grandfather, who'd taught college-level mathmatics, took me off alone for a few hours each day to observe me and test me in his special field of knowledge. My parents knew I had a basic aptitude for numbers, but they didn't know to what degree. My grandfather, also a doctor, knew all the professional theories and diagnoses regarding my learning disabilities. Now he determined to find out for himself how intelligent I was.

The first day he began by teaching me a form of binary code, and counting in the base-two number system, the basic numerical language used in electronic circuitry and all modern computers. To his amazement, I acquired a working understanding of the basic concepts in our first thirty-minute session. His visible excitement told me I'd done something remarkable and completely unexpected. Our little game of numbers turned out to be a dramatic event.

After that first lesson, he sat down with me over the next few days to see how far he could take me. In that time, I transitioned from base two through base sixteen and was able to add and subtract within base. He told my parents my ability to grasp and utilize the various conceptual ideas of binary-to-hexadecimal code was far beyond my age and grade level, indicating "genius qualities." He said many of his college students had trouble grasping these concepts as quickly as

I did. It was all the more remarkable given my substandard performance in almost every other area of learning.

I was excited by my success. Yet to my disappointment, it meant virtually nothing when I returned to class. My newly discovered facility for numbers didn't erase the list of defects and disabilities compiled by the experts who had tested me, and the basic subjects of my grade level remained beyond my grasp.

I wanted desperately to meet the expectations of my parents and teachers, and to feel part of the world. I wanted to rise to challenges and succeed. I wanted to learn the same subjects as the other kids and to be competent like them. I didn't want to be criticized, punished, written off, and left behind. But that increasingly happened to me.

I wasn't athletic, my social skills were clumsy, and my scholastic performance was poor, but I did succeed in one area—fighting. In our semirural school, fights were an almost daily ritual for establishing pecking-order dominance. I managed to earn the respect of my peers in a few well-chosen confrontations, mostly in response to someone else's aggression. I never picked a fight or fought anyone who didn't deserve it. I fought only bullies for hurting or intimidating me or other weaker kids.

My years of combat with Emerson had accustomed me to fighting and also instilled in me deep sympathy for underdogs and outrage toward bullies. Despite being small and uncoordinated, I had fighting experience few kids had and a reckless intensity other kids found intimidating. Fear, violence, pain, and blood didn't frighten me. I was willing to take on anyone and never lost a fight. No matter how it started, the other kid would always eventually quit when I hurt him enough. Still, most kids and adults who knew me saw me as a kind and friendly boy—and mostly I was.

My first school fight occurred in my first year of second grade. Another second-grade class from a tough neighborhood had temporarily relocated to our school while their building was being renovated. There were a few bullies among them. When the toughest one started picking on one of my classmates, I stepped in. He was heavyset, much bigger than me. I wasn't proficient with my fists, but I'd learned a trick with Emerson: I'd take punches, throw a few myself, move in close, then lunge and grab my opponent in a headlock. Once I got him, he was mine. I'd squeeze until he couldn't breathe. Every kid, no matter how big, gave up when he couldn't breathe. In that first fight, I got the bully in a headlock and squeezed until he gave up. That's how I won all my fights.

Defeating the toughest kid from a tough Chicago neighborhood established my reputation. I didn't need to fight again that year. After that first fight, I could intimidate any bully and back him down without coming to blows. That victory, which won me sudden status and the admiration of my classmates, gave me a thrilling self-esteem I'd never felt before. It compensated somewhat for the low self-esteem my learning disabilities created.

Failing second grade that year was a turning point, the beginning of a downward spiral. It set in motion a completely new course in my life—one I didn't want to take but was powerless to change. The following year, despite my best efforts, I continued to fall behind the other kids, all a year younger than me but still smarter than me. With a sinking feeling, I watched them learn, succeed, and leave me behind academically. My second year of second grade was worse than the first. My classmates were acutely aware that I was older and unable to keep up with them academically. My closest friends, the co-op kids I'd known since nursery school, were now a grade ahead of me.

That year I had a terrible nightmare that evoked the profound sense of isolation simmering inside me. In the dream, a kid who seemed like me wandered aimlessly around the school playground, a blank look on his face and a big, snakelike worm wriggling out of a hole in the top of his head. Although the other kids seemed not to notice him as he wandered zombielike in their midst, they maintained a ten-foot circle of space around him at all times.

I'd been seeing my psychiatrist twice a week for nearly a year, but nothing good had come from our sessions. I felt from him no sense of caring, compassion, or interest in me as a person; just a cool, impersonal detachment and a sense of being judged. I thought he was an idiot, and I refused to talk to him. He periodically fell asleep during our sessions. I did too. I'd nap on the couch or climb into the toy cabinet, close the door, and doze in the dark. My parents didn't know what happened in our sessions. The psychiatrist made various excuses for my lack of progress. I believe he was the one who advised my mother to threaten me with the possibility of institutionalization.

Under his supervision, my parents' behavior toward me changed. I only realized years later how troubled, even anguished, they were by the strict rules the doctor established as a condition for working with me. I misinterpreted their hesitation and frustration as disapproval and anger. My mother had always followed her instincts with me, often against professional wisdom. But as she helplessly watched me falling farther behind, she lost faith in her own instincts. Blindly following the advice of a doctor she didn't trust placed a subtle wedge between us and plunged her into a private hell. I didn't know she'd lost faith in her instincts. I thought she'd lost faith in me.

At the end of that year I should have been held back again, but the school staff realized that I wasn't going to learn and that I couldn't continue repeating second grade forever. Though I could barely read or write, they promoted me to third grade. After that, my teachers passed me along, year after year, through the rest of elementary school, and I believed I really was moving forward.

4

Fighting My Way to the Bottom

The specters of illiteracy and hopeless disability began to haunt me when I failed second grade. The threat of ending up in a mental institution triggered deep anxiety and an urgency about my future. How would I earn a living and take care of myself when I grew up? Would I be a valued member of society or find myself alone and isolated as an adult? What job could I get if I couldn't read and write? If I couldn't learn the things I needed to pass second grade, how could I learn all the things I needed to know in order to live and function in the world? But one thing I wished for above all else troubled me: would I ever be able to have a family and provide for them?

Several things became clear to me. My mother couldn't protect me, I didn't know how to take care of myself, and I had to learn how to learn. I had to figure out how to become independent and to develop the necessary skills to manage my own life.

My fears provided a powerful motivation to become independent. I began to distance myself from all of my family members except for Neil. I stopped telling my parents I loved them. I questioned their decisions to see if they matched my own perceptions. I asked to be sent away to school. When they added a ground-floor bedroom on the far side of the house, away from the other bedrooms, I asked if I could move there. They let me. This literally gave me a distance from my family and a sense of being on my own, which I needed.

My mother, realizing I had to become more independent, also began distancing herself from me. While providing basic care, she became noticeably detached. She let me take risks to learn the consequences of my decisions. At times, I interpreted her lack of concern and detachment from my activities as abandonment and neglect. Mostly, I appreciated my newfound freedom.

In fifth grade, I stumbled into a possible vocation that held the promise of success and gave me more of the self-esteem I desperately needed. I had a terrible sweet tooth and frequently brought candy to school. My classmates often asked me to share but wanted more than I could afford, so I offered to buy candy for them. After figuring out what they wanted, I started bringing extra candy with me and charging them for it. So began my career in sales. More kids found out and wanted to buy my candy too. I started buying larger quantities and selling it for a profit.

Penny candy was big in those days, and nickel packs of gum with five strips. I put gum in a bag with penny candy and sold two pieces for a nickel—or three pieces for good friends. I bought nickel candy bars and sold them for ten cents. I noticed the most popular items and refined my inventory accordingly. I never understood why kids bought candy from me for more than they could buy it on their own. But they seemed to like buying from me, and I did a steady business. Every day before school, at recess, and during lunch, a crowd of kids gathered around me. I kept the candy in a book satchel I rigged with a makeshift alarm. It was my first invention and my first venture into electronics. I wired a battery and buzzer together in my dad's workshop and attached it to the handle. Unless you opened the satchel in a precise way, the buzzer would go off.

I tried to keep my business low-key but never tried to hide what I was doing. When my parents and teachers became aware of my candy selling, they didn't seem to mind because it wasn't causing problems. I was learning a lot about business through hands-on experience. I soon had a fairly profitable business, which dramatically increased when I began manufacturing and marketing my own product. I dipped toothpicks in cinnamon oil and sold cinnamon toothpicks. To advertise, I walked around with a cinnamon toothpick stuck between my teeth and passed out samples. My cinnamon toothpicks became a popular local fad. I got so busy I hired my good friend Larry as my sales rep. Then I decided to expand my territory and hired kids from other schools, including the local junior high school, to sell my toothpicks. By the end of the year, I had a steady business with four salespeople. We were all making a profit. I was a highly motivated entrepreneur.

For the first time, I began to believe in my future. I was learning through experience what I'd never learned from schoolbooks and chalkboard scribbling. I had good people skills, marketing savvy, and a knack for sales. I learned to purchase products people liked, how much I could mark up the price, how to sell, and how to motivate other people to sell for me. I also learned financial self-discipline. I didn't spend my profits frivolously or squander them by eating my products. And I learned how to keep personal money separate from business money by paying myself a salary.

I saved all my profits except for the money I put back into the business. I had a plan. I was saving a nest egg for the future. My goal of achieving independence now seemed realistic. I believed I could become a successful businessman and achieve my bottom-line goal of not ending up in a mental institution. And maybe, just maybe, I could have a family.

Academically, nothing changed. There I was still lost and struggling, unable to spell many first-grade words. I could spell a few three-letter words but no four-letter words. Fearing public humiliation, I never tried to answer questions in class. When teachers called on me, I made jokes to try to cover up and to avoid looking stupid. I was a class clown. But I was making money. I was finally succeeding at something. And it felt great.

* * *

At age ten, in 1964, I began going to Circle Pines Summer Camp near Kalamazoo, Michigan. Circle Pines was designed to provide underprivileged city kids and middle-class kids with a shared summer camp experience at a very low cost. They accomplished this by incorporating hard work into the daily camp activities. We did the usual things like swimming, hiking, campfires, singing, and storytelling, but we also did real work. For a few hours each day, we dug ditches, cleared brush, hauled stones, and put in roads. We even built a couple of cabins. The camp counselors instructed and supervised our work. We learned practical skills that most kids never learn at camp.

At Circle Pines, I shared a small cabin with Robert, who would become a good friend. Robert was a year and a half older and lived on Chicago's South Side. His knack for flirting with girls he didn't know earned him the camp nickname Casanova. It was a skill I wanted to learn. I'd grown up around girls at the co-op. I never went through the typical "not liking girls" stage. I felt comfortable with girls. I trusted and liked talking to the girls I knew. But approaching girls I didn't know and striking up a conversation was different. Robert and I became camp buddies, with girls being a key topic of conversation between us. One night, the topic turned into personal exploration with two girls we really liked and flirted with a few times.

After a campfire gathering of scary storytelling, Robert and I walked back to our cabin. To our surprise, we found the girls hiding in our sleeping bags. We ended up in the sleeping bags with them and stayed up late, talking and holding them through the night. This first physical experience with a girl left me feeling close and connected.

My first personal experience with an Eastern culture also occurred at camp. I saw one kid in our cabin chanting the mantra *Namyohorengekyo*. The tone and repetition intrigued me. He was a very calm, responsible kid with more common sense than most of us. When I expressed interest, he showed me how to do it. I practiced chanting twice a day for several months, then periodically, but a sense of its potential value stuck with me.

When summer camp ended, I started taking subway trains into Chicago to visit Robert. Venturing alone into the city made me aware of my limited possibilities in my sequestered co-op world. My mother encouraged these solo excursions. She and my father often drove me to the train station, eleven miles from our house. "I don't want you to grow up being a naïve suburban kid," she said. "I want you to know the world and to be able to get around in it." If my mother thought I ought to know or be able to do something, I believed her and tried to meet her expectations as if my future depended on it. But there was more to these outings for me; I felt drawn to an edge of anxiety and fear when I ventured into the greater world.

It wasn't the familiar anxiety of my daily life. I'd always felt anxious about going to school, about the shame and humiliation of failing, about being excluded and left behind. Now I'd found a new, exciting edge of fear, involving risk, danger, and plunging into the unknown world "out there." My future independence required this sense of urgency and drive; I had an obsessive need to step beyond my comfort zone, confront my fears, and push beyond them. Traveling the subway trains and venturing alone into the city of Chicago satisfied all these needs. I wanted to see if I could make myself do things I was afraid to do and then repeat them until I could do them without fear. At first, just going on the trains alone accomplished this. Then it was talking to girls on the train, even while their parents were sitting next to them, or talking to bums and crazy people on the train. By repeatedly pushing myself beyond my fears, I was going places and doing things the kids I knew would never dare.

When I stepped onto the subway, I entered a new world. I was exploring, looking for something missing in my familiar world: for opportunities, challenges, adventure; for other kids like me who were different, who struggled and didn't fit in; for a place where I *did* fit in. I wanted to see how far beyond my edge I could go, to discover what I could or couldn't do, to find out who I could be if I dared. I discovered that in taking risks, fear wasn't a final barrier. The secret to overcoming fear was to repeat what was fearful until it became familiar. I'd take unreasonable risks if I thought I might break through to some new level of strength, resilience, or independence.

I also wanted to understand good and evil and the meaning of life, though I didn't think of it with those words. I was curious and hungry for experience, knowledge, and truth. Were there rules to live by, or was it dog eat dog? Would I be able to make it on my own out there? For a few hours? A day? A lifetime? I wanted to see what kind of people were out there, what they did, how they lived. I wanted to see people who made it, who succeeded, and people who failed, who were beaten down and had become what I was afraid I might become. All this motivated me, made me feel alive and aware.

My father subtly encouraged my new adventuring. One time, he gave me a rare, uncharacteristic glimpse into his own difficult childhood. He told me how he'd run away from home as a kid and gotten his first job at a local circus. They began teaching him how to be a fire-eater and sword-swallower. He gave me a demonstration. Dousing his hands with lighter fluid, he lit them on fire, let them burn briefly, then put them out. Then he lit a cigarette and put it out on his tongue. He did both without getting burned. Then he got a silver butter knife, held it by the edge of the handle, leaned his head back, and slid the knife down into his throat until it disappeared. He said he could put a sword down into his stomach without getting hurt. I was the only one he showed these things to. I think he understood the struggle my life was. He was letting me know that he'd also struggled in his youth and that some of us have to do things to survive that others might not understand.

My dyslexia was a recurring problem on public transit. I almost always got lost at some point—getting onto the wrong train, getting off at the wrong stop, forgetting directions and the names of the stations where I wanted to get off. I couldn't read the signs. I had to ask strangers for directions and help. For my first few trips, my mother wrote down my itinerary on a piece of paper, with the names of the stations and the number of stops in between. I couldn't read it, but if I got lost or confused, I'd show the paper to strangers and ask them to read it to me. Someone would usually let me know how many stops to my station, or if I'd already passed it, how to get back on the right train.

Asking for help didn't always work. Sometimes people told me how many stops to my station, but I'd lose count. Or if they named the stop, I'd forget the name by the time the train arrived at that station. Every trip was, to some degree, a disorienting ordeal that triggered anxiety and confusion, as well as excitement. A couple of times I rode around lost for hours, getting off at wrong stops and onto wrong trains, ending up at the end of the line on the north side of Chicago. More than once my mother had to drive all the way out to the Skokie Station to get me.

Yet my excursions were sometimes about simple fun, hanging out with friends and meeting girls. Robert lived near the end of the subway line on the South Side. We'd leave our houses around the same time, catch a train, and meet somewhere in the middle, usually at the White Sox Baseball Park. Once I learned the route it was easy. For lunch we'd buy hot dogs, which I often paid for since Robert was poor. Our primary goal was to flirt with girls our age, who were usually with their parents. When we saw girls we liked, we'd try to talk with them. Sometimes we'd serenade them with absurd love songs we made up. Robert would take out his recorder—a miniature flute he always had with him—and play a melody while I sang the words. If that went well, we'd start little conversations to try to get to know them. We never expected anything beyond that. Most parents saw us as harmless kids doing silly stuff to get girls' attention and were amused. The girls usually liked the attention.

We took the trains everywhere, exploring as much of the city as possible in the hours before I had to return home. Robert and I got lost together a few times, and got mugged more than once. The first mugging occurred when we got off at the wrong stop, near Midway Airport, not a good neighborhood for two young white boys traveling alone. The territory belonged to the infamous Blackstone Rangers, the largest youth gang in America back in the 1960s, predecessor of the Bloods and the Crips.

Standing on the elevated platform as the train pulled away, we saw six black kids running up the stairs toward us. When they jumped the turnstile and headed straight at us, I knew they weren't running to catch a train. I always carried a pocketknife in case of trouble, but unless I knew my life was in danger I wasn't about to pull it on a gang of six kids, all bigger and several years older than I was. They grabbed us and demanded our money. I gave them what I had, except for what was in my shoe. One of them took a ring I was wearing. Robert resisted and got slugged hard on the side of his head near his left eye. It swelled into a huge lump. Later, he could rest his recorder on the lump and his left ear without it falling off. When I told my mother about getting ripped off, she said matter-of-factly, "Well, you've got to be more careful than that."

*   *   *

On my sixth-grade year, my personal tutoring ended, and instead of going outside during recess, I went to a special ed class as a volunteer assisting "retarded" kids. I felt an impulse to help kids I imagined were struggling more than I was. I felt funny going to the class, though. Having a learning disability was difficult enough; I didn't want people to think I might be "retarded" too. Yet caring for these kids each day was truly fulfilling. I came to love them and kept in touch with some of them for years after.

I was still doing my candy-and-cinnamon-toothpick business, but near the end of the year, my business came to a sudden end. When the principal of the junior high I'd be attending the next year learned of several boys selling cinnamon toothpicks in his school, he talked to them and found out they all worked for me. He knew who I was because he knew my mother well. As the psychologist for our school district, she had helped him with troubled kids in his school.

He called one evening just before dinner. My mother answered the phone, and they spoke briefly. Then she called me over, handing me the phone with her hand covering the mouthpiece, "Why is the principal of Jackson Junior High calling you?" she whispered with a scowl.

I had no idea. I shrugged with a puzzled look and took the phone. "Hello?"

"Hello, David. This is Principal Schultz of Jackson Junior High." His voice was stern. "Are you selling cinnamon tooth-picks to students in my school?" He was clearly unhappy about it.

"Um…yeah."

"Well, David, you'd better stop immediately. And I don't mean just in my school. I mean stop altogether. If you don't, you won't be allowed to attend my school next year. Students aren't supposed to conduct business of any kind on school property—in *any* school."

"Okay, I'll stop."

"Good. I'll speak to your mother now."

That was it. My youthful business career was over, temporarily. Deeply disappointed, I handed the phone back to my mother and went to my room. Once again, it seemed the world was cutting off any possibility for me to succeed.

The next year, when I started seventh grade, all my disabilities were suddenly magnified. It was 1967. For years, I'd been passed along from grade to grade, despite my failure to learn the basics in each grade. I knew I was way behind, but because I'd been passed along, I imagined that my classmates believed I wasn't hopelessly far behind. I wasn't a very good student, but, hey, I was passing, right? But now the rules changed. I would not be passed undeservedly up the ladder anymore. Now I was expected to learn—or to flunk. Years behind my peers academically, I was put into the remedial classes, for the "slow" kids. But even there I was unable to keep up.

After being held back in second grade, I'd formed a whole new group of school friends. I hung out with good kids, normal kids, smart kids. Now I'd been put in remedial classes and another parting of the ways began. Another group of former classmates and friends were going on without me again, learning things I'd probably never learn, moving confidently toward normal, conventional, probably successful lives. They'd graduate, go to college, get well-paying jobs, have families, and enjoy lives of effortless freedom and fulfillment. But I was stuck in a remedial classes with misfits and bullies, with the slow, damaged, dysfunctional kids.

I had felt detached from my own classmates, who were younger than me and had their own bonds together. Now I was in a special class, a remedial class, falling behind everyone there as well. It was suddenly obvious to me how far behind and how *stupid* I really was. I'd try to read, slowly sounding out the words, but I couldn't understand what I read. My anxiety over being exposed as a dummy in front of all of my friends was overwhelming. I dreaded the loss of their respect and perhaps their friendship too. My future was threatened again, in doubt more than ever. I was plagued by chronic insomnia and an inescapable sense of doom.

The teacher's misguided attempts to help me in my English class spelling bees proved humiliating. She'd save the simplest words for me. "Okay, David, *candy.*" I'd sound out the word in my mind, searching for letters that matched the sounds: k...n...d. Saying the letters together out loud sounded like *kandy* to me, but the other students' laughter told me I hadn't even come close. This would have been bad in early grade school, but I was in eighth grade! I sat in my seat, flushed with embarrassment, acting like I'd blown it off on purpose. It was bad enough being exposed in front of the class for not knowing the most basic things they'd all learned years before, *but this was a remedial class!* The more incidents like this happened, the more I felt the other kids pulling away. It was painful and humiliating, and I became more and more isolated. Now, every day at school was more frightening and anxiety-provoking than getting mugged by Blackstone Rangers in Chicago.

Most kids and adults viewed remedial classes as a warehouse for "problem kids," kids who couldn't fit in or function in a normal class. Many of them truly *were* the worst kids—bullies, punks, and thieves—often psychologically disturbed and emotionally damaged, not just unable to function academically but socially too. Looking at some of these kids, I saw eventual prison or early death ahead. Yet as messed up as many of them were, they were all way ahead of me academically. I wasn't even close to their level. I had severe learning disabilities, not severe psychological or emotional problems. I knew I wasn't like them, but the school system seemed to see no distinction between them and me. We'd been placed on the same track. I feared I might end up just like them or worse. And that was unacceptable! I fought against it every way I could, and in a class of bullies and troubled kids, that meant physical fights as well.

At first I tried reaching out to some of them, even the meanest and worst among them. A few became my friends. But to those who interpreted my friendly overtures as weakness, I became an object of ridicule. First, they gave me a hard time. Then they started to pick on me. When I nixed that by fighting back, they ignored me. I began feeling angry and mean myself. Even there, I was the alien, the outsider, the misfit. So I established a personal code of ethics: I'd be nice to the nice kids, a son of a bitch to the bullies, and a protector of the picked-on. I wouldn't steal or purposely harm others. I appointed myself class sheriff based on my code, my skill and fury as a fighter, my willingness to escalate the level of violence, and my lack of fear. More than once, I made a bully I'd beaten apologize to his victim as I stood quietly a few feet away. I hoped their shame would stop them, though it didn't always.

I never picked fights out of meanness; I only fought to stop a bully in progress. I got along with most of the kids most of the time. Students and teachers noticed that I got into fights with the troublemakers, which fueled the perception of me as a troublemaker too. And that perception began to grow.

5

The Trip

My mother was always taking me to the newest cutting-edge specialist for testing and to try out the newest theory or program. When I was twelve, I began experiencing episodes related to a "neurosensory processing disorder" diagnosed by one specialist. Almost daily, I instinctively shut down, withdrawing internally into a kind of tunnel vision, with a dulling of tactile, visual, and audio perception. When severe, the shutting down occurred with a *chuh-chunk* feeling or sound. These episodes worsened in the seventh grade. A few times I shut myself in my room and didn't come out for two or three days. But near the end of that difficult year, grace entered my life.

While riding my bike one day, I saw Jane, a co-op friend, standing in her front yard and talking with a girl I'd never seen before. Jane was black, and the other girl was white. This would have been an unusual sight in most neighborhoods, but not in our co-op. I stopped to say hi to Jane and to meet her friend, Joy. Joy immediately impressed me. She was beautiful, with long, vibrant red hair and a radiant smile. The three of us talked for several minutes, and then I continued on my way. The next day Jane told me Joy liked me, and she gave me Joy's phone number. I called Joy, and we had a long conversation. Thus began a close friendship that would become my first real relationship.

I couldn't understand why Joy was interested in me. She was a popular girl, with a lot of friends. She was smart, beautiful, confident, and could have had any guy she wanted. She was also two years older and three grades ahead of me. She attended high school.

Joy was involved in the theater department at her school, helping to build and to paint sets for school plays. As our friendship grew, I started helping her prepare sets for the shows. That's how I began hanging out with her crowd. Joy's world was very different from mine. Her friends, mostly jocks and students involved in the school theater, came from families ranging from conservative to reactionary to racist. The theater kids tended to be good students with school spirit who didn't drink or get into trouble. The jocks drank, fought, and got into some trouble.

Joy was unconventional. She hungered for something deeper than the conservative world of her parents. A kid with long hair from an antiwar, liberal family living in an interracial community, I symbolized a new world. Joy liked me for who I was. I was a nice kid, a good talker, and a good listener. We talked about everything—school, music, politics, sex, our feelings and problems, our hopes and fears. She said I really understood her, that I made her feel comfortable, that she could tell me anything, and that she always felt good being around me.

I felt safe enough with Joy to tell her everything about myself, knowing she'd understand and keep it confidential. She listened without judgment, seemed to understand my inner conflicts, and never gave me advice or answers. I told her about my learning disabilities, my inability to read, and my conflict with Emerson, which had mostly subsided. I shared my fears about my future, even told her about my suicide option. But there was one thing I didn't tell her, something I couldn't verbalize: how I wanted the intimacy of a wife and family in my future more than anything but could never respect myself unless I could provide for them—and if I couldn't respect myself, I couldn't live with myself.

Besides Joy, I'd only shared my suicide option with two school kids after hearing them talk about wanting to commit suicide. I quickly realized that was a mistake. They saw suicide as a cool idea, but I didn't get how feeling doomed to an unhappy life and planning to die was cool. I'd have given anything to be normal, to have a life that worked and hope for a decent future.

My suicide plan made Joy sad. She really cared about me. From time to time, she asked how I was doing, but mostly we talked about her life and I listened, cared, and offered suggestions. Talking to others about their struggles distracted me from my own troubles and helped me feel less isolated.

Joy's extremely conservative father hated her seeing a longhaired kid with learning disabilities, who lived in the liberal, racially mixed co-op. He'd ground her for weeks at a time for seeing me. Deep down I knew our relationship wouldn't last. Our worlds were so different. We'd eventually separate and go in different directions. Yet I was okay with whatever happened because I believed I wouldn't live very long. My suicide plan gave me a detachment in relationships, an indifference to common concerns that occupied most kids, and a sense of freedom, especially with my friends. This allowed me to open up emotionally with my close friends and to be present and loving in ways most kids seemed to avoid. It also caused problems.

One evening after dinner, my mother said she'd heard I was planning to commit suicide. Even worse, she'd heard it from my school principal. The two students I foolishly shared my plan with told our social studies teacher about their suicide plan. They told the teacher I was also planning to kill myself.

This wasn't completely unexpected news to my mother, though the source of it came as a shock. My parents knew the struggle my life had always been and that it had worsened in the past year. I'd told my mother more than once I didn't want to be alive and that I blamed her and Dad for bringing me into the world. Once I realized how much this hurt her, I'd stopped saying it. But until now, she didn't know I might seriously be planning to kill myself. When she asked me, I confessed that I'd thought about it a lot. I didn't tell her about my mercury stash. I told her how much pressure I felt at school, how depressed I was about not being able to learn like other kids, and how much I hated remedial class. I talked about my insomnia and how bleak my future looked. After that, nearly every night at dinner, my mother anxiously asked me how I was doing.

I knew my parents loved me. We'd always been closer than most teenagers and parents. They'd tried to give me more freedom, always respecting my privacy and never pressing me for information. My mother had always told me she loved me. Now she told me she'd do anything she could for me and get me whatever help I needed. What she couldn't tell me was how I could ever have a future worth living. My mother took me to see my old psychiatrist, and another therapist, but nothing these experts said deflected my drift toward suicide.

When word of my suicide plan got around school and the co-op, some of the adults tried to help. Mostly, they asked me seemingly pointless questions and offered comments I found unhelpful, such as "You don't even know what life is yet" and "You're too young to know what you're doing" and even worse "Childhood is the best time of life!" If that last statement was true, I *really* had little to look forward to, making suicide more appealing.

My social studies teacher was genuinely concerned about me and often asked me how I was doing. Several times, she suggested I talk to a priest she knew in a church near the school. Feeling desperate, and partly to please her, I finally accepted her offer. My teacher spoke to the priest about me in advance and scheduled an appointment for me to see him after school one day. Having talked to many psychiatrists, psychologists, doctors, and various other experts, I didn't expect much from a priest.

As soon as I entered the church, my perspective changed. I gazed around at the brilliant stained-glass windows depicting biblical scenes, beneath a large dome and giant arched ceiling. The eerie atmosphere, with a palpable presence—as if inhabited by ghosts or spirits—stirred a flood of unexpected feelings in me. There was a power here I didn't understand.

I had no formal religious upbringing and was uncomfortable with religious formalities. My mother, born into Christianity, didn't go to church, and my Jewish father didn't go to temple. No religion was practiced or promoted in my home. My only exposure to formal religion was a few scattered childhood visits to churches and synagogues.

I didn't know where to look for the priest, so I stood waiting, absorbed in the atmosphere. A couple of minutes passed. Then I heard a voice say, "David, is that you?"

I whirled around to see a tall man dressed in black behind me. He had wavy black hair and wore a white collar. The white collar caught my gaze first, and then my eyes fastened on his thin face. It was a tough face to read: serious but pleasant and without much expression. He was younger than I thought he'd be. I nodded.

"Come with me," he said.

I followed him into a small office at the back of the church. We sat down in comfortable chairs, facing each other a few feet apart. He started with basic chitchat. I barely responded. I wasn't good at small talk; it seemed meaningless and made me uncomfortable. Then he asked why I'd come.

"My teacher told me to come," I said.

"What's going on? Is there anything I might be able to help you with?"

I was starting to feel really uncomfortable, like I was wasting my time. But since I didn't want to be there any longer than I had to, I decided I might as well get right to it.

"I don't want to live in my life the way it is," I began. "I have no control over anything in it. Everything seems unfair and pointless, like it's all about winning meaningless games or survival of the fittest. I don't have the skills to succeed or to survive."

Then I told him I thought the world was messed up—the Vietnam War, the nuclear threat, and superficial, self-centered people running everything. It seemed that truth had little relevance and being a good person was a luxury for people who fit in and that some of the so-called bad people were just good people caught in bad situations. I told him I was unwilling to live without self-respect, as one of the desperate who had to fight over scraps left behind by the more fortunate, being judged by people who knew nothing about desperation—as if being judgmental could keep them safe. It was easier to judge than to think.

"I don't want to be part of it," I said. "How come I can see through all the bullshit, but I'm the stupid one? I've had to fight my whole life, but I keep falling farther behind. I don't think I have what it takes to get ahead. My brother does. He's all about himself and what he can get for himself. When I was little, I used to think I'd rather be dead than become like him. I'm tired. I'm past tired. If I have to keep fighting just to survive, it isn't worth it. I'd rather be dead."

He listened attentively until I was finished. Then he sat quietly for a minute, looking thoughtful. Finally, he started talking. He told me I was struggling on two parallel paths in search of happiness and meaning. One was an external path in the world, involving things like learning to read, becoming more functional, having relationships, finding an occupation, and being of service to the world. He said he could see my dilemma and didn't know if a practical path would ever work out for me. That path wasn't his specialty. I felt a sense of trust hearing this. I saw that he sincerely wanted to help me.

I'd learned that people don't understand your situation, your peculiar angst, by having you explain it to them. People only understand your suffering through their own life experience. I can tell when someone knows suffering, has really let it touch them. They're not quick to judge, and this was very important to me. This priest truly seemed to understand suffering. He clearly understood me. So I hoped he'd have a real answer, even if it was that there is no answer.

His specialty, he told me, was the second, more important path—the only path to true happiness—and it was inside me. He called it an "existential search." He said he'd never talked to someone my age about this path. He said only God's gift of pain and struggle forced someone to look beneath the surface of life and that many people never have to ask themselves these deeper questions. The answers to existential questions are personal and spiritual, he said, and his job was to help people find these answers. But ultimately it was up to me.

Then he summarized what I'd told him in a nutshell in a way that clarified for me my own thoughts and feelings about myself and about my predicament. His words made more sense to me than anything the therapists and psychologists had told me. He was hitting the mark. God's gift of pain and struggle, the existential search, the only path to true happiness—he was on to something.

I sat up straight and asked, "What's the answer? How do I find it?"

He looked at me for a moment and then said, "It's both simple and hard. You must realize that you're fundamentally a sinner and accept Jesus Christ as your savior."

My heart sank when I heard that. I thought, *You can't be serious!*

"What do you mean I'm fundamentally a sinner?" I asked.

"We're all sinners," he said, "and we must believe in Jesus, who offers salvation."

It sounded too simple. I wished it were that simple and that I could believe it, but I couldn't. Maybe I was missing something. But I wanted to understand what he meant. Trying to be respectful, I asked him, "So what do I do? How do I believe in something I don't believe in?"

"Only those who believe in Jesus can be saved. Pray for God's grace and forgiveness. Let's pray. I'll pray with you."

He leaned forward in his chair, put his hands together, closed his eyes, and began to pray in a low, soft voice.

It was hard for me to follow him. My mind was racing: *Is believing in Jesus really the answer? How can I believe in something that doesn't seem true or make any sense to me? Can something I don't believe in, that doesn't make sense to me, actually be the solution to my problems?*

I believed that Jesus was a transcendent being. I also knew that people did horrible things in his name. According to this priest, Christians would be saved, while good, kind, honest people—Jews, atheists, and anyone else who didn't believe in Jesus—would be damned to hell. It didn't make sense. Wasn't the kind of person I was and what was in my heart more important than whatever I believed about Jesus? I couldn't believe in the solution this priest was offering me—that the answer to all my problems was simply to ask for forgiveness and believe in Jesus. He was sincere, but maybe he didn't really have an answer. Maybe he was just trying to give me hope.

He finished praying, and it was over. Nothing had changed that I could feel. I thanked him, got up, and walked out of the room, the same person, with the same problems as when I walked in. In the following days, I thought a lot about what he'd said. So many of his words seemed right to me, but I still couldn't believe God would damn to hell everyone who didn't believe in Jesus. The world was messed up enough already. I didn't think people were fundamentally bad, evil, or deserved to go to hell. We were all just trying to live and survive any way we could. Somehow all the insanity of the world came out of that.

Of all the people I spoke to, Joy gave me the best advice. One day, after I'd been discussing the possibility of suicide, she said, "Promise me you won't decide while you're unhappy. You can't do something like this when you're unhappy." This made sense to me. I decided to give her idea every chance and agreed not to kill myself when I was feeling depressed or hopeless.

But nothing changed. The daily pressures and stresses of school, chronic insomnia, failure and humiliation, living in a cruel, indifferent, crazy world, feeling defective, invisible, stupid, and estranged, all of it made me feel increasingly pessimistic and depressed. I was slipping deeper into myself and disconnecting further from life.

My parents watched me anxiously.

❋   ❋   ❋

A year earlier, on April 4, 1968, Martin Luther King Jr. was assassinated. I admired King's strength and pacifism. And he once said: "He who passively accepts evil is as much involved as he who helps to perpetrate it."

Not long after my conversation with the priest, a series of school incidents changed things for me. It started when I entered the boys' bathroom to find a punk from my remedial class pushing a smaller kid against the wall saying, "Eat it, or I'll smash your face in!"

The smaller kid, cowering in front of the punk, began eating a stick of chalk. Sudden rage rose within me, toward everyone, toward the whole rotten system I felt trapped in. I'd been bullied by Emerson and others. I'd been ignored and ridiculed for years. I'd seen kids and adults do mean things to each other for no reason, sometimes just for sport. Maybe something was fundamentally wrong with people, with human nature. Maybe I couldn't do anything to change that, but I could make this punk pay right now for his actions.

I went over and shoved him hard. He lost his balance and crashed into the steam heater. His head bleeding, he took off running. But I wasn't finished. I needed to teach the smaller kid a lesson. I glared at him, feeling a mixture of concern for his welfare and contempt for his lack of backbone. "Are you so scared of getting hit that you'll eat chalk?" I asked him. "Why don't you get pissed off and hit him back? Why don't you stand up for yourself?" Then I said, "Is this really so bad?" and gave him a hard slap upside his head. In that moment, I felt that kids who got bullied and didn't try to fight back were part of the problem. In my experience, it was the passivity that haunted you later; it was debilitating and shaming. Fighting back gave you dignity, even if you lost and got hurt. At least you had your pride and didn't have to live in shame and regret. Nobody should eat chalk.

Later that day, as I walked down the hall between classes, I saw the punk I'd shoved against the heater in the bathroom. As we passed each other, he struck me in the ribs with his books, knocking the wind out of me. I wanted to hit him, but I couldn't breathe. I tried to grab his collar, but the pain was so intense I had to let him go. I bent over, gasping, and put my hands on my thighs. I found out later he'd stuck a piece of wood from shop class in his books. I had three broken ribs.

During my next class, the principal called me into his office. As soon as I walked in, I could tell he was angry. He'd heard about the bullying incident in the bathroom, probably from the kid I'd protected and then slapped. The excruciating pain in my ribs made it hard to breath or stand up straight. He thought I was slouching disrespectfully. At one point, he got mad and started yelling in my face. He poked his finger in my chest just above my injured ribs. Instinctively, I shoved him back, and he went ballistic. He rushed at me, and I panicked and punched him in the face, shocking him and scaring me.

I was kicked out of school for two weeks, but I didn't care anymore. I'd had enough. Two weeks later, the day before I returned to school, I went to a gathering at a co-op house. For some of the older, more socially aware kids in the surrounding area, the co-op offered a refuge from racism and intolerance. I'd been hanging out with this expanded crowd. Most of them were a few years older than me. We'd sit around playing music, talking about the social and political issues of the day and our life struggles. Someone had some weed that night, and we smoked several joints. Drugs were just starting to creep into our scene, but none of us were regular users. I'd smoked weed for the first time at Circle Pines Camp when I was twelve. I didn't feel stoned then, just happier than usual. I'd concluded that weed could help me be happy, but I didn't try it again until I was fourteen. I smoked weed a few times since then, which gave me a certain status in the group. I felt a quiet pride at being accepted into a group of older kids I'd always admired.

The high I experienced that night was different than I'd felt before. Waves of euphoria washed over me. I felt incredibly happy, for no apparent reason. I hadn't felt this happy in a very long time. All evening I was smiling and laughing joyously.

I got home late, feeling fantastic. Everyone had gone to bed. At one point, I went into the bathroom and looked into the mirror. My face looked pasty and a little bit weird. Yet I looked happy! Looking at myself in the mirror, I recalled my promise to Joy not to make a decision about suicide from an unhappy place. I realized I might never feel this happy again. Maybe this was the best time to decide if I really wanted to live or die. Looking at my reflection, into my own eyes, I asked myself, "Do you still want to commit suicide?"

I thought about it for a moment and realized I really did want out of here. I didn't want to live my shitty life. I didn't want to return to the hell school had become for me. I didn't want to go through the ordeal of dying, but it seemed better than my probable future. It would be so much easier to end it now, to disappear and be done with it once and for all. Just thinking about it brought a profound sense of relief, a peace of mind. So I answered myself in the mirror, "Shit, yeah."

I meant it. I felt an assuredness, a confidence in my decision. I wasn't feeling sadness or self-pity, wasn't being reactive or trying to hurt anyone. It felt right. I was tired of the struggle. My future looked hopeless. I'd waited seven years. Now it was time. Joy was right. I was glad I'd waited for this moment. Everything had fallen into place. Strangely, one of the happiest moments of my life was the moment I chose to end it.

I went back to my room, looking forward to my death, but not looking forward to what I had to *do* in order to die. I went to the central air intake duct next to my room, reached into the inside corner and withdrew an old friend, the glass tube of mercury. I'd moved it through a series of hiding places over the years, because I feared my parents finding it and taking it from me. This thought always triggered anxiety in me, and I'd think, *Maybe I should take it right away.* Then I'd take it from its hiding place and swirl it around in the tube, just to look at it and make sure it was still there, to remind myself of my plan, and to make it real again. Each time I held the mercury, I felt a sobering chill; I was holding my death in my own hands. It made me feel alive and powerful.

Before taking the mercury, I needed the final ingredient: Valium. I walked softly across the house to the bathroom. There, in my parents' medicine cabinet, was a cardboard container stacked with rows of small drawers, each drawer labeled in pencil. I scanned the rows of drawers for one starting with the letter *V.* There weren't any! For a moment I thought I'd have to do this without Valium. Then I looked at some bottles off to the side, studying the labels carefully. One started with the letters *V-a-l.* I had to sound it out in my head a few times. This had to be it. I opened the bottle and poured all but a few of the tablets into my hand. There must have been forty or fifty, probably enough to kill me and at least enough to put me out so I wouldn't feel the pain from the mercury poisoning.

I snuck back to my room and closed the door. Holding the tube of mercury, I felt a thrill of anticipation. At long last, the moment had come. This was the most important, the most real thing I'd ever do. I removed the rubber stopper, poured some of the mercury into my cupped hand and gently rolled the heavy, quivering silver liquid from side to side. I couldn't take my eyes off it. It was cold and heavy as lead. I knew just holding it in my hand could make me sick. That didn't matter now. Holding my guaranteed death in the palm of my hand, I felt again the sense of power and control I'd felt when I first made the decision to kill myself seven years before.

Carefully, I put the mercury back into the glass tube and swirled it around in the bottom. It was alive. It was my friend. Its promise to me was godlike. Once I swallowed it, everything would change. My problems would be over. I would leave the earth. All I needed now was the courage to act.

But first, I had to think it through one last time. I had to be certain. My action would have real consequences. I wanted to make sure I understood all the implications, that this was what I really wanted to do. I didn't want to act now and then in the next moment be full of regrets—when it was too late. I paused to reflect for several moments. Finally, I was sure. I was ready.

First I swallowed a handful of Valium with water. I waited a few minutes. Then I picked up the test tube, swirling the mercury one more time. I felt a momentary sadness over the imminent loss of my family and friends. But the sense of anticipation in knowing I was about to be liberated from my life quickly returned.

I lifted the tube to my mouth, tipped it back, and emptied it. I'd always imagined holding it in my mouth and savoring it before swallowing, but there was no need to swallow, no effort required because gravity did the trick. I felt a momentary shock as the cold, liquid metal, as if of its own volition, rolled across my tongue and slipped down my throat. It seemed to know where it wanted to go to fulfill its predestined purpose. I felt the cool, heavy mercury slide all the way down to the bottom of my stomach. I swayed from side to side, and it rolled around in my belly, the way it had in the test tube.

It was done. I looked around my bedroom for the last time, at the desk lamp, the bookshelves, my stereo and the records I loved. Then, to make it all real, I said out loud, "I'm dead. It's just a matter of time." I was already feeling woozy from the effects of the Valium. I hoped I'd timed this right. I braced for a possibly violent, painful death to come.

Man, I thought. *What a fucking trip!*

6

Devil Eyes

Friday, April 6, 1969. I'm lying on my back. I'm weak, and my body feels unbelievably heavy. I smell antiseptic odors and hear people's indistinguishable mumblings and bustling about, the constant beeping of electronic machines, and other sounds I can't make out.

I can't open my eyes; my eyelids feel heavier than lead. I can't lift my head. Something like a seat belt is strapped across my forehead. My wrists are strapped down at my sides, with another strap across my chest, and my ankles are strapped down too. I barely manage to open my eyes. The light is harsh, and my vision is blurry. A pattern of small holes on a white surface comes into focus. I'm looking at white ceiling tiles and fluorescent lights.

I strain my neck, force my shoulders into the bed, and manage to raise my head just enough to make out my surroundings. I'm in a small curtained enclosure. Through the opening I see nurses moving around, scurrying back and forth. A couple of them are busy behind a tall desk in the area directly in front of me. I try to take it all in before my head falls back. I'm achy and exhausted, my mind in a fog. I don't know where I am or how I got here. I lie still, trying to make sense of what's going on. Then it hits me.

I'm in a hospital. Oh shit! I'm alive. It didn't work. What happened?

I experience a profound sinking feeling. Now I have to go back to my life and deal with the same crap, the same people, every minute of every day. I struggle to get up again. *Why am I strapped down?* I try pulling on one strap at a time, to see how strong they are. First I try to bend one leg, then the other, then my arms, then my chest, then my head again. Each time I pull or push I feel sharp pains around the straps. Now I push through the pain against my wrist straps, trying with all my strength to force myself into a sitting position. As I strain to get free, I feel an intense pressure in my eyes, as if they're about to burst. Frustrated and desperate, I begin flailing in slow motion, pulling weakly on all the straps in turn.

A nurse arrives at my bedside. She's tall, thin, black, fortyish, with a fluffy Afro. Her face has a worn look but a kind expression, as if she's seen tough times but managed not to become jaded or judgmental. I like her immediately. She puts her hand reassuringly on my chest.

"It's okay, honey; just lie there," she says. "You'll feel more like yourself in a little while, once the Valium you took wears off. You're going to be okay. Do you understand?"

I nod as much as the head restraint will allow.

"How old are you, hon?"

"Fourteen," I mumble hoarsely.

"Do you know what city we're in?"

I think about it for a second. "Chicago?"

"That's right. You're in the ICU at Cook County Hospital. They brought you in late last night. Are you ready to have a couple of visitors?"

I close my eyes without responding.

"Your mother will be right back. She's very worried about you. She went to pick up a change of clothes for you."

I shrug my shoulders.

"There's also a beautiful redheaded girl here to see you." She emphasizes the word *beautiful*, maybe to see if this will help cheer me up. "She says she's your girlfriend. She's under visiting age and not in your immediate family, but she seems to really care about you. She begged us to let her visit you. If you'd like, we can make an exception in her case."

I look up at her and pull against the wrist straps, a request for her to remove them. I wince at the hot sting of wrist burns. I'm beginning to feel pain all over my body, in my muscles, even in my bones. I wonder if it's mercury damage. *How can I still be alive?*

"Okay," she says. "But I need you to promise if I take off your restraints, you won't cause me any problems."

I nod, but her expression hardens, and she asks sternly, "Are you sure? You put up quite a fight earlier in the ambulance. You pulled out one of your ankle restraints. You pulled out of your wrist restraints twice and tore out the IV lines and the tubes they were using to pump your stomach. You also injured one of the officers who was with you. He had to go to the emergency room. I *really* need you to promise me. You need to say it."

"I promise," I say. It hurts to talk. My throat is raw and sore, and my voice sounds gravelly.

She pauses for a moment. Then her face relaxes, and her voice becomes nurturing again. "All right. I just wanted to make sure."

She unbuckles the strap across my forehead, then the straps holding down my ankles, then the strap across my chest. She pauses, a little uncertain, then says, "You be good now, okay?"

I nod, and she removes the straps holding down my wrists. "Okay, there you go."

What a relief to have those straps off! I start to move my arms and legs. My whole body feels sore and stiff. As I rub my wrist, the nurse pours me a small cup of water from a pitcher on a small table next to my bed and hands it to me. I drink it all. The cool water temporarily soothes my throat.

"How long am I going to be here?"

"We're not sure. I'll get someone to change your sheets. Your mother should be back any minute."

Two nurses in light blue pinstriped uniforms come in to change the sheets, damp from my wet clothes after I pulled out the IV. When I start to get up, the first nurse, about nineteen and kind of cute, smiles and says, "Stay there. Don't get up; you're still too groggy."

Usually I'd have enjoyed the attention, but I figure her smile is a smile of pity. I'm embarrassed to have a pretty girl see me like this. I'm finally coming out of the fog. The nurses finish changing the sheets. As they turn to leave, the second nurse says, "Your mother should be back any minute. She's been here for hours."

But I'm not ready to see her. How could I be ready? Last night I thought I'd never have to face her, or anybody else, ever again. I know

I've hurt her. There's nothing I can say or do to take away her pain. This is going to be hard. However bad things were before, I've made a worse mess of them now. I feel trapped and more hopeless than ever. Everything I do just makes things worse.

Now my mother walks into the room in a hurry, holding a paper bag. She looks exhausted, but there's no emotion on her face. Her clothes are rumpled. She hands the bag to the nurse, then goes to her knitting bag and stuffs her knitting inside. She must have been knitting beside me for hours, waiting for me to wake up. She avoids looking at me, scanning the room with a cool expression. Things are worse than I thought. I have a terrible feeling that she wants nothing to do with me. Pursing her lips, she says, in a dull monotone, "How are you doing, David?"

I don't know what to say, so I say nothing. Now she looks at me, but I avoid her gaze. "David, I asked you a question."

"I don't know."

It occurs to me that she's the staff psychologist for my school district. This has to be a professional and a personal blow for her. I stare down at the bed sheets, feeling like shit. I don't want to deal with this right now. I can't look at her. I wonder if I'll ever want to make eye contact with her again. I just want this to end. She finishes packing her bag and starts to leave.

"Joy is here to see you," she says. "I'll tell her you can see her now." She turns and leaves through the curtains, without our having made any eye contact.

I'm curious to know what's in the bag. The friendly nurse walks in, and I ask her.

"A change of clothes," she says.

That's right; the other nurse already told me. I'm still groggy. I close my eyes and wonder how this went so horribly wrong after years of planning. How did I botch this up? I'm alive, and things are worse than ever. I blew my one big chance.

I could never put my mother through that again. I didn't kill myself, but I've killed something in her. Nothing will ever be the same between us. I didn't mean to hurt her; I just wanted to stop the pain.

I feel betrayed by the mercury, my most trusted friend. All these years I'd depended on it. It had been with me, a part of me, for half of my life. Knowing it was there made life easier to bear. Then at the crucial moment, it let me down. I feel more alone than ever before.

Joy walks into the room, beautiful as always. Neither of us knows what to say. She gives me a big smile and blushes a little. I can tell she's feeling self-conscious.

"Hi, David," she says.

"Hi, Joy. You look great."

Reaching my bedside, she catches a better look at me. Her smile fades. Now she looks scared.

"Your eyes—they look creepy. I mean, *really* creepy."

"What do you mean?"

"The whites of your eyes are totally red. They look like they're bleeding."

"Bleeding?"

"They're bloody. Do they hurt?" She leans down for a closer look. I almost think she's going to try to touch one of them. "They make you look evil. Like the devil." She pulls away from me with a funny look.

Now I want a mirror to see what I look like. *I look like the devil?* Joy is a devout Christian. I wonder if my suicide attempt and my devil eyes will change the way she feels about me.

"They don't feel different," I say.

"Really?"

"Yeah, I'm fine. I'm sorry you have to be involved. Thanks for coming. It's good to see you."

"They're only letting me see you for a minute."

"I know."

"What's going to happen now?"

"I don't know. I didn't think it would go like this. I thought I'd be gone."

"Well, I'm glad you're here." She sounds concerned. "I mean . . . you know how I feel about this." She bends down, kisses me gently on the lips, and says, "I love you."

"Me too," I reply lamely.

"I'd better go."

She walks to the exit, turns to give me a little wave; then she's gone.

As soon as she's out of sight, I call to a passing nurse for a mirror. She brings me one, and I take a good look at my eyes. There's no white left in them; they're completely red. Joy was right. I do look scary. What was going to happen now? Everyone in my family will probably react differently. Mom is already emotionally distancing herself from me. I hope I haven't messed things up too bad with Dad. Neil is only ten. This must be hitting him hard. I don't think he'll be able to understand something like this, and I can't explain it to him. I'll try to make it up to him somehow. Emerson will probably have some goddamn opinion.

Now Mom returns and stands at the foot of my bed looking tired but determined. "David, you need to get dressed and get ready to go. I've got Neil with me. He's waiting alone in the car."

"I can just leave?"

"Yes, but we need to hurry."

She goes outside to wait. The Valium has mostly worn off. There must have been a lot left in my system after they pumped my stomach. I'm a little wobbly, but I feel stronger now. I get up and walk a few steps.

The friendly nurse returns, hands me the paper bag with my clothes, then asks in a whisper, "Why did you do it?"

It. I realize people don't want to say the words *kill yourself* or *suicide* to someone who's just attempted it.

"You have a wonderful family and a gorgeous girlfriend."

Her tone is almost chiding. I don't know what to tell her, so I just say, "I don't know."

It's complicated. There's no one reason. It's nobody's fault. My parents are wonderful people who did their best. All my life I've watched them agonize over how to help me. Now everything is so difficult and complicated. I can't untangle it, fix it, or sort it out. Suicide seemed such a simple solution.

Maybe I was born into the wrong family? Both my parents' families are well-educated overachievers: doctors, pharmacists, and lawyers. Every bit of wall space in our house—in the rooms, the halls, the closets, even my room—is lined with tall bookshelves filled with books. Those books have both fascinated and tormented me all my life.

I take off my dirty clothes, put on clean clothes, stuff my dirty T-shirt and jeans into the bag, and step through the curtains, where my mother is waiting.

"Okay," I say.

I follow her down the hallway to the elevators. She's walking fast. Outside the hospital, we slow down and walk to the car. Neil is waiting patiently in the front seat. He seems small and vulnerable. He looks at me, bewildered, as I climb into the back. Then he turns his head to peek at me over the front seat. It's like he's trying to figure out if the brother he's always known and loved is still here. He can't take his eyes off of my eyes. I must look like I've come back from the dead.

"Are they okay?" he asks.

"I think so," I tell him.

"Your brother is okay," Mom says curtly. "During the struggle last night, he broke blood vessels around the whites of his eyes. He'll look normal in a couple of weeks."

Mom has always talked to us like we're adults, but it's odd to hear her talk to Neil that way about this. On the drive, Neil never takes his eyes off me. He asks me occasional questions. Each time, Mom breaks in to answer, as if I'm not to talk to him directly. I stare at the back of her head as she drives. Her shoulders are stiff. She looks like she's barely holding it together. I've permanently broken her trust. It never occurred to me that I might live and have to face her like this.

I stare out the window at the passing trees, my mind full of questions I dare not ask. *Why aren't I dead? How did they find me?* My memories of last night after swallowing the mercury are hazy. I search my mind, and flashes come to me. I remember lying down with the Valium coming on. I have vague images of police coming into my bedroom and me flying into a rage. The last thing I recall was getting up from my bed and rushing at them, shouting, "What the fuck are you doing here? I'm going to kill you!" I wanted them out of my room. They weren't supposed to be there. A week before, I'd taken the train into Chicago to attend a peace rally. The police started clubbing the demonstrators, turning it into a riot. I got caught in the crowd and clubbed upside the head. The police entering my room triggered all my rage.

The nurse said I put a cop in the emergency room. I hope he's okay. He was trying to help me. But I can't ask my mom if he's okay. I can't ask her anything about last night—how she found me, why the mercury didn't work. I'll probably find out later, one way or another.

Now she makes an unexpected turn onto the Dan Ryan Expressway. This isn't the way home.

"Where are we going?" I'm a bit alarmed.

"I'm taking you to another hospital," she says matter-of-factly.

Her body is stiff, and her eyes are glued to the road. I bolt forward in the seat.

"What hospital?"

"Lake Forest."

My stomach sinks. Lake Forest is a mental hospital. I try to keep my voice calm, to control the rising panic.

"Why are you taking me there?"

Is she done with me? She warned me in second grade I might end up here. Was this it? I can't blame her. Her life would be so much easier without me. But I don't want to go.

"When someone has done what you've done, you have to be evaluated in a psychiatric hospital." Her voice is calm and flat; she's trying to be patient with me. "Besides, you injured a police officer last night. He agreed not to press charges if we had you committed for evaluation."

"For how long?"

"I'm not sure. It's a very good private hospital. A psychiatrist friend of mine has hospital privileges there. He can work with you as an inpatient. I'm working with him to get you out in two weeks, depending on how you do. Do you understand?"

"Not exactly." I slump back in the seat.

"The less trouble you are, the sooner you'll get out. It's up to you. If you have to be hospitalized for more than thirty days, our insurance may not cover the costs. That means you'll have to transfer to a public facility. I promise none of us wants that. I worked very hard to get you into this hospital, where I know someone. They'll be watching you closely. So, David, it's important that you. . ."

I tune her out, lost in my paranoid thoughts. *What if she isn't telling me everything? What if she's wrong about how long I'm going to be locked up? Who knows what will happen once I'm in? One slip, and I could be held there indefinitely. Maybe in a few years I'll be calling it home. I'd rather be dead.*

"What if I don't want to go there?" I ask.

"David, I'm not going to get into a fight with you if you refuse to go right now." She spoke fiercely, cutting to the point like cold steel. "But one way or another, you're going to end up in a hospital. You're very lucky. There's a waiting list here, and I was able to get you a bed. If you don't go here now under your own power, you'll be sent somewhere else later, maybe somewhere much worse. This is an expensive private hospital. Your best chance is to go in here now if you want to get out anytime soon."

I detect no empathy in her voice or manner. None. She's never spoken to me like this before or acted like she had to protect Neil from me. She's not just mad. It's more like she's written me off, like she's circling the wagons to protect the family, but I'm on the outside.

"Okay," I say.

I owe her at least that much. I've caused enough problems already. I think she still loves me, but I'm not sure she likes me anymore. Maybe I'm two different people to her now: the son she's always known and loved and the boy in the backseat who tried to kill her son. Right now, she's speaking to the killer.

My mother and I had lost something then. Something we'd never get back.

7

The Mental Hospital

Mom turned off the freeway. We drove through a housing development of new homes with newly mowed lawns and small trees in front. We passed several strip malls and eventually made a left turn into the hospital parking lot. The structure looked like any nondescript two-story office building.

In movies and TV shows, mental hospitals were usually old, Gothic-looking brick buildings with green lawns, sterile rooms, and hallways where insane patients sat catatonic, wandered about like aimless zombies, talked and gestured wildly to themselves or imaginary people, or erupted in random fits of violence. Men in white uniforms kept strict order, subduing unruly patients by tying them up in straitjackets, dragging them off to padded rooms, immobilizing them with powerful drugs, administering shock treatments or, worse, lobotomies.

Man, I really fucked this whole thing up!

My mind was full of questions. *What will happen now? In the next hour? The next day? The next week? How long will they keep me here? What kind of people will I meet? Will I have to return to my old life when I get out? What about school? What about clothes and toiletries?*

My mother pulled into the emergency ambulance bay at the back entrance. Before she even turned off the ignition, two large male orderlies in white uniforms appeared and stationed themselves on either side of our car. Both had crew cuts and looked like soldiers. This wasn't a movie. My fears were fast becoming reality. A woman in regular dress clothes stood in the entrance.

"Is that David?" she called out.

My mother didn't respond, didn't look up, didn't move. She

sat frozen, face forward, her hands on the wheel, her head bowed. I realized she was crying silently. All the fight drained from my body.

"Is that David?" the woman called out again, a little louder. Now the men made their move. One, a big guy with a small chin, stepped in to block the car door opposite me, in case I tried to use it to escape. The other guy, slightly smaller, opened my door and stood in the gap, waiting for me to get out. They clearly had this choreographed with military precision. Neither spoke, yet their bearing and impassive faces issued a clear warning: don't make trouble.

I got out. In a flash, the bigger man was around the car, and I was standing in between them. They didn't need to lay a hand on me; I went peacefully. As we passed through the entrance to the hospital, a nurse joined the rear of our parade. I turned my head to look back at her and saw a metallic object in her right hand. It was a large, old-fashioned stainless steel syringe with metal loops for finger grips— emergency backup in case I got out of control. I would see a lot more of that shiny syringe.

As they walked me through the building, I tried to guess which room was mine. What kind of people would be on my ward? Were there any patients like me who couldn't read? How many locked doors would stand between my room and freedom? How many patients were doomed to spend their lives here? How many had come for a temporary stay that became permanent?

As we approached a metal door with large hinges, the nurse stepped to the front, unlocked the door, and opened it. Suddenly I didn't want to go in. When that door closed behind us, I'd be locked in. I tried to turn around and look back, but firm hands grabbed me high under each arm and lifted me off the floor. I squirmed and resisted, but only my legs moved. The two orderlies carried me inside. I heard a loud *chuh-chunk* as the metal door closed and locked behind us. Then they lowered me to the ground, and we continued walking through the seemingly endless hallways.

I was paying close attention to everything. The doors were painted a 1950s avocado green, and the linoleum floor was dark and worn. I noted every turn in the hallways and every door, trying to memorize the path we were taking. I noted specific details and tried to visualize how it would look going in the opposite direction. We continued down a hallway through another locked door. The nurse opened it with a key, closed it behind us, and it locked automatically with the same disturbing *chuh-chunk* sound. Then we walked up a dim stairwell, went through another locked door. *Chuh-chunk.* Then down another hallway and through another locked door. *Chuh-chunk.* By now I'd given up trying to memorize the route. I'd never be able to remember my way out.

We arrived at a large main room with a nurse's station in the middle and two hallways extending off each end. Nurses moved busily around, and patients milled about randomly. The two orderlies released my arms as we passed through the nurses' station. We followed the nurse with the syringe down one of the hallways, finally arriving at a surprisingly bright second-story room. I looked around my room. *You fucking idiot*, I thought. I hated myself. I'd failed in everything I ever did. Now the biggest fuckup of my life had gotten me here, the last place in the world I ever wanted to be.

Two thick glass windows embedded with chicken wire faced a parking lot and the suburban view beyond. Two single beds rested against a wall in opposite corners. A lanky guy about eighteen, strikingly handsome, with long blond hair, followed us into the room. He seemed completely normal to me. He was my roommate, Philip. I wondered why he was here.

Next they took me to the main common room. We weren't allowed in our room during waking hours without supervision. I sat on a couch, contemplating the events of the last twenty-four hours. Finally, I was able to relax and accept my situation.

That night I lay awake for hours, unable to fall asleep. Something had changed in me. I'd faced my death. I'd acted to end my own life. I'd believed it was all over and accepted it. I'd crossed another line. I could feel it. I knew the difference between life and death. I could choose to live, or I could choose to die. It was up to me. All I had to do was decide and then act.

The fear of being hopelessly trapped, which had been with me for years, was gone. I felt a calm confidence. But I still needed to get out of here. The fear of ending up in a mental institution hadn't disappeared. Whatever I wanted to do about my life, I couldn't do it from in here.

Instinctively, I began considering again how I might kill myself when I got out. I began to plan my suicide in the far-off future. I picked the age of twenty-seven. If I didn't get my life together by then, it was pretty much over anyway. That would give me time to separate from everyone close to me, so they wouldn't be as affected. However I did it, I'd make it look like an accident, something like swerving off a cliff. But that was risky. I might survive the attempt and be crippled. Still, I had thirteen years to figure something out.

Resolving the problem, at least theoretically, gave me a sense of relief and a feeling of control over my life again. It also reminded me how badly I'd hurt the people I cared about. It brought up the question of whether my life even belonged to me. Did I owe it to others to stay alive even if I wanted to die? Should I sacrifice my happiness for the sake of others, living an unwanted life in a personal hell just to avoid hurting people who love me? Was my life even my own?

Lying there calmly, locked in a room in a mental hospital at the end of a series of hallways, behind a series of bolted doors, I wondered: *What is the purpose of my life? Of any life? Who am I? What am I? What in the hell is existence anyway?* I realized I didn't know. My parents and teachers, the doctors and experts I'd seen, the priest I'd talked to, none of them knew. They pretended to know. But nobody knew. These were total mysteries.

As I considered this, I felt my awareness shifting. *I had no idea who I was.* The fear and anger vibrating inside me for years, dissolved. I felt a pleasant sensation of energy radiating throughout my body. The constant mental chatter I'd always thought of as "me" subsided, and I fell into an awareness of a peaceful silence. I'd lost all control and along with it my desperate identification with my mind and its tortured thoughts. My hopes and desires for the future had been based on ideas—thoughts—that seemed to promise my only hope for survival. These hopes had been a result of my fears. My biggest fear from the age of seven was of being institutionalized. Now I'd realized my worst fear, yet I was left with a simple, grateful enjoyment of being and a loving desire to serve. I had no hope for the future, yet I felt a most unexpected sense of relief. Giving up hope wasn't a sad thing or a loss of anything. It was a relief. Hope was a burden that kept me living in the future, struggling for control, fighting situations beyond my control, trying to escape the painful sense of myself. But there was no escape until I gave up and let go.

A feeling of profound contentment and peace washed over me. I felt as if I was seeing things clearly for the first time in my life. Life suddenly seemed simple. I was still locked in the same room. I still had the same learning disabilities and the same human problems. I still had no skills to deal with my life and my future. The world was still the same crazy place where all the usual crap would continue. But now none of this bothered me. I no longer minded any of it. I was completely okay with things exactly as they were. I felt happy, free, contented. I felt as if I had come home. It occurred to me that I was in a mental hospital, and maybe I'd gone crazy—but even this thought didn't disturb my sense of peace. At last, I was able to fall asleep.

This experience was important to me. It was the first time in my life I felt truly happy in myself and as myself. This happiness wasn't dependent on weed, circumstances, relationships, things, or pleasing other people. Until now I had no idea this kind of happiness existed. This kind of happiness could make life worth living.

The next morning, Philip, my roommate, didn't get up with the wake-up call. When a nurse came in and found him still lying in bed, he threw a cup of water at her. To me, it seemed an annoying but harmless prank. But the nurse ran out and returned moments later with the metal syringe and two large orderlies. They grabbed Philip and held him down as he struggled and screamed, "No! I don't want to go! No! I'm sorry!"

It was too late. The nurse shot him up with whatever was in the syringe, and the orderlies dragged him out of bed, out of the room,

and down the hall. Philip's belongings remained in my room. I asked
the orderly if he'd be back and where they'd taken him. He said Philip
was in "isolation"—I later learned this meant a padded room—and
that he didn't know when he'd be back. I never saw Philip again. But
now I had a private room.

* * *

I could barely make out the garbled message over the intercom,
calling me to the nurses' station. Maybe I'd finally find out what was
going on. I'd been here a week now and hadn't yet met with the
doctor, hadn't been evaluated or given any information about my
situation. I'd had no communication from the outside world. And
no nurse or attendant I'd spoken to had any idea what was going to
happen to me.

When I got to the station, the nurse told me to go into the room
just off the common room to wait for the psychiatrist. It was a small
room. Two chairs faced each other in the middle, and two bad paint-
ings of flowers, probably done in art therapy by a patient, hung on
the walls. I sat down in a straight-back chair with a cloth covering. I
assumed the plush, high-back chair was the doctor's.

Over the course of the week, the calm, clear awareness that had
come over me the first night had slowly dissipated. But the fear and
rage hadn't returned. My past and future started to have meaning for
me again. My mood and state of mind were once again dependent on
my circumstances—which didn't look good.

I knew the psychiatrist would ask me about my suicide attempt.
I had to be very careful how I explained it to him and assure him I
didn't plan on any future attempts. I had to be 100 percent convincing
rather than 100 percent honest. You couldn't be honest in a place like
this, not if you hoped to get out.

A woman's long, shrill scream suddenly interrupted my thoughts.
It sounded like she was in pain. I knew all the screamers in this ward,
and this wasn't one of them. A few minutes later the psychiatrist, Dr.
Lahe, came into the room. He introduced himself, shook my hand,
and sat down in the opposite chair. Dr. Lahe was the person who'd

helped my mother get me into the hospital. They'd been fellow students and friends back in medical school. He had a rough complexion, like a blue-collar worker, but a friendly face and smile. He wore a black suit with his jacket unbuttoned and a white dress shirt with an open collar and no tie. His shirt wasn't completely tucked in all the way around. I liked him right away.

"Okay, David, I don't have much time, but I'd like to get a quick history."

"Who was screaming?" I asked him.

He shrugged, then opened the file on his lap, and started shuffling through the papers, which I assumed were about me.

"What do you want to know?" I asked.

"Well," he looked up at me, "have you ever seen a psychiatrist before?"

"Yeah. I saw one twice a week from the end of my first year of second grade until sixth grade."

"Do you know what for?" He pulled a sheet from my file.

"Sort of. They gave me an IQ test because I was flunking second grade. My mom said I got a really high score in abstract thinking but a really low score in linear thinking. They said such a big variation in IQ was very rare, and I must have psychological problems."

Dr. Lahe jotted a few notes as I spoke.

"You seem to know a lot about this," he said. "Do you recall what the test involved?"

"I've had tests of all kinds since I can remember. I think those were tests with cards and blocks—the little red and white ones. I was supposed to duplicate the patterns they showed me on the cards." I was feeling more relaxed but a bit impatient. "When am I going to get out of here?"

"Well, that's the question, isn't it?" he said. "That depends on how you do here in the hospital and how forthright you are with me now."

I nodded. I figured I needed to tell him just enough to persuade him I was being honest but not enough to get me into more trouble than I was already in.

"How am I doing so far?" I asked him.

"I don't know. You'd know better than me. How is it going?"

"It seems like things are going well. I feel okay. I haven't made any trouble. I just want to get out of here."

"Let's finish with your history." He opened his notebook to a fresh page. "What led up to your suicide attempt?"

"My whole life." It sounded like an exaggeration, but it wasn't.

"Why don't you start with what led up to your being kicked out of school. Tell me whatever you think is important."

I told Dr. Lahe how seeing the punk in the bathroom making the kid eat chalk filled me with rage, how the kid's fear and submissiveness tipped me over the edge, how I'd shoved the punk against the heater and slapped the kid upside his head, how the punk had broken my ribs in the hall and the principal had poked me there and it hurt so bad I couldn't breathe, and how I'd punched him and gotten kicked out of school for two weeks. Then I told Dr. Lahe what I'd told the priest in the church, about my fears of never having a normal life or being able to take care of myself, how the world seemed messed up and I couldn't change it, and how I was so tired and frustrated I didn't want to play its games.

I talked for several minutes. Dr. Lahe listened attentively and seemed interested in what I was saying. When I was finished, I looked at him to see if I was making sense and if he understood. He reached down into his briefcase and pulled out a cardboard pack of small cigars. Then he looked at me thoughtfully, extracting a cellophane-wrapped cigar from the pack.

"So you think things are hopeless?" he asked.

"Yeah, for me. Don't you?"

A series of three shrill screams sounded again outside the room. It was the same woman shouting, "No! No! No!" Dr. Lahe seemed a little annoyed as he carefully unwrapped his cigar.

"It doesn't matter what I believe," he said.

Now I thought he was being rude. I felt irritated.

"If you were honest with yourself, you'd see how hopeless my life is," I said.

I immediately regretted my words. I might have gone too far. I didn't want to sound depressed or suicidal. I wanted to see if he could help me, but I didn't want to have to stay here for long.

Dr. Lahe lit the cigar, took a long drag, leaned back, and exhaled the smoke toward the ceiling in a fast-moving stream that gathered into a large cloud above my head. Then he looked at me expectantly, waiting for me to continue. He held up his cigar and asked, "Is this a problem?"

I shrugged. "I guess not." It wasn't true—I hated tobacco smoke. My face must have given me away.

"Do you smoke?" he asked.

"No."

"Your brother told your mother you smoke marijuana."

I shrugged again.

"So you just don't smoke cigarettes?"

"Never tried one. The smell of them makes me sick. I've never tried coffee either. And I don't like alcohol."

He tipped his head to the side as if he was thinking and waited for me to continue.

"When I go back to school, it's going to be worse than ever," I said.

Dr. Lahe silently puffed on his cigar, watching me, listening with interest.

"Everyone else gets to have a normal life," I continued.

"So how does that make you feel?"

"Like I'm being punished. Sometimes I wish I was too stupid to understand my situation."

"Your mother told me you have learning disabilities—difficulty reading, things like that. Do you think that means you can't have a normal life?"

"It has so far," I said. Suddenly I felt a lump in my throat. Tears welled in my eyes. I didn't want to do that here.

"What's your worst fear?" he asked.

"That I'll end up here, permanently. That's what my mom told me when I was seven, when they still kept 'retarded' people in these places."

"Is that when you started thinking about suicide?"

"Yeah. That's when I got the mercury ready. Suicide's been in the back of my mind ever since. I still can't figure out why it didn't work. It's supposed to be poison, and it seemed like I took a lot."

"There are different kinds of mercury," Dr. Lahe said. "Liquid mercury is too dense to dissolve in the bloodstream. If they hadn't pumped your stomach, it would've passed right through you."

"Oh . . ." All those years planning to kill myself, hiding the mercury in various places, and it wasn't even dangerous. I felt like an idiot.

"Do you think you'll ever try something like this again?"

"No fucking way," I lied. "It just hurts the people I care about. I didn't realize what it would do to them." As stupid as it sounded, it was actually the truth. He seemed to accept it.

"Well, David, our time's up," he said. "I have to see another patient now. We'll talk again soon."

"Sure."

I got up and headed for the door. On my way out, I heard the lady scream again. The sound was coming from the other side of the door to the left of the common meeting room. I'd learn that was the ward with the padded isolation rooms where Philip went, the place no one wanted to go.

8

Is This It?

I sat on the couch in the recreation room with the other regulars. My mind was in chaos, and I was grateful for the company and the constant blaring of the TV. The medication they made me take each day didn't seem to do much. I didn't know what it was, and the staff wouldn't tell me. They weren't uppers or downers. Meanwhile, the slow passing of time wore away the profound clarity and peace of mind I'd felt my first night.

I wanted to get high, but it wasn't an option. I tried to trade my meds for some of the other patient's meds, but they apparently knew what I was taking and no one wanted any of it.

The worst part was being kept in the dark about how long I'd be here, not knowing when or if I'd ever get out. Except for the pills and the brief visit with Dr. Lahe, I'd received no treatment of any kind. My experience was one of nonstop boredom, with rare moments of over-the-top excitement when someone acted out unexpectedly and got dragged away by the staff.

Other than Philip, whom I hadn't seen since he'd been dragged away, no other teens lived on my ward; it was mostly the zombie and shock-treatment types. But there were two older teens in the art therapy class I attended twice a week. I tried hanging out with these two druggies, thinking we had something in common, that they'd be more sane and cooler than the other patients. But we had almost nothing in common. They had no social or political awareness and no interest in meaningful conversation. Their shared big thrill was sniffing lighter fluid in the music room.

With nothing to do, I spent much of my time playing with a deck of cards, teaching myself to shuffle. I found mindless shuffling soothing. Philip never returned. I assumed he was in solitary in some padded cell. At least I had a room to myself.

A few of the patients were fine to hang out with, but most of them really were too crazy to talk to. I knew I was screwed up, but I wasn't insane, at least not the way they were. Some patients were here to get clean and sober from drugs or alcohol, and some were here because they were truly crazy. It wasn't easy to tell the difference. Some patients seemed perfectly sane for days at a time, then went suddenly and completely nuts. It seemed to occur in cycles. Everyone there was unpredictable. They were all interesting.

Rosie, a woman in her early thirties who looked like a normal housewife, had been sent there for violently attacking her husband. She seemed sorry for whatever she'd done to him. I never learned what it was, but it was serious enough to land her in a mental institution. I couldn't understand why her husband would let her attack him. I figured he must be a weak guy. Rosie didn't look that strong.

Things picked up for me when Sheryl, a cute girl a little older than me, transferred to my ward. She'd been in a while and knew the ropes. She seemed nice, and we flirted a bit. One afternoon she invited me to sneak off with her. I followed her through the halls to an out-of-the-way bathroom. She climbed into the bathtub, lay down on a towel, and invited me to join her. We stopped just short of having sex. We fooled around a little more over the next few days. I wished I hadn't. When I told her I might be leaving, she started following me everywhere, constantly watching me. It was nerve-racking. I was afraid she'd tell someone we'd fooled around, and I wouldn't be released.

Sheryl was more messed up than I realized. I didn't judge her; I was in the same mental institution for attempted suicide. But I was now in a big dilemma about girls. After my suicide attempt, I knew I couldn't be with normal, sweet girls with suburban expectations any-more—like Joy—but only be with someone as damaged as I was.

Joy loved me, but she thought I was going to hell for not believing in Jesus. It broke my heart. Why did people cling to dogmatic beliefs in fear instead of trusting what their hearts told be true about others? I'd suffered this my whole life. No one in my life fully accepted the fact that I lacked the skills to function in their world. They weren't helping me by denying my reality and offering me false hopes. They were judging me falsely.

My decision to commit suicide reflected my clarity that I'd rather die than become the person I'd have to be in order to survive in the world I was being forced to live in. To survive, I'd have to become a person no one would like. I'd have to live on the fringes of society. Who knew how far I'd have to go? I'd become a criminal out of sheer necessity, and the people who wanted me to live would think I had chosen to become such a person. That hurt the most. The person I would have liked and hoped to become died when I attempted suicide. Now, if I were ever going to have a girlfriend, it would have to be someone who was as damaged as I was. Of course, I couldn't tell any of this to Dr. Lahe.

I was still waiting for my second visit with Dr. Lahe to find out what was going on. I'd had no contact with him after our first session. I had no idea what his assessment of me was or when I might be able to go home. I thought maybe I'd blown it by being so candid with him. Finally, two weeks into my stay, I was called in to see him again. I knew I had to be more careful about what I said this time. He started the session by talking about my relationship with Emerson.

"Your mother tells me you and your older brother don't get along at all," he said. "In fact, she said your fights get pretty awful."

"Yeah, we don't get along." I was trying to play my cards close to my chest, but I'd never been good at that. Soon I was telling him everything about Emerson and me, even how I'd almost killed Emerson with the screwdriver. "That scared me," I said.

Dr. Lahe looked at me calmly, smoking one of his little cigars. "You mean almost killing your brother?"

"Yeah. I can't believe how hard I threw it. I felt like I'd crossed a line and could never go back."

"Everyone can be pushed too far, David. It's good that it scared you. It tells me you're not a sociopath."

It was a huge relief to hear that. That was my secret fear. "It's weird," I said. "I hate Emerson and I'm afraid of him, but I envy him too. He knows all about music, books, TV shows—everything. He's really smart. He understands the world and how it works in ways I never will."

"So, you admire him?"

"I guess, in a way. But it's mixed. I hate people like Emerson who are all about themselves and hurt other people, but I envy them because they can fit in and pass tests and get ahead in life. They're one of the reasons I wanted to check out . . . you know, permanently. But now Emerson admires me."

"How is that?" Dr. Lahe's interest perked up.

"He told me that until a few years ago he didn't think of me as human. Now he thinks I'm cool because I smoked dope and I've had more experience with girls than him. He treats me almost . . . I don't know . . . with respect."

"So what are you going to do when you go back to school?"

Back to school? It sounded as if I might be getting out of here after all. Dr. Lahe hadn't mentioned Sheryl, so he probably didn't know about her and me. I hoped he wouldn't find out before they let me out.

"I don't know. I'm not going to do any better academically. I've tried as hard as I can, and I still never learn. I guess I've got to get tougher. I'll probably have to survive in the streets."

"Do you think being tough is helping you or hindering you?"

"I don't know. Probably both. If you're not tough, you get taken advantage of. You've got to be able to take care of yourself. But some people start thinking you're a troublemaker. Like my principal. But I'm not a troublemaker."

Dr. Lahe puffed thoughtfully on his cigar. I could tell he was listening. I decided to ask the main question on my mind.

"When do you think I'll get out of here?"

"Do you still want to commit suicide?"

"No."

"Good, because you're going home now. I wanted to talk to you once more to get a sense of how you're doing. I think you're ready. Your father is waiting out front. The staff has already packed your things. Good luck, David." Dr. Lahe sat up straight and tamped his cigar out in the ashtray on the table.

The session was over. I was in shock. I was glad to be getting out, but I didn't feel especially prepared to go back into the world. Other than two sessions with Dr. Lahe, I hadn't gotten any real help here. I'd been warehoused for two weeks. One thing I did get was an absolute commitment to never set foot in a place like this again.

As I left the little office, I saw my dad in his work suit, standing by the nurses' station chatting with the nurses. He was handsome, about five feet seven, with jet-black hair, and a bit of a belly. With freedom so close, I suddenly felt desperate to get out of there. As I went up to him, he turned and gave me a serious look, but he was truly happy to see me. I was so happy to see him.

"Hi, Dad."

"Hi, David," he held up a bag. "I'm taking you home." A white-uniformed orderly led us silently through the labyrinth of hallways and locked doors to the exit. I stepped out into the sunlight.

I hadn't seen or talked to my Dad since "the event" that had changed everything. Mom had changed, treating me like I wasn't me anymore. I didn't know if Dad would be the same. The whole time in the hospital I worried about how he'd be when I saw him. Was he angry, disappointed, hurt? Was he tired of me and my problems? Was he done with me? Had he written me off as a hopeless case? I didn't know. As we walked silently to the car, the tension was palpable. We got into the car and both opened our windows. Dad was looking out, straight ahead, at the sunny suburban landscape.

"Wow," he said, "what a beautiful day." He sat for a moment, not moving; he had a special way of relieving the discomfort in almost any situation. Then he turned to me. "How are you doing?"

"I don't know. Okay, I guess."

His simple warmth was reassuring. It was just like him.

"I'm glad to have you back and coming home." He paused and said, "Your mother and I want to help you, but we don't know how. We need your help, David. You're going to have to tell us what you need."

I think I was in shock. The idea of having to face everyone after what I'd done and all the trouble I'd caused felt overwhelming. Other than that, I didn't really know what I was feeling.

"Okay, I'll try." I paused. "I'm sorry."

Turning back to start the car, he said, in the way I loved about him, "That looks like a fun place, but how about we do all we can to keep you out of there?"

* * *

It was good to get out and go home. I felt shaky and very disoriented at first. Returning home from the hospital took adjusting. I noticed my family and friends watching me to see how I was doing. Attempting suicide had changed things in me and in the people around me. No one knew how to act around me. They seemed both cautious and unusually attentive, as if they wanted to help but were afraid to set me off. I didn't want to deal with people. I spent most of my time alone in my room listening to music. But I did hang out with my old friends after they got out of school.

I felt stuck. The knowledge that I had no future was like a cloud hanging over my head. But for now I wasn't in school, and nothing was required of me. This was a huge relief. I started living in the moment with no plans or consideration for the future. I wanted to see if I could be happy right now, the way I'd felt that first night in the hospital. If I could just do that, then I'd see if it could become something more. This was a newfound freedom after spending years fighting against a world that seemed reluctant to accept me and make room for me.

I felt very uneasy about returning to school and to life without my closest friend, liquid mercury. I was afraid the other kids would look down on me as a pathetic loser or avoid me out of awkwardness, pity, or fear. The school recommended home tutoring. That seemed the simplest solution. My parents didn't want me to be under any pressure; they just wanted me to be safe and happy. I didn't want to go back and face my peers after my failed suicide attempt. How pathetic to screw up your own suicide!

Although I was going to be home-schooled, I couldn't hide out at home like a coward. I knew I had to go back. It was part personal pride and part morbid curiosity. I had to find out what people thought of me, what they were saying about me. If I didn't go back, people would think I was just a crazy loser kid who'd tried to kill himself and was put in a mental institution. I was afraid I might begin to think that myself.

But another, more compelling part was a desire to face my fears. Most of my life I'd felt compelled to face my fears, including the fear of intense pain. At eleven, I'd slid into a pane of glass, severing the muscle in the front of my thigh, which pulled back like a snapped rubber band, revealing the bone underneath. I was bleeding profusely, and the pain began to overwhelm me. Despite the intense pain and fear, I couldn't stop staring at the bone. I reached in, grabbed it, and shook it, as if I could conquer the pain that way. Now, returning to school and the circumstances that drove me to suicide, felt similar to my reaction to that childhood injury. So I told my mother I wanted to go back to school.

When I finally went back, I acted as if nothing had happened, as if I didn't have a care in the world. But word had gotten out. Everyone knew I'd done drugs, tried to kill myself, and been put in a mental institution. Kids turned to stare at me when I walked through the hallway. My fears of being shunned, ignored, or pitied turned out quite the opposite. People thought I was cool! I was a topic of gossip. The fact that I'd been struggling at the bottom of the remedial class didn't matter. Suddenly I had a reputation. Everything about me now fit my new image. I was a co-op kid; that made me a radical. I was a fighter; that made me tough. I had long hair; that made me a "freak." I was the only known drug user; that made me an outlaw. Even my lack of social skills didn't matter. It was all part of my new, strange antihero mystique. Now I got invited to parties I wouldn't have been invited to before.

More surprising, I was suddenly a girl magnet. Girls who'd never looked at me now came up to me to talk and to flirt. They wanted to be with me. They even came to my front door to meet me. Hanging out with me, a supposedly desperate and dangerous character, apparently granted them a kind of rebel status. It bothered me, but I liked the attention.

Even kids from other schools had heard about me. One night at a friend's house, I was introduced to a high school kid I'd never met. He gave me a look and said, "Oh, you're David Patten?" He was impressed. That happened several times. I got a kick out of it, but it made me distrust people. If I hadn't tried to kill myself, they wouldn't have been interested in me or have wanted to hang out with me. Who I really was didn't actually matter to them. I was the druggy, dangerous suicide kid. I didn't get the glamour of it. To highlight the absurdity, one kid who'd been declaring he was going to commit suicide now resented me, as if I'd stolen his thunder.

The social scene at school and my dubious antihero status got old fast. Also, I couldn't stand the manipulation and deception going on constantly among the most popular kids. I couldn't play the game. I'd spend all day Sunday dreading school on Monday, sometimes throwing up from the anticipation. I finally decided I'd rather be home tutored after all. My mother contacted the school and made the arrangements. No doubt the school principal was relieved.

Though I felt more isolated than ever, I became more decisive and self-directed and felt a new sense of urgency and energy. I wasn't in constant rage anymore. But I was still mad at the world and its intolerance of me, so I wanted to find intolerance and fight it wherever I could. I wanted to do new things, to experience more. I wanted to get stoned more. I wanted to hang out with people who talked about important things, who were more political and passionate about what really mattered in life. Having been raised in the co-op, I was already politically aware. And it was 1969. The Vietnam War had united my generation in opposition to war. The Civil Rights Movement had exposed the brutal oppression of millions of American citizens of color and given us a model of courageous rebellion against hypocrisy and injustice. Rock music, weed, LSD, the assassinations of the Kennedys and Martin Luther King Jr. had radicalized, redefined, and disillusioned the values of my generation.

Being home tutored and no longer in school, I let my hair grow down near the middle of my back. Even high school kids in Chicago had a dress code. I was one of few kids with such long hair, who could dress however they wanted. I was still smaller than average, but I seemed confident and older than my age. This enabled me to get into nightclubs most high school seniors couldn't get into.

I still rode the trains into the city to see Robert and my circle of Chicago friends. They knew nothing of my suicide attempt, so I didn't have to deal with weird reactions from them. I'd cooled my contact with Joy after coming home. We were still friends, but she was no longer my girlfriend. We rarely talked. I still hung out with the old crowd. The ones I'd gotten high with the night I took the mercury were three or four years older than me and had known me most of my life. Some of them had been Emerson's friends, but Emerson had gone off to college. Despite our age difference, they welcomed me into the group and accepted me for who I was.

We hung out, got drunk and stoned together, talked, and listened to music. Getting high was our ritual and an important part of our friendship. We did a lot of weed, acid, and mescaline together. We'd stay up all night talking about life, the war, music, politics, and how we thought the world should be. We were rejecting the world around us and embracing a new world with different values, one that included drugs, music, and altered perceptions.

Many of my peers and friends were open, curious, thoughtful people who never did drugs. There was no peer pressure in my crowd to get high. Yet drugs seemed to make it easier to connect at deeper levels. Some of us who got stoned became more open and real. At times, our minds opened and our awareness expanded in remarkable ways. But the positive effect faded in those who used drugs frequently, to be replaced over time by a dulling of awareness, a sapping of motivation, and a disintegration of their personalities. It was a lesson I would learn at great cost.

Drugs were still hard to come by in the suburbs. Since I could score through my Chicago connections, I became the main supplier for my crowd. This gave me a new kind of status. I'd take the train to

Chicago's South Side, score some weed, acid, or mescaline, and take the train home again. Sometimes friends drove me there to score. My transition from drug user to dealer happened the way my candy business did in fourth grade: as favors to friends. Word gradually spread that I was a reliable source of quality weed. More people started coming to me, begging me to score for them. I did, reluctantly at first, mostly as favors. Then I thought since I was taking a risk, I might as well make a profit. Soon I was doing a brisk, profitable business. It was the cinnamon-toothpick model all over again. At fifteen, I was buying two kilos a month. By age seventeen, I'd be buying twenty-five pounds at a time.

I was smoking a lot of weed and enjoying the company of my friends, but the joyous high I'd experienced on the night of my attempted suicide was a one-time deal. Now, getting high was just a temporary relief from unhappiness, a distraction from my fucked-up life and my fucked-up mind. I knew I was killing time, but what else was I going to do? When the high faded, I was the same anxious, pessimistic, unhappy person. The habit became a way of life and finally a trap it would take me years to get out of. I'd learn the hard way that habits are deceptively easy to start and nearly impossible to escape. Meanwhile, my future looked as bleak as ever.

9

Central Y

At fifteen, my parents started giving me a monthly living allowance, a family tradition designed to teach us kids responsibility with money. Once it started, we had to buy our own clothes, school supplies, and other basic necessities. If we went broke before the end of the month, we experienced the consequences of poor money management.

I bought school supplies and other necessities, but not new clothes, which felt uncomfortable. I wore my old clothes until they fell apart or no longer fit, which my parents didn't like. Any money left over at the end of the month I put in my safe for the future. As clothes were the primary expense, I tended to have a lot of money left over. My parents finally decided I wasn't ready for the responsibility, and the allowance stopped. But I'd soon be making more money than they'd ever give me.

I still noticed the impact of my suicide attempt on my relationship with my parents. My mother was very concerned about me and my education, and very reserved with me. My joking relationship with my dad returned, but it wasn't the same.

My academic difficulties in school persisted. I decided to take the school district up on its offer to pay for private tutoring. They didn't want me back in school any more than I wanted to be there. They hired a woman to come in and work with me a few hours a day, five days a week. She covered the required material and quizzed me orally. There was no reading. After several months of tutoring, I passed the eighth grade through oral exams.

I received my eighth-grade diploma in the mail that summer and immediately enrolled in summer school at Chicago's Central YMCA

High School to get an early start on my freshman year. Central Y was a continuation school designed to teach students enough basics to graduate from high school. Located in the financial district in the Chicago Loop, it seemed the right fit for me. Classes ran year-round, and by attending the full schedule, I could graduate in three years instead of four. That was my plan.

I had to get to and from Central Y on my own via the Northwestern Train System. I took the morning train in, went to classes, and took the train home at the end of each day. I knew the days of the week and most of the months of the year, just not always in order and not always in real time. This caused me a few logistical problems.

Central Y, partially funded by a federal government project, was part of a concerted federal effort to deal with an overwhelming and growing gang problem. It was designed to help gang kids and other troubled youth get their high school diplomas, get back on track, and gain a foothold in the "legitimate" world. Many of the students had done time in juvenile hall or jail. Some were on probation. Many came straight out of Charlietown, the infamous juvenile detention center in St. Charles, Illinois.

The local Chicago community was proud of Central Y for the educational opportunity it offered underprivileged, marginalized kids. It was a noble idea, a last-chance school for kids who couldn't fit in or were too dangerous to put in the normal public school system. This mix of underprivileged juvenile delinquents, criminal misfits, drug addicts, and undiagnosed learning-disabled or psychologically borderline kids made Central Y a risky venture. Some took full advantage of the opportunity. Many didn't. The odds were against them, and the predictable failures far outnumbered the worthwhile successes.

Most of the students were from poor, crime-ridden neighborhoods and broken or extremely dysfunctional families marred by alcoholism, addiction, abuse, or neglect. Gang members from different tribes or factions comprised much of the student body. Unspoken rules and protocols governed interactions between groups, with racial tension simmering at the core of it all. It was the era of the Black Panthers, the Nation of Islam, the Black Power movement, and the

Watts race riots in Los Angeles. Between classes, the halls of Central Y were a sea of bright colors, long leather coats, bulging Afros, pimp hats, and black berets bobbing to a strut-and-bounce walk.

The YMCA owned the building and rented four floors to the school. One classroom was on the first floor, the rest were on the tenth and eleventh floors, with the cafeteria on the fourth floor. The rest was YMCA and YMCA office space, so there were a lot of "suits" in the building.

On one of my first days at school, a white kid sitting next to me in class warned me to use only the main elevators and to avoid the back stairways and back elevators. From the way he said it, I think he was mugged there. I soon learned that the front stairs were rarely used and the hallways, and even the classrooms, could be dangerous.

An unspoken rule was that whites could use the school cafeteria from noon to twelve thirty, and then we had to clear out. The rest of the time was for blacks only. By the time we got our sandwiches and drinks, it was often a quarter past twelve or later, so we rarely went. We'd bring lunch or buy food and eat outside in the street. In winter, we ate in Chicago's subterranean maze of tunnels, basements, and stairwells.

At that time, well-organized youth gangs, like the Chicago South Side's Blackstone Rangers, were escalating in most major cities. The Blackstone Rangers comprised Central Y's largest group. In their prime, they were the largest gang in the United States, estimated to be ten times larger than the Chicago police force. They were a major problem for Chicago and a large part of the student population of Central Y. Gangs were a source of stress and fear for kids like me who were not affiliated with a gang and therefore unprotected. Nonaffiliated kids included loners; longhaired counterculture, often politically radical rebels; and "freaks" like myself who liked to listen to music and get high.

Another force in Central Y was the Black Coalition. The coalition wasn't a gang but a student group formed to address race issues in school. The syndicate kids, with short, greased-back hair and black leather jackets, also were not to be messed with. Many were full-fledged criminals, more eager to graduate into the Chicago Italian syndicate than to get a high school diploma. One top "connected" kid was the son of a major syndicate figure from Chicago's North Side. His father hired him a personal bodyguard, a Blackstone Ranger called Chappy, a fierce-looking giant in his late teens, about six feet ten, weighing several hundred pounds. Chappy escorted him everywhere and sat beside him during classes. I never figured out how, given the racial tension, a Blackstone Ranger ended up a bodyguard for a white syndicate kid. The grapevine said there was some kind of political arrangement between adults of the two groups.

Mutual understandings between black and white gangs kept a measured peace between them, allowing them to operate their various criminal enterprises—drug dealing, burglary, fencing, robbery—without going to war with one another. Chicago's defining characteristic—in politics and crime—was tightly run, strictly enforced hierarchical organization. That was apparent even at Central Y, where the major Chicago syndicates mentored their protégés. Central Y, the educational bottom of the public school system, was a graduate school for future criminals and gang leaders. There was no place lower I could go. I figured if I survived in this world, I could survive almost anywhere.

Most Central Y students were older than average high school age, with the majority between seventeen and twenty, and a fraction in their mid to late twenties and early thirties. The older students tended to be more serious about getting high school diplomas. Some of the white kids were from working-class immigrant families, including second- and third-generation Russian, Polish, and Irish kids. I was shocked to learn that some of my new schoolmates lived in areas of the city like Polack Hill, so poor their houses had no indoor plumbing.

There were foreign students too, who'd come to America to find a better life. I got to know one guy, a political refugee from Guatemala, who'd come to the U.S. through Amnesty International. Almost thirty, he'd been imprisoned and tortured by the Guatemalan government for alleged communist activities, which meant anything from political dissent to being in the wrong place at the wrong time. He had ugly scars on his face from being tortured. He told me how government death squads had tortured and "disappeared" thousands of citizens, mostly peasants and laborers, and how the urban poor lived in tin-and-cardboard houses.

Being young, white, short, Jewish, and suburban made me a natural target for a host of unsavory Central Y characters. With only a handful of whites in school, I had no natural allies, so I did everything I could to fit in and look tough. It was a very different world from the co-op community I'd been raised in but still preferable to my previous school situation. Central Y was more honest, and my lack of sophisticated social skills didn't present the same problems. Students were more real because their problems were more real. We didn't pretend to like each other here. When someone said he was going to kill you, he meant it. There was nothing to decipher or decode. In confrontational situations, my bluntness and tendency to say what I thought without the normal filters worked in my favor.

As dangerous as it was, I felt less threatened than I had at regular school. I no longer experienced the dread-filled Sunday nights, and I walked through the halls on Monday without feeling the tightness in my chest. I'd always heard that fearful people became easy prey because they showed their weakness. That wasn't true here. Fearful people were targets, but more because they couldn't be trusted and were unpredictable. They might do anything—stab you in the back, rat you out, or explode in your face. They were targeted because they were cowards. I was scared, but I could stand up to a threat and back it up with action.

Central Y's plainclothes armed security guards were off-duty police officers, intimidating and tough moonlighting members of "King Richard" Daley's infamous Blue Knights. They patrolled the halls with holstered guns, the safeties always off, and with handcuffs dangling from their belts. You could tell they trusted only one another. Given the environment, you couldn't blame them.

These were tense, politically polarized times. Chicago was a hotbed of political dissent, with antiwar protests going on for several years. The riots at the Chicago Democratic Convention in August 1968 were a recent and vivid memory. Mayor Daley, notoriously authoritarian and intolerant of dissent, ruled the city with an iron hand. The hair-trigger Chicago police, quick to use their clubs and draw their guns, had a fondness for tear gas. The air was frequently thick with "Chicago cologne."

The infamous Chicago Seven Trial was a current event, with daily protests held outside the courthouse, not far from Central Y. Some of us freaks went there on our lunch break to watch the protests. After the announcement that American war casualties had exceeded thirty thousand, Mayor Daley put twelve thousand police officers on twelve-hour shifts to deal with escalating protests.

I attended many antiwar protests, put up posters announcing marches, led chants, and saw many riots. On several occasions I ran with tear-gassed crowds from the cops, and twice I was among those caught and clubbed. I hated the police and the brutality they represented, and I hated the Vietnam War and all it stood for.

I also attended meetings of the Students for a Democratic Society, otherwise known as SDS, and participated in their nonviolent protests. I stopped going after the Weathermen came on the scene; they started disrupting meetings and actively provoking police to violence at peace demonstrations. Their violent philosophy and tactics, even against peaceful protesters, enraged me. My politically aware circle of friends felt the Weathermen were turning the public against the antiwar movement by linking it to violence and anarchy. I'd been in many school fights, but politically I was a pacifist.

❋ ❋ ❋

I didn't have to go to political protests to find violence and anarchy. At Central Y, anything could happen anytime and anyplace. You were only safe within sight of one of the armed security guards. Even the "suits" who worked on the other floors were occasionally mugged by Central Y students.

It took time to learn the rules at Central Y. I'd grown up in an interracial community with no racial tension and virtually no crime, where, with few exceptions, everyone trusted one another and got along together. But none of that had any value here. What prepared me for this new environment were my fighting skills and feral instincts, my experiences riding the trains into Chicago, and my familiarity with drugs.

Until now, drug dealing consisted of buying ounces of weed as favors for friends. Now, people with major drug and organized crime connections surrounded me. Sensing opportunity, I quickly found my way to the dealers. I only bought from those I thought could be friends. This strategy took discipline and limited my contacts and opportunities, but it kept me from getting busted or ripped off. At the end of the first week of that summer semester, I scored two thousand Dexedrine tabs—Mother's Little Helpers—standard housewife-prescription speed, considered nonaddictive at the time.

One Friday afternoon, I took the tenth-floor stairway to my next class on the eleventh floor. I always carried a switchblade in a long, thin pocket that a friend had sewn into the right knee of my pants. If I fully bent my knee, the tip popped up for easy access. I also carried a leather pouch with six 35 mm rolls of film on my belt. I was an amateur photographer with a darkroom at home, but these film rolls weren't for taking pictures. I'd devised a foolproof method for stashing dope. I cut the tails off the rolls before developing the negatives, then taped them jutting out from inside the empty rolls so they looked like new rolls. Each roll in my pouch contained ten to twenty hits of speed. It worked in the field. More than once while hanging out with friends on the South Side, cops had shoved us against a wall and searched us all. They never checked the fake film rolls.

Now, rounding the halfway curve between the tenth and eleventh floors, I looked up and saw three black guys waiting on the upper landing. They looked right at me, like they were waiting for me. I immediately stopped. I knew right away I was in trouble. The guy in front wore a loud yellow button-up shirt. The guy next to him wore a thick gold chain around his neck.

As they started down the stairs toward me, I turned and ran, taking two steps at a time. Before I reached the tenth-floor landing, the door opened and two more black guys with conked hair entered the stairwell. They saw me and started toward me. I backed up a few steps and stopped, holding on to the banister so I could see both ways. Now Yellow Shirt and Gold Chain came rushing around the stairway with the third guy right behind them. Gold Chain, a tall, sullen-faced guy a few years older than me, reached me first. He grabbed my arm in a firm grip. He looked really familiar. Then I recognized him from first-period English Lit class. We'd never exchanged a glance until now. But he clearly knew who I was. Now Yellow Shirt, also several years older and several inches taller than me, was standing in front of me. He leaned down right in my face.

"What d'ya got?" he demanded, almost casually.

"What do you mean?" I gave a puzzled look.

His cold eyes fixed me with unnerving intensity. Without warning, he palmed me hard in the chest, knocking me back against the banister.

"Don't fuck with me," he said in the same monotone. "We know you're selling."

Caught offguard, I stalled weakly. "Selling what?" I asked stupidly. They knew what I had. I'd been selling it in school all week. I felt completely stupid and scared as hell. Yellow Shirt was a freaky dude, with his cold eyes and unnatural calm. I knew he saw right through me. He was no punk. A punk had to overcome some level of fear, some inner hesitation, and muster the intensity to act. Yellow Shirt had a sociopath's calmness. He didn't need to muster anything; he was already there. His kind of guy could slip a knife in you and walk away with no change of expression. He scared the hell out of me.

I looked up at him, completely tongue-tied. He stared at me, like he was giving me one last chance to come clean. The conked-hair guys hovered a couple of steps below, watching. Then they came up and stood beside Yellow Shirt. One of them reached in and pulled on my film pouch.

"What's in here?"

"Just film," I said. I opened the pouch, exposing the dummy film rolls.

"Let me see that, asshole," one of the conked-hairs said, grabbing at the pouch.

I pushed his hand away, closed the pouch, and his friend reached in and tried to grab it. Yellow Shirt angrily knocked away his hand, growling,

"That's my shit!"

"Hey! Hey!" Gold Chain shouted at the conk-haired guys who were apparently working freelance. I was the focus of a scavenger hunt. It was almost comical, except for the fix I was in, and Gold Chain's painful two-fisted grip on my arm. The third guy stood behind Gold Chain, out of my line of sight.

Gold Chain and the two conked-hairs seemed agitated. Yellow Shirt stood like the calm center of the storm. Then, with a firm sweep of his arm, not even glancing at them, he shoved the two intruders away from me. His eyes remained fixed on me.

"Give me the dope," he said.

I didn't respond. I wasn't giving them my dope. And saying nothing seemed better than saying something stupid again and pissing him off worse. Maybe the chaos of the situation would work to my benefit. Maybe the conked-hairs would do something stupid and provoke him. I almost hoped they'd reach for me again. But they didn't. They were like jackals, hungrily eyeing the lion's kill, afraid to attack but unwilling to leave. "I'm done talking," snarled Yellow Shirt. "Give us what you've got."

His voice was truly threatening. The fifty hits of speed in my film rolls wasn't a lot to lose, but I absolutely refused to give it to them. If I caved in now, my reputation as an easy mark would be set. It would be open season on me. Instinctively, I glanced back over my shoulder, down the long stairwell, ten floors to the bottom. I looked back at Yellow Shirt and kept my mouth shut. He nodded slightly.

"Have it your way."

Now the third guy with Yellow Shirt and Gold Chain came out of the background and grabbed one of my legs. Suddenly my legs were high in the air, my left shoulder blade was resting on the banister, and I felt myself sliding backward like I was going down a chute. I grabbed the banister and clung to it with a death grip. Then one of the conked-hair freelancers reached in, grabbed my other leg, and tilted me farther back. As they lifted my legs higher, I felt myself sliding backward over the banister. I clung to it with both hands in a panic and started kicking violently, aiming at their heads. If it weren't for Gold Chain's grip on my shoulder, I'd have gone over. I landed a couple of kicks at the conked-hair holding my leg, and he let go and backed away. My head and shoulder were now over the edge, and the third guy still had my other leg. I looked down the center shaft at the banister spiraling below, ten floors to the bottom. I couldn't believe they'd throw me over for a few pills. But surrendering my dope was not an option.

"Let go of me, you assholes!" I shouted at the top of my lungs. "Let me fucking go!"

Gold Chain, still gripping my arm, was forcing me over the banister, while the third guy tried to hold my kicking legs still and lift them higher. Yellow Shirt stepped back and calmly watched. They now seemed to prefer throwing me down the stairwell to scoring my stash. I managed to land a couple more kicks, but the force of each kick made it harder for me to keep my grip on the banister. Finally, the third guy dropped my leg. I now had both feet on the stairs again. They were really pissed off, cursing at me in a fury, like I should have let them throw me over. Then the third guy and a conked-hair grabbed my legs again, lifted them up, and tried one more time to shove me over the railing. I gripped the banister again, more weakly now. Yellow Shirt returned, leaned into me, and tried to pry my hands off the banister. I knew I was about to go over. Then I saw his neck right next to me.

"Wait a minute!" I screamed. "I'll give it to you, all right? You can have it!"

They paused, still holding my legs, and I saw my chance. I let go of the banister, grabbed Yellow Shirt in a headlock and squeezed his neck as hard as I could. It was the last thing any of them expected. I had him in a vice grip, my ear pressed to the back of his head. I was now more pissed off than scared. If I went over the railing, he was coming with me. What did I have to lose? I planned to kill myself later anyway. This way I'd do some good by ridding the world of a sociopath on my way out.

Yellow Shirt struggled furiously but couldn't get away. He flailed at me with his fists but couldn't do much damage. I was kicking like a wild man, yelling into Yellow Shirt's ear, "You're coming with me, asshole! You're coming with me!"

Gold Chain pummeled me in the ribs and shoulder, but rushing on adrenaline, I felt no pain. Suddenly they put my legs back down. Yellow Shirt stopped fighting. He leaned against me, breathing hard in my ear. No one was grabbing or hitting me. Were they tired? Had they decided I was telling the truth? Had my willingness to die changed the equation? I let go of Yellow Shirt's neck; I couldn't hold on forever. To my surprise, he backed away. Then they all went down the steps and disappeared through the tenth-floor doorway.

I sat down on the stairs, breathing hard, trying to calm down, an unbelievable amount of adrenaline still flooding through me. I was relieved, exhilarated, puzzled, and scared as hell all at the same time. *Fuck this!* I thought. *I'm gonna quit. I'm not cut out for this place.*

But I didn't quit. I went home for the weekend and decided to go back and face them on Monday morning. It was partly pride—I didn't want them to think they'd beaten me and scared me off. It was also practical. Central Y, dangerous as it was, was my best chance for a high school diploma. My parents had told me if I quit school they'd kick me out. In a way, the challenge of Central Y appealed to me. It was a boot camp to toughen me up and hone my street smarts, a place to learn how the world I'd have to live in really worked.

I entered the building on Monday morning gripped with fear. I'd be seeing Gold Chain in my English Lit class. At some point, I'd run into Yellow Shirt and the conked-hair guys in the halls. Either I'd proven myself to them and they'd leave me alone, or I'd totally pissed them off and they'd be looking for me. But I'd be dealing with Gold Chain first.

He was sitting at a long table in the back of the room when I walked into class. We saw each other but played it cool, neither of us acknowledging the other. I grabbed one of the cheap metal folding chairs, put it next to him, a little too close, and sat down. The tension between us was electric. Neither of us looked over. After a few moments, I leaned back casually, staring straight ahead, then glanced over at him.

"Hey, what's up?" I said.

He seemed confused and on the spot, like he didn't know what to make of me. A guy he'd tried to rip off and kill three days ago was sitting next to him making small talk, like nothing had happened. He tried to ignore me, but I wasn't going away. A passive truce, just pretending nothing had happened, wasn't good enough. I had to know if I needed to constantly watch my back, so I had to make direct contact and get him to acknowledge me. If you know someone, and they know you, it's a little harder for them to rip you off, stick a knife in you, throw you over a stairwell, or whatever.

"Looks like this class has a lot of reading," I said to Gold Chain. "I fucking hate reading."

He stared sullenly ahead, still trying to ignore me. I could tell he was flustered. "Do you like writing reports and stuff?" I continued.

He sort of glanced over and grunted, "No."

A monosyllabic reply was progress. I kept going. "Me neither. This class is going to be a pain in the ass, huh?"

"Yeah, I guess."

Wow, he was warming up. To my surprise, he volunteered more. "Have you taken any math classes with Graham?"

"Yeah, I have algebra with him," I said.

"Is it a pretty tough class?" he asked.

"Not too bad," I said.

He paused, like he was thinking of what to say next. *What do you know?* I thought. *We're having an actual conversation.*

"But he gives a lot of homework, huh?"

"Yeah," I said, "that's a drag." Then, in a friendly way, I said, "Hey, I'm David. What's your name?"

I knew I'd never remember his name if he told me. It didn't matter. I didn't plan on becoming best friends; I just wanted to get off his hit list.

He grunted and said lamely, "I don't know."

I let that one hang in the air. His reluctance was understand-able. He'd tried to rip me off and kill me; he didn't want me to know who he was. Maybe I was trying to get something on him. Maybe *I* was the potential psycho now. I was fucking with his head. It might make me a less appealing target in the future. Next time, they'd rip off somebody else who was less of a pain in the ass. I was definitely putting him on the spot. I sat there, waiting, keeping the pressure on. I figured he'd either get angry or give in. Then some-thing shifted. Maybe he figured I could find out anyway. We were in the same class. Maybe he just felt stupid telling me he didn't know his own name.

"Benny," he said, or something like it.

I forgot it before class ended. I knew then he wouldn't try to rip me off again. So I pushed him further. "Cool," I said. Then I looked directly at him, making sure to use his name. "So, Benny, you and your buddies jumped me a few days ago. What the fuck was that about?"

We both knew perfectly well what it was about. They'd wanted my dope. But now we'd had an amiable chat, and I was cashing in on our new acquaintance status.

He looked at the floor for a moment, then answered sullenly, "I don't know."

Wow, he actually seemed embarrassed, like he knew he'd done something wrong. At least he wasn't a psychopath.

"Did I do something to you?"

"Nah."

"Okay." I paused, feeling the need for a little more reassurance. "Are you going to try and rip me off again?" I tried to just sound curi-ous.

"Nah."

"Cool." Mission accomplished. I'd shifted the balance of power. He looked up slightly in my direction. I decided to change the subject. "Hey, man, do you know where I can get some good weed?"

"No, not really," he said

I already had some weed. I just wanted to lighten the moment with that no-hard-feelings touch. "I know about some stuff coming in, in a few days, if you're interested."

"I don't know. I may have some by then," he said.

"Well, let me know if you need some. I'll see what I can do."

"Sure," he said.

This last part was diplomatic bullshit. We wouldn't be doing business together. I wasn't tough enough to stop him from hurting me if he wanted to. But I realized I didn't have to be the toughest guy. I just needed to be more of a pain in the ass to rip off than the next guy. That helped take some of the pressure off.

I shifted my attention to Mr. Brown, who stood facing our mostly uninterested class, talking about *Catcher in the Rye,* our first reading assignment. Benny leaned down and rustled in his backpack. A second later he sat up and handed me a paper cup with half of a shot of gold liquid in the bottom. I took a sniff; it was whiskey. He lightly bumped his cup against mine and we both drank.

After class, Benny and I nodded to each other on the way out. We weren't exactly friends after that, but we had a "How's it going?" relationship in class and a nodding relationship in the halls. He never bothered me again. Neither did Yellow Shirt or the other guys, who studiously ignored me whenever we passed each other in the halls.

As the summer session ended, I wasn't happy at Central Y. It was dangerous, and I wasn't learning much, academically at least. My mother looked around and found an experimental high school with about forty students, located on the second floor of an old monastery, five miles from my house. Dr. Lahe's daughter and some of my old friends were enrolled there. It wasn't a remedial or continuation school, but it was small and teachers could work more closely with students than in public school. The school also encouraged greater student input, so the curriculum would better reflect their needs and interests and stimulate more active participation. It wasn't accredited, but it was working toward accreditation and seemed sure to get it.

I started in the fall and encountered the usual problems. I couldn't keep up with the rest of the class, and the teachers didn't know how to deal with my learning disabilities. Grades weren't based on conventional tests but on an independently written report. Because of my severe dyslexia, no written test could accurately reflect my actual grasp of the material. I tried to persuade them to grade me on my actual grasp of the material, not on my skewed test scores, but the school was unwilling to make any exceptions. I dropped out after a few weeks, immensely frustrated. I later learned that after electing the school's prom king and queen that year, the students held an informal tongue-in-cheek vote for other school titles. I was no longer attending, but I was voted "least likely to survive."

I still wanted to get a high school diploma. So, the next semester, I went back to Central Y.

10

Survival is an Education

I noticed right away things were different at Central Y. The black kids always had their own social politics to deal with—pressure to join a gang, which gang to join, or not. There were a lot more whites now. It seemed Central Y had become cool to many public school whites. It offered more choices, more interesting and edgy classes, and more freedom. More whites meant new cliques with new social pressures to be cool. I had no interest in that game. The school was safer for whites now, but not for me. More people knew my business, and some kids talked too much.

I continued dealing, carefully and discreetly, keeping an eye out for trouble. I never carried more product than I could afford to lose and didn't put myself in vulnerable situations with people I didn't trust. Business picked up week by week.

My buying connections were nongang-affiliated, longhaired freaks with major drug contacts, who scored the best marijuana and psychedelics. When they were dry, so was I, and nearly everyone else. Shipments of various drugs came in randomly. Supply depended on smuggling, adding an element of unpredictability.

The big Chicago syndicates weren't yet trafficking in pot and psychedelics, so Central Y's syndicate gangs weren't dealing them. Syndicate operations were mostly vice, burglary, and car theft. That would change as recreational drugs went mainstream and became hugely profitable.

I came to know a few Blackstone Rangers and a couple of Superfly characters who dealt cocaine and heroin—drugs I stayed away from. As with my candy-and-toothpick business, I didn't consume my inventory. I paid myself a little, stashed a chunk for a nest egg, and put the rest back into the business.

A few months after the stairwell incident, I was sitting in Mr. Brown's English class when the classroom door opened and Chappy, the syndicate kid's giant bodyguard, walked in. The entire class turned to him, and the room went absolutely silent. No one, including Mr. Brown, said a word. Chappy looked around, his eyes locked onto me, and he walked over to my chair and stood looking down at me from his great height.

"You need to come with me."

He sounded firm but not threatening. I couldn't think of any reason he'd come for me. We'd never exchanged a word. Maybe his boss, the Near North Side syndicate leader, had sent him to get me. I had no reason to think I was in trouble. But I was definitely nervous. I got up from my chair. Chappy was in charge, and he wasn't a guy you said no to. I followed him to the door. A gentleman, he opened it and let me go first.

I stepped outside and stopped in my tracks. About fifty black students were milling in the hall, their angry faces turned in my direction. I heard ominous, indecipherable murmuring. I had no idea what I'd done. I gazed into the angry crowd, way past nervous, approaching full-blown panic.

Chappy grabbed me by the shirt collar with his meaty hand like a rag doll and shoved me against the wall. Holding me firmly by the collar with one hand, he put his other hand on my chest and glared down at me. His slightly red eyes looked crazy. His breath stank from a mixture of alcohol and halitosis. Suddenly he was one angry motherfucker.

The elevators were to my left, the back exit to the alley was to my right, but the crowd blocked my access to both. Chappy turned and looked around the hall, and it went deathly quiet, like he was about to give a speech.

What the hell did I do? I wondered. *Where's a fucking cop when you need him?*

"I want you to meet the Black Coalition," said Chappy in a deep bass voice, swinging his right palm away from my chest in a sweeping gesture, as if introducing me to the crowd.

The angry murmuring started up again, and the crowd surged slightly forward. Chappy kept his grip on my collar. He turned back to me; his crazed, bloodshot eyes stared into mine. "I'm going to kill you, you little white piece of shit!" he announced in a loud, convincing snarl. A chill traveled down my spine all the way to my toes.

Oh shit! This is going to hurt, I thought. *What did I do?*

I was a lightweight compared to most of these guys. I didn't know them. I'd never done anything to them. It made no sense.

"Do him!" someone called out.

Others chimed in with equally encouraging words. Chappy turned back to the crowd, loosening his grip on my shirt, and I seized the moment. I ducked down, twisted away, jammed my shoulder into the heavy classroom door, and slipped through the gap into the room.

I darted between the tables to the far side of the room. Students jumped up from their desks and ran as Black Coalition members swarmed through the door into the room. Chappy stepped inside, looked around, and fixed his eyes on me. Mr. Brown was out of his chair, heading for the door.

It was pandemonium, with scuffling feet and the clatter, scrape, and crash of chairs and tables being overturned. With a sinking feeling, I watched Mr. Brown force his way through the crowded doorway, followed by seven or eight students. He was a hero leading them to safety, but I felt completely abandoned.

I looked around for Chappy. He was no longer standing near the door. Glancing behind me, I saw him wading through a maze of fleeing students and overturned desks and chairs. Twenty or so students still in the room were migrating toward the far wall. If Chappy was going to kill me, he'd have to do it in front of witnesses. And he'd have to catch me first.

I managed to evade him by running into a tangle of chairs and tables. The Black Coalition guys now hovered in a crowd along the wall by the door. They didn't know what to do. Being in a brightly lit classroom full of frightened students was different from gathering in a dimly lit hallway.

Suddenly the pandemonium subsided, and an unnatural calm fell over the room, as if everyone had come to their senses. I kept my eye on Chappy, twenty feet away, separated from me by a table and some chairs. He had one eye on me and was arguing with several coalition members about what to do with me. Chappy wanted to kick my ass right there, but they were saying take me out to the alley and do it there.

At that point, two school security cops burst into the room, guns drawn. They glanced around, quickly assessing the situation. One of them shouted, "Nobody move!" I zeroed in on them with some anxiety. These were off-duty cops. If they searched me and found my dope, I could be sent to Charlietown until I was eighteen and maybe jail after that. With my attention on them, I didn't notice Chappy backing away from the cops, toward me. Then he was standing near me. Suddenly he lunged and swung his thick fist at my head. I dodged, and he struck the wooden curtain behind me that divided the room in half, splintering a section.

Hearing Chappy's fist crash into the wood, the cops instantly pointed their guns at him. One cop yelled at him to freeze, and the other yelled at me to back away. I did, greatly relieved, looking like the short, scared white kid I was. Soon the cops quarantined the coalition members against the wall and began ushering the rest of us out of the room. As soon as I was out of the room, I left school and caught the train home.

* * *

I decided I'd never go back to Central Y. For the second time in less than six months, someone had tried to kill me. But by the time I got home, I'd changed my mind again. I still wanted a diploma. And I had nowhere else to go and no other plan.

I returned the next morning, just after the first class had started. The halls were empty. Instead of going to class, I went around and checked various classrooms for friends who might know what was behind the Chappy incident. After a few conversations, the story came together. It turned out to be a misunderstanding based on a junkie's lie.

The morning Chappy came to get me, a girl named Violet had nodded out on heroin in class. The teacher knew she was on something and took her to the principal. When the principal asked her what she'd taken and where she got it, she said a short white guy with long curly hair cornered her in the elevator and shot her up with heroin. I was the only guy in school who fit the description.

Violet had blamed me to avoid getting in trouble for using. When they took her to the hospital, the doctor found multiple track marks on her arm and she admitted shooting herself up. But word had already spread that I'd shot up Violet, and Chappy was already coming after me. Chappy learned the truth from the security cops who took him to the office for questioning. He wasn't happy. He looked like a fool in front of everybody.

The incident worked to my favor. No one felt bad about it; mostly they thought it was funny. And I bantered with them about it, "Yeah, he's lucky he didn't catch me. I woulda kicked his ass." Being able to joke about serious matters was a useful survival skill. The incident broke the ice between us. Many Black Coalition members now recognized me in the halls, occasionally nodding in a familiar, good-humored way.

It also helped that I didn't talk to the cops about Chappy. I was earning some respect at Central Y, not as a tough guy but as a reliable guy who fought back, minded his own business, kept his mouth shut, and wouldn't give up his dope. Now some notable people acknowledged me as I walked through the halls. One day as I passed the head of the Blackstone Rangers at Central Y, he called to his friend, "Watch out for my buddy Patten here; this motherfucker thinks he can fly." I figured that was about the banister. I had no idea he knew who I was. I was no longer the suburban white kid. I had a minor reputation, but a reputation nonetheless.

Being known by this crowd was a plus for my dealing. My drug contacts expanded, and new Blackstone Ranger contacts opened up, including a couple of Superfly guys, who otherwise never would have had anything to do with someone so young. This improved rep also lifted my self-esteem.

* * *

In the end, at Central Y, I learned more from gang protocol, criminal mentality, and feral survival strategies than from any of the subjects in my classes. It's like what people say about prison: it doesn't rehabilitate you; it makes you a better criminal. If not for my learning disabilities, I might have left with a high school diploma. Instead, I became a better survivor and dealer with better connections. That unexpected education would prove useful to me in the next few years. It even benefitted others, including my logic teacher, Mr. Scofield.

One day I walked into Mr. Scofield's class, but he wasn't there. At twenty minutes past, he still hadn't showed up and students started leaving. I stared out the window, bored. At half past, only one other guy and I remained. I was about to leave when Mr. Scofield walked into the room.

I had a decent relationship with most of my teachers. I wasn't passing their classes, but I was polite and well behaved. A few of them knew I struggled with learning disabilities and could tell I really was trying to learn and do well. Most of them weren't very good teachers. No one wanted to teach in this underpaid, high-stress war zone. You didn't end up teaching here without a reason. If you were here, it meant you couldn't get a job anywhere else. And I mean anywhere else. Some of the teachers had been fired from other schools, some were just bad teachers who didn't seem to care about their students, and one or two were actually senile.

Mr. Scofield wasn't one of those teachers. An antiwar pacifist, he'd become a teacher to avoid Vietnam. He really cared about his subject and his students and tried hard to do a good job. He was a decent guy, and I could tell he liked me.

"Hey, Mr. Scofield." I grinned as he came in. "Party last night?"

He looked grim. "No. Someone broke into my apartment yesterday. They trashed it and took everything. I just finished cleaning up the mess."

"What did they take?" asked the other student.

"Everything electronic—my stereo system, my typewriter, even my crappy alarm clock. Whatever looked like it might be worth anything is gone. The police said I probably won't get it back."

I felt bad for him. Then it occurred to me the burglary had to be the work of a syndicate guy I knew. I'd learned at Central Y that the Chicago criminal scene was disciplined and well organized. Major syndicate gangs controlled what went down in Chicago proper and oversaw the junior syndicate gangs. Every guy in every gang, juniors and majors, had a modus operandi and designated territory and never operated outside his area. You couldn't do a burglary or fence stolen goods in Chicago if you weren't connected. You'd be infringing on someone else's territory, which would be a mistake. By now I knew the different gangs and their territories. It made me think.

Our school had two syndicate gangs. One specialized in stolen cars, especially Corvettes, and operated in Chicago proper. The other, specializing in residential break-ins and stolen home electronics, operated exclusively on the Near North Side. They were the likely suspects.

"Where do you live, Mr. Scofield?" I asked.

He looked at me suspiciously. "Why do you need to know that?"

"I have an idea. I might be able to help you."

He looked at me warily. Finally, he said, "Rogers Park."

"Near North Side. Let me go check something out with a friend."

He nodded. "Sure."

He didn't have anything to lose: he'd already lost his stuff, and the cops couldn't help him. I had no clout with the Near North Side syndicate, but my friend Rick was in the gang. They usually hung out on the eleventh floor. I headed upstairs looking for Rick. It didn't take long to find him. I told him I needed to talk with him, and we walked over to the back stairwell.

"What's up?" he asked.

"You know Mr. Scofield—he teaches logic class?"

"Yeah."

"Someone ripped off his apartment yesterday. He lives in Rogers Park. That's your guys' territory, right?"

"Oh, I think I see where you're going with this."

"Yeah. Scofield's a decent guy. I'm trying to help him out. What do you think?"

"I don't know. Wait here. Let me check something out." Rick went back to his buddies and returned a few minutes later wearing a poker face. Then he gave me a little grin. "I'll need his address," he said.

I could tell he was pleased to be able to help me out. He was basically a good guy and wanted to show me he could make things happen.

"That's great, man! I'll go get it."

"Can't promise anything," he said as I was leaving, "but I'll see what I can do."

I ran down the back stairs to the classroom. Mr. Scofield was standing at a table, talking with the other student. He looked up as I came over.

"So?" he asked.

"Hey, Mr. Scofield, I need your address."

He gave me an incredulous look. "I just got ripped off. Why should I give you my address?"

"I'm trying to help you get your stuff back. They're checking to see if they can get it back, but they need your address to figure it out. They already took everything anyway, right?"

"I suppose you're right."

He took a piece of paper from his satchel and wrote down his address. I took the paper and ran back up to the eleventh floor. I went up to Rick, who was talking to his buddies, and handed him the paper.

"Here it is."

The guys eyed me with interest. They knew who I was and seemed interested in helping me recover the stolen goods for my teacher. Rick handed the address to the main guy. He looked at it, then looked up at me, gave a little nod, and shrugged as if to say "We'll see."

I nodded and left, heading to my next class. But I began to feel apprehensive about the whole thing. I hadn't thought it through. I was trying to help Mr. Scofield get his stuff back, but I was also asking the Near North Side syndicate for a favor. I began to worry about what I might owe them in return.

The next day when I walked into logic class, Mr. Scofield greeted me with a cheerful nod and a smile. Had he gotten his stuff back already? I sat down at a corner table, alone. He finished talking to the class, gave a reading assignment, and came over to me.

"Thanks, David," he said quietly.

"What happened?"

"When I got home last night, all my stuff was piled up at my front door.

"Really? Oh, man, that's fantastic!" I was surprised it had happened so fast.

"Yeah. Please thank your friend for me. Tell him and whoever helped him they can sign up for any of my classes and they'll get an A. They don't even have to show up. That goes for you too, David."

I passed Mr. Scofield's offer on to Rick. He was impressed. I'd fulfilled my quid pro quo for the North Side syndicate and was on its radar. I wasn't "connected," but we had a connection. Some of them now acknowledged me in the halls. Curious, I asked Rick if Mr. Scofield's stuff had been safe left outside his door in the hall.

"David, you don't get it!" he said. "That's our territory. I guarantee no one would dare take it. It was as safe there as it would have been in his apartment."

A few days later, I introduced Rick and one of his syndicate guys to Mr. Scofield, who made good on his offer of a guaranteed A in his class. I didn't take him up on the offer. I had my own moral compass. I needed to actually learn in order to function in the real world.

It finally became clear to me I wasn't going to graduate from Central Y or any other school. It was the same story: I couldn't pass my classes because I couldn't pass written tests. I did hone my ability to live a double life and to keep my two worlds separate. At the end of every school day, I took the train home, had dinner with my parents and Neil, and then hung out with my friends, laughing, talking, and getting high. I'd tell them some of my adventures, but I couldn't explain what I went through each day as a short, white, suburban, learning-disabled kid in a mostly black, inner-city, gang-infested continuation school. My family and friends never saw the darker side of me that came out when that shit hit the fan. They never saw the tough attitude and persona I cultivated to survive as a drug dealer at Central Y. Or maybe I just wanted to believe that. But the only person I could really talk to about these things and who seemed to understand them—and me—was my new friend, Donna.

So, I left Central Y with a life-experience degree in survival and drug dealing. I had a knack for it. Apparently, that was where my future lay.

11

Guarding the Fountain

One cold Chicago night, I went out with Bob and Annie, two good friends from the crowd I now hung out with. They were both eighteen, three years older than me. We drove around the city in Bob's Volkswagen bug, smoking a joint and trying to decide where to go for the evening. Bob wanted to go to Lolly's, a nightclub where blues bands played. I was only fifteen, but with my long, frizzy hair, wispy mustache, and fake ID, I could pass for twenty-one.

To meet girls my own age, I'd go to the Coffee House, a local teenage hangout in a church basement. That's where we finally decided to go. Bob parked strategically in the church parking lot for a quick getaway if necessary. I'd scored some dope that afternoon and was holding two ounces of hash cut with black-tar heroin. Things had changed a lot in the short time since I'd started smoking pot. More people were doing drugs, and more narcs now infiltrated various scenes where drugs were bought, sold, and consumed. Selling to someone you didn't know was risky. I had friends busted with an ounce of weed doing time in federal prison. And there were guys looking to rip you off.

I never sold drugs at the Coffee House. It wasn't a drug crowd. The Coffee House hosted an interesting mix of trendy kids with hippie ambitions and little political awareness; suburban kids in bell-bottoms who liked pop music, tried to act cool, and talked about dope; "good" kids, usually church members, who stayed in the front of the room and refilled the punch bowl and plates of stale cookies; the more interesting oddball crowd that hung out in the back of the room where it was darker; and the random punks who'd show up and make trouble. Jocks and greasers never came; it wasn't their scene. I usually ran into some of my old public-school friends. And there were always pretty girls. That was the main reason I went.

Bob and Annie stopped to smoke a cigarette out front before going in. I didn't smoke and went inside to get out of the cold. I stood at the top of the steps overlooking the large basement room, checking out the scene, seeing who was there and what was happening.

The folding table at the bottom of the stairs was lined with the usual plates of cookies and rows of little Dixie cups filled with bright red punch. Nearly a hundred teenagers milled around the main room amid rows of folding tables and scattered folding chairs. They gathered in various cliques, laughing and talking. Steppenwolf blared out of loudspeakers.

As I scanned the room, a girl caught my eye. I'd never seen her before. Tall and thin, she stood alone next to the drinking fountain, her feet touching together and her arms folded behind her back. She wore an embroidered peasant-style shirt and bell-bottom jeans. Her long brown hair hung down in front of her face, and two big brown eyes with dark circles under them peered out through the strands. From the dark circles and her thin frame, I pegged her as a speed freak. She looked like a lost little girl, but she was definitely cute.

I knew I had to talk to her, so I headed for the drinking fountain. As I got closer, I saw she was really pretty. I leaned down to drink from the fountain, standing right next to her, and heard a feathery voice say, "Please . . ."

I lifted my head and looked up at her. Was she talking to me? Her head turned toward me. Through the gaps in her hair, I saw fear in her eyes. I could feel it in my gut. I felt an immediate empathetic bond. What was she so afraid of?

"What?" I asked her.

"Please, don't . . ." she said in the same soft voice.

I didn't understand. "Don't what?"

"The fountain—it's broken."

I turned the chrome knob. The water flowed just fine. "It works okay." I gave her a puzzled look.

She shrugged and lowered her eyes. "They told me to guard it."

"What?" I furrowed my brow. Someone was messing with her. "Who?"

She nodded nervously toward the main room. I looked over and saw two smirking, shorthaired punks sitting at a table thirty feet away, watching us. One was a white guy; the other was a sullen-looking Native American kid. They looked about eighteen. I looked back at her and saw something I'd missed in that first glance: she knew a level of fear most people never experience, the kind that never goes away, that lives in the same house with you. I wanted to help her.

I looked at the two guys watching us with smarmy looks. Rage boiled inside me. I wanted to get in their faces, teach them a lesson—maybe hurt them. I locked eyes with the white guy. He held my gaze for about ten seconds, then looked away, trying to laugh it off. Then I looked at the Native American kid. He glared at me and didn't look away. He was the alpha of the two. I could have left them alone and stayed with the girl, but I wanted to know what they were up to and why.

I hated bullies who picked on weaker kids; it triggered rage in me. It made me want to go after them. I felt it now.

I glanced around, looking for Bob. If something started, it wouldn't hurt to have backup. I didn't see him. He was probably out front with Annie. It was just me then.

"I'll be right back," I told the girl.

I walked up to the two guys, staring them down. I'd had plenty of experience with punks. I never bothered to bluff; when you're short, it only makes you look weak. A lot of guys back down if they sense you're ready to go all the way. When I was ready and aching to hurt someone, most guys could tell it was for real.

"Are you guys fucking with her?" I asked bluntly.

"We thought it was funny," the white guy said sheepishly.

When they both leaned back a bit, I knew they weren't up for a fight. It was already over. I'd won. But I stayed put. There was no way I was going to walk away until I knew what was behind their game.

"She's pretty, and she wanted white cross," Alpha said.

That confirmed my suspicion about her. White cross was a potent methamphetamine. These sick punks were testing her to see what she'd do for some speed. I wondered what they might try next.

"Just fucking leave her alone," I snarled. "You ever talk to her again, I'll find you. You understand?"

They didn't say anything, so I turned and started back toward the girl. She was still standing by the water fountain, watching me. It flashed through my mind how stupid I was for inserting myself into other people's problems when I couldn't even solve my own. I'd been doing it since kindergarten, when I started protecting the little co-op girl from her crazy John Bircher father.

When I reached the girl, she looked at me shyly and then looked down at the floor. I stood close, but not too close, careful to respect her space.

"Are you okay?"

"Muhmmm . . ."

It wasn't much of an answer. Maybe she'd thought those guys were going to get her some speed, and now I'd ruined it for her. I looked at her, but she didn't seem upset. She didn't seem much of anything. She had a ghostly presence. It was almost like she wasn't there.

"Are you sure you're all right?"

"Yeah."

"You won't look at me. Am I making you uncomfortable? You want me to leave?"

She looked up and made eye contact. "No."

Then I saw a little smile. The fear was gone from her eyes. They were soft now. My heart started beating faster.

"My name's David. What's your name?"

"Donna."

Now Bob and Annie came down the stairs toward Donna and me. I introduced them, and they exchanged casual but friendly greetings. I decided to move things forward.

"Hey, Donna, Bob's parents are gone for the weekend. We're going to his house to get high. You wanna come? I'll make sure you get home whenever you need to."

She looked at me shyly and said in a small voice, "Yeah."

I reached out and took her by the hand. We left the Coffee House and walked through the chilly evening air toward Bob's Volkswagen bug. I felt high and alive holding Donna's hand; my mind and emotions raced. I glanced at her several times before we got to the car. Each time she looked more beautiful. Anna came up to Donna, and as they whispered back and forth, I quietly asked Bob if he could make sure Donna got home on time.

"No problem," he said.

Donna and I got into the back seat, and Annie and Bob got in front. We left the church parking lot with Sly and the Family Stone playing on the local underground radio station. I felt an energetic connection with Donna—definitely chemistry. I hoped she felt it too.

Donna and I talked about music—rock bands we liked, albums we had, concerts we'd been to. At one point, I impulsively told her how glad I was to have met her. She gave me a shy little smile, and I knew she liked me. When I leaned in to kiss her, she responded willingly, without holding back.

"Bob, don't forget to stop at the drugstore," Annie said.

"What for?" Bob asked.

"We need birth control gel, remember?" she sounded annoyed and amused.

"Oh, yeah," said Bob.

I was completely caught off guard. Was Donna in on this? Was Annie just speaking for herself? I glanced furtively at Donna, and she gave me a sweet, shy smile of apparent consent. This was unbelievable. When had they come up with this plan? It must have been on the walk to the car. I found it easy to be with girls and talk to them, but I was inexperienced sexually. Donna seemed relaxed and confident about sex. That surprised me; she seemed so shy and introverted.

Bob pulled into a drugstore parking lot. Annie asked him for money, and he handed her a five-dollar bill from his wallet. Not knowing how much Donna needed, I gave her a ten-dollar bill. Annie saw it and began razzing Bob about only giving her a five.

"Well, I'm not a big-time dope dealer like David," Bob grinned.

I didn't like Bob saying that in front of Donna, but it was done.

Annie and Donna went in together and came out ten minutes later, giggling and holding their purchases. I liked seeing Donna light-hearted and laughing. When they got into the car, Annie was holding an instructional pamphlet for the contraceptive jelly.

"Hey, you guys need to make sure you know how much gel to use. Bob never does it right." She giggled. "David, read them to us—Bob's driving."

She waved the instructions at me, laughing like it was a funny joke. But it wasn't funny, because I couldn't read.

Then Bob said, "Come on, Annie! You know David can't read."

Fuck! I cringed in the dark. That was the last thing I wanted Donna to know. I grabbed the instructions and stuffed them into my coat pocket.

"I'll read them later," I said tersely.

Annie saw how embarrassed and angry I was. She felt bad about it, but the damage was done.

"I'll read them," she said apologetically.

I just wanted the moment to be over and the subject dropped. I shook my head and said, "Don't."

"Okay," she said in a subdued voice.

Annie turned around to face the front. The laughter had stopped. The car was silent except for the music on the radio. I was afraid to look at Donna, afraid of what she must think of me now. Moments later, I started the conversation again, trying to act like nothing had happened, ignoring the churning in my gut. Donna seemed the same as before. When we were almost at Bob's house, she leaned against me and put her head on my shoulder. Maybe everything was okay after all. I put my arm around her, and she relaxed into me. As we pulled into Bob's driveway, I leaned over and kissed her again. She responded, kissing me warmly, her lips melting into mine.

Donna seemed different from any girl I'd ever met before. In the short time I'd known her, I hadn't detected any capacity in her for self-inspection. This would usually make me mistrust someone. But I also saw no signs of judgment, dishonesty, or maliciousness in her. And she had a soft, sweet innocence. It was a combination I'd never experienced in anyone before. She intrigued and intimidated me. I thought about her asking those guys back at the church for speed. I wondered if she was high on something now.

Bob pulled into the driveway of his house, and we went inside and sat down in the living room. In one corner of the room was a rabbit in a small cage. I felt sorry for it having to live like that.

"Why don't you let the rabbit out for a while?" I suggested.

Bob just grinned at me and said, "Let's get stoned."

He pulled a bag of weed and some rolling papers from his pocket and tossed them to me. I took the two-ounce block of hash from my pocket, picked off a small chunk, crumbled it into the weed, and rolled a perfect joint. Donna watched intently. She didn't seem impressed by my superior rolling abilities. I could tell she'd seen it all before. She definitely wasn't naïve.

In the middle of the joint, Bob got up and let the rabbit out of the cage. It hopped around, but not like a regular rabbit. Its hind legs flew up and out, arching over its back. A couple of times it flipped over, landed on its back, then scrambled upright again, facing the opposite direction. We all watched in amazement through increasingly stoned eyes.

At one point Donna said softly, "He said he's going to run away."

"Who said?" Annie asked.

"The rabbit," Donna said.

Bob and Annie laughed. I looked at Donna, staring sadly at the rabbit, and realized she wasn't joking. I didn't know what to make of her. Finally, we all got up, very stoned, and headed for the bedrooms. I took Donna by the hand and led her down the hall toward the guest bedroom. I was excited, but the prospect of being with someone more experienced was intimidating. I entered the guest room, leaving the light off. The streetlight cast a dim light into the room.

Donna followed me in, dropping her purse by the door. In that moment, she seemed older than her years. She found the directions for the gel. I suddenly felt anxious, as if the moment was about to be ruined. Usually, when people found out I couldn't read, they didn't know how to handle it. They acted incredulous or became awkward or condescending. But Donna didn't seem the least bit fazed. She went to the window and read them aloud by the streetlight's glow. I joined her there. It felt intensely intimate, standing beside this beautiful girl I barely knew while she read birth control directions out loud.

"Annie's right to read this. I don't use that much gel," she said. She was about a year older than me, but her familiarity with diaphragms seemed unusually mature. It made her more mysterious and a little intimidating. Then she gave me an impish smile. Suddenly everything seemed natural. The tension in me was gone. I was so relieved. I felt good about myself with her.

She took the diaphragm and gel into the bathroom. When she returned, she casually took off her shirt and pants, leaving them on the floor. She got on the bed in her bra and panties, her hair half covering her eyes. She was thin and her ribs showed, but she was incredibly beautiful.

I stripped down to my underwear, and we climbed under the sheet and blanket, escaping the cold. Her arms were covered with goose bumps. I made a joke about it, and we laughed together. Then we kissed. Lying next to her, everything seemed uncomplicated.

She seemed to take things as they were, accept them without analysis and move on, something I had a hard time doing. Between the two of us, I was definitely the complicated one. I couldn't let go of things that bothered me, stop my thoughts from racing, or just be in the moment. She had no problem with me being an illiterate drug dealer. I didn't feel judged by her. I lay holding her, fretting over her eccentricities. Questions popped into my mind: *How much speed does she use? What does it mean that she thought the rabbit was talking to her?* I felt I needed to know what was going on with her if we were going to be intimate.

"You like speed?" I tried to sound casual.

"Yeah, I guess." She sighed.

I pulled her to me. She kissed me again, but her body went limp. I sensed her ambivalence. Did she want to have sex? As I touched her more intimately, her body stiffened. She was giving very confusing signals.

"I'm on my period," she said softly.

I took that as a signal to back off. Now she seemed vulnerable and confused. I wasn't going to press her. I was happy just to lie together and talk.

I couldn't get the rabbit remark out of my mind. I knew if you did too much speed you started to lose touch with reality. It could even make you psychotic. I'd met some truly crazy speed freaks before. I liked Donna. I felt a protective concern for her. I didn't want to take advantage of her.

"Do you do a lot of speed?" I asked.

She brushed off the question with another kiss, so I let it go. I stroked her hair, ran my hand down her stomach, and let my fingers play lightly across her ribs. She instantly recoiled, as if I'd touched her with a lit cigarette. Suddenly, she pressed her hands together like she was praying. She looked up at me with terror in her eyes, nearly in tears, pleading, "Please don't...please don't..."

She repeated this several times, though I'd stopped immediately.

"Okay, I'm sorry." I didn't know what I'd done. I pulled her gently to me and held her tense, shivering body.

"What's wrong?" I asked.

She relaxed a little and pressed her face against my neck. We were silent for a while. I wondered if she was manipulating me. I wanted to know more about her.

Finally, reluctantly, she obliged my curiosity and started talking about her life in a stoned stream-of-consciousness ramble that lasted well over an hour. I glanced at the clock periodically, because she told me she had to be home by eleven.

I learned a lot about Donna that night. She had five brothers and sisters and strict Italian Catholic parents. Her family was extremely dysfunctional. Her father drank, emotionally and physically abused his wife and kids, especially Donna, and moved his family every year or two to get promotions in his high-powered sales job. Donna had lived in fear of him most of her life. He flew into wild rages and hit her with his fists and openhanded slaps, leaving large bruises on her body. Sometimes he tickled her, ignoring her desperate pleas, until she passed out. That's why my accidentally tickling her ribs triggered her.

Because of all this, Donna had never formed deep or lasting friendships. She didn't trust people. She'd been getting high since she was twelve. Her father thought she was straight when she was stoned and stoned when she was straight. Because he beat her when he thought she was stoned, she got stoned as often as possible. She talked so openly. I felt her and what it all meant to her.

Her story disturbed me and filled me with overwhelming empathy and anger about her abuse. Getting to know her—her head and her heart—made her more of an enigma. She totally fascinated me. A strong desire to protect her filled my heart.

When it was time for her to go home, we lay quietly for a few minutes, holding each other in the dim streetlight bleeding through the blinds. My feelings were poignant and sweet. It was like the lull before a spring storm, when the air is cool, the sky turns dark, the wind is blowing gently, and the world takes on a magical glow.

Donna and I exchanged phone numbers in the car on the way to her house. She placed the slip of paper with my number into her purse as if it were treasure. When Bob pulled to a stop in front of her house, Donna and I hugged and kissed goodbye. As she walked up to her front door, I saw the drapes part in the living room window. When she reached the front porch, the light went on, the door opened, and her father stood there. He didn't let her in, instead stood yelling at her while she cowered in front of him. Then he stepped aside and let her pass. I could still hear him yelling as he closed the door. The magical glow I'd been feeling wasn't the lull before a spring storm but the eerie calm that precedes a tornado.

12

A Life Raft

After the night we dropped Donna off at her house, her father wouldn't let her go out for a week. I called her every day when I got home from Central Y. I couldn't wait to see her.

We arranged to meet a block from her house the next Saturday afternoon. Donna lived a couple of miles away. I got there a little early and stood waiting on the corner in the chilly autumn air, watching her front door. Finally, it opened. She came out, and I waved from a block away. She started walking toward me, her head tilted down, and her hands shoved into the pockets of her winter coat. Her bell-bottoms accentuated her long, slender legs, and her long, brown hair hung down over her face. She looked beautiful, awkward, and mysterious.

As she drew near, she seemed uncertain, so I went to meet her. I put my arm around her and pulled her gently to me, giving her a reassuring hug. It felt so good to hold her. We walked slowly, making small talk, taking almost an hour to reach the co-op. We came in the back way, walking through the fields near the edge of the property until we got to my house. Donna was nervous about meeting my mother. It took a few minutes for me to make her feel comfortable about going in. Finally, we went in.

As we walked past my mother, sitting at the kitchen table drinking her coffee, I said, "Hi, Mom! This is Donna. She's a friend."

"Hello, Donna!" Mom greeted her with a big smile. "Good to meet you."

"Hi, Mrs. Patten," Donna mumbled shyly, her head down.

We went through the family room and moved past the large, heavy wooden door into my bedroom. That door afforded a sense of protection, as well as soundproofing. My bedroom was actually two adjoining rooms, more a living quarters. I hung out mostly in the front room and slept in the back room.

"This is my hangout room," I said. "My bedroom is through there." I pointed at the second door. "Make yourself comfortable. That's my couch and chair, my desk, my stereo and record collection. You can check out my records if you want."

She went over to my desk and started looking through the clutter. Then she saw my pride and joy: an AR, belt-driven, state-of-the-art turntable and speakers, and my collection of almost a hundred rock albums. She looked through the albums and handed me Buffalo Springfield. While she sat down in my big slouch chair, I put the record on, turning the volume low. Then I sat down behind her and softly pulled her back so she was leaning with her back against my chest.

"Finally, we're alone together," I whispered in her ear, kissing her ear and neck. She didn't seem to mind.

"I'm off my period," she said. "It ended last Tuesday."

"Oh, good," I said, a little surprised. Then I felt like I'd said something stupid. But she turned around, leaned forward, put her arms around me, and we started kissing. She was so sweetly open. I leaned back, and she maneuvered her body so she was lying on top of me. We made out until the record stopped.

"I'll turn the record over," I said.

As I moved her off my lap to get up, I lightly bumped her lower back. She jerked away, cringing with a whimper, but tried to hide it.

"What's wrong?"

"It's sore," she said.

I carefully helped her to a sitting position, then lifted the back of her blouse to look. She had two fist-sized bruises on her lower back.

"What happened? Those weren't there Friday night."

"No," she said, almost apologetically.

"Do you have any other bruises?"

She hesitated, then pointed at her left upper arm. I lifted the left sleeve and saw the bruise around her skinny bicep, where someone very strong had grabbed her and squeezed hard.

"What happened?"

"My dad got mad," she said softly.

"Any more bruises?" I asked.

She shook her head no. I was furious at her father. The worst part was she seemed to think it was her fault. Seeing the anger in my face frightened her.

"When did he do this?"

"Last Friday night."

The night we met. My heart sank. Her father had seen me and taken it out on her. I knew it wasn't my fault, but I felt responsible. I didn't know what I could do to help her, but right then I decided I'd do whatever I could to make sure he never hit her again.

"Why?" I asked.

"He said I was high."

I kept asking her questions about her father until she finally opened up. She told me things that made me sick.

"When I was eleven he came into my room one night really drunk. He climbed in my bed and started…you know."

"What did you do?"

"I screamed and got out of bed. When he came after me, I climbed out the window onto the ledge. My mom came in, and they both started yelling at me to come back inside. They acted like I was the problem. He didn't try it again. But after that, I never felt safe around him, and he started beating me more."

"Is there anything you can do to stop him?" I felt like a jerk for asking. If she could have done something, she would have done it long ago. She changed the subject.

"Do you want to get some speed?" she asked with big puppy eyes. "Please?"

I didn't know what to say. I didn't like that she used speed and wasn't about to feed a bad habit. I mostly dealt non-addictive drugs, like pot, hash, and psychedelics. The kind of speed I sold at Central Y was considered no more addictive than coffee. Her big eyes bored into me with what I read as the anxiety of withdrawal.

"I don't think I can," I said.

"I can pay you back if that's what you're worried about."

"Do you have a job?" I tried distracting her by changing the subject.

"I model sometimes for catalogs."

"Really? How much does that pay?"

"Forty-five an hour."

"Wow. That's more than my dad makes."

"I don't work regularly. It comes and goes. So can we get some speed?"

"Look, Donna, I really don't know how I can get you any speed right now." I could have, but I wasn't going to. She was disappointed. "Let's just stay here. We can smoke pot, listen to music—just be together. Do you want to get high?" She nodded.

I wondered how hard-core she was. Did she shoot up or just do pills? Was she an addict, did she just like it, or think it was cool? I loaded the pipe, took a toke, and handed it to her. As she reached for it, I scanned her arms for tracks. I didn't see any. She took a long toke and handed the pipe back.

"Do you shoot up?" I asked her.

"Sometimes," she said, holding her toke. "Just meth."

"Where do you shoot? Your arms look clean."

She exhaled a stream of thick smoke. "My ankles. No one looks there."

"Can I see?"

She shrugged, then pulled up her bell-bottoms, and pulled one sock down below her ankles. I leaned down for a closer look and saw tracks in the delicate area inside and just below her ankle. Some looked recent; some were old scars. She was definitely a hard-core speed freak. I hated the idea of her shooting up. The more I learned about Donna, the more worried I became about her. She pulled her socks back up.

"When was the last time you shot up?" I asked.

"Yesterday morning. It was the last of my stash. I don't have any money or connections here."

"Hmm…"

We finished the pipe in silence. I felt anxious. Speed withdrawal could be real bad. The second day was a lot harder than the first, and the third day was the worst.

I asked her if she was hungry. She asked if I had any sweets. I went to the kitchen, got a piece of white cake and a Coke from the fridge, came back, and put them on the floor next to her. Then I lay down on the couch. A few minutes later, she came and lay next to me, her head on my chest. We held each other for a while.

"Are you going to stay with me?" she asked plaintively.

"Yeah, sure," I said. Then I realized I wasn't sure what she meant. Tonight? Forever? "What do you mean?" I asked.

"You can't ever leave me. I need you to always be with me."

"You mean by your side?"

"Yeah."

"I can't be with you every minute of every day. But I'll be there for you when you need me."

"I need you with me all the time."

She had a childlike way of drifting into unreality—like she had with the talking rabbit. I wanted to be there for her but didn't want to promise what was impossible. So I changed the subject.

"When did you start doing speed?" I asked.

"When I was twelve. My boyfriend, Eric, shot me up the first time. I didn't want to. He made me. But when it came on, I loved it."

"How old was he?"

"Twenty-one. My father hated him. He was always calling the police on him. Eric got busted for possession a year ago. They shortened his sentence on the condition that he join the army when he gets out. He's in boot camp now. My father moved us here from Minnesota a couple of months ago. Partly because he got a promotion, but partly to get away from Eric."

"You're father moved out of state to get away from your boyfriend?"

"Eric's a pretty intense guy. I think my father's afraid of him. He didn't beat me nearly as much when I was seeing Eric."

Then she dropped a bomb. "We're still engaged. He's coming to see me in a couple of weeks."

"What?" I was astonished.

"He gets out of boot camp on leave in three weeks. He's riding his motorcycle out to see me."

This was getting stranger by the minute. She spoke in a calm, matter-of-fact voice, like this was normal

"What the hell do you mean you're engaged? Why are you here with me?"

She cringed and gave me a worried look, like she thought I was going to hit her.

"I really like you, David. I want to be with you."

"Then you need to break up with him! Do you want to stay with him?" I was really confused.

"No, not anymore."

"Then call him and break the engagement."

"But . . . I still have the ring. He's gonna want his ring back."

I looked at her in disbelief. "So mail his ring back."

She was getting more uncomfortable by the second. She stared at the wall, worry wrinkles creasing her forehead. "It's not that easy. I'm afraid of him."

I could see she was really was afraid.

"He gave me two miscarriages," she blurted.

"What? How did he do that?"

"He'd punch me in the stomach and take me dirt bikeriding on really rough trails until I finally miscarried."

"Both times?"

"Yeah."

I couldn't believe what I was hearing.

"He said we couldn't afford to have the babies," she explained. "He didn't think they were his, and even if they were, he could have gotten arrested for statutory rape."

"Whose else would they have belonged to?"

"I don't know," she said, watching me intently. "I don't want to say."

I wondered what it was she didn't want to tell me. Then it hit me:

he'd made her a prostitute. "Shit!" I said. "That fucking asshole!"

"He made me," she said in a small scared voice and began crying.

"Why didn't you break up with him?"

"I tried to a few times. He just says no and comes back. Besides, if I don't marry him, I don't know how I'll get out of the house before I'm eighteen. I can't live with my dad anymore. At least Eric takes care of me."

"Are you serious? He's worse than your dad!"

"No, he's not. He doesn't hit me as much. There's nothing I can do anyway. He's coming for me."

She seemed completely resigned. This was crazy. But she was so vulnerable that I couldn't just leave her in this situation.

"If you knew you were safe and Eric couldn't hurt you, would you break up with him?"

"Definitely! I want to be with you."

"Would you want to break up with him even if it wasn't for me?"

"Yes, but I want to be with you."

"You're absolutely sure?"

"Absolutely."

"Good. So, we have to figure out how to keep you safe. I promise I'll protect you, Donna. I'll keep you safe."

"How?"

I didn't know. I had no plan.

"I'll figure it out. I promise."

We lay, holding each other, her head on my chest. Dusk fell outside, and the room grew darker. I had a sinking feeling. Eric was as bad and dangerous as the worst Central Y sociopaths. He wasn't going to like it when he found out I'd stolen his girlfriend. I'd been in dangerous situations before, but this definitely upped the ante. I hated the war, but I hoped they'd ship Eric straight from boot camp to Vietnam.

I had to come up with a plan to keep Donna safe. She'd have to break up with Eric and kick her speed habit. I couldn't be with a speed freak. I wondered if her bizarre behavior was due to long-term speed use. I hoped that was it, that if she got clean, she'd return to some degree of normalcy—unless she was screwed up before, and the speed made it worse. Either way, I still wanted to be with her. After all, who was I to judge her? I was as screwed up in my own way as she was. My problems felt too big for anyone to help me, so people stood on the sidelines judging me, as if that was helpful. I wouldn't do that to Donna. I wouldn't abandon her. I'd stand beside her and do everything I could to take care of her.

"Have you thought about getting off speed?" I asked her.

"Yeah, someday. But not right now."

"Why not?"

"I'm not ready for that."

"How would you get ready? If you want to kick it now, I promise I'll stay with you the whole time. You're already one day clean, right?"

"I don't know. I don't want to think about it now." She tensed up.

"Are you going to leave me if I don't quit?" she asked a few moments later.

"No."

"Good."

I could tell she took that as a commitment. Quitting cold turkey was scary. I didn't want to pressure her or freak her out. She was so fragile, clearly terrified of abandonment, but I couldn't help her unless she quit. So I said, "But I don't see how we can have an ongoing relationship if you don't quit."

It sounded like double-talk even to me. She didn't respond, and I didn't say anything more.

"Can you stay the night?" I asked her.

"Yeah. But what about your parents?"

"I'll take you out the front door, you can say goodbye to my mom, then I'll sneak you in through the back door to my room. What about your parents? Can you work it out?"

"Yeah. I'll say I'm staying at a girlfriend's. I'd better call soon."

Donna called her mom from my room and worked it out. Then I took her out past my mom and snuck her back into my room as planned. I left the lights off, and we cuddled to Buffalo Springfield, side two. Donna seemed more relaxed now. We made out a little and talked a little. At one point, when I asked again if she'd consider quitting speed, she immediately tensed up.

"Why do I have to quit speed? I just want to be with you. Don't leave me alone. Please don't leave me alone." She started crying uncontrollably. "Promise you'll never leave me, that you'll always stay with me."

"I'm not leaving you, Donna. I'm right here. I'm not going anywhere." I held her close and rocked her. "But I really want you to get clean. It'll make everything better. I promise."

Finally, she agreed. "Okay, I'll quit for you, as long as you never leave me."

"Don't worry. I don't know about never, but everything's going to work out."

It grew darker outside. Her face looked so vulnerable and sweet by the faint light of the stereo. I held her, stroking her hair, telling her everything would be all right. I half believed it myself.

After a while, she went to use the bathroom. On her way back, she stopped at my desk. I saw her reach down and pick something up. I heard a familiar click and saw, by the light of the stereo, a metallic flash in her hand. I got up immediately with a weird feeling. She'd opened my three-inch pocketknife. I went over and saw her calmly pressing the blade into the soft flesh above the inside of her elbow.

I lunged for the knife, the blade caught the edge of my palm with a sharp sting, and she began struggling with ferocious desperation. It was surreal. We'd been so connected and intimate only moments before, and now she was a completely different person. I struggled to stop her from hurting herself, while she thrashed wildly with unbelievable strength—as if I was attacking *her*!

She still had the knife. Gripping her hand, I maneuvered it behind her, reached my other arm around, and pulled her to me. Now I had both arms around her and control of the knife. My hand was bleeding, but I couldn't let her go. If I did, I didn't know who she'd use the knife on.

I pried the knife from her hand and tossed it away. In the struggle, we both lost our balance. Gripping her tightly, I tried to soften our fall by landing on my shoulder and elbow. Still, she struggled furiously. Every few minutes, she'd go limp. Then we'd lie panting, catching our breath, saying nothing, and then she'd start up again, trying to kick and bite me, hitting her head against me or against the floor. During one break, I managed to tear a strip from my sleeve and wrap my hand. This went on for a couple of hours.

At last, she began to calm down. We were both exhausted and covered with sweat. I relaxed my grip but was still on guard. We lay there quietly for a while. Over the next half hour, she slowly softened. Then she was back, the tender, fragile girl I knew. She gently wiggled around in my arms, turning to face me, and went limp with her head on my chest, crying silently. We lay there for hours, holding each other. The open knife lay on the floor a few feet away. It was a relief when she finally fell asleep in my arms. Eventually, I drifted off too.

Dawn came. The sun rising over the distant trees shone through the window of the outside door to my bedroom. I felt desperation and intimacy in our embrace—and a new wariness inside. I didn't understand her. I was in way over my head. But I wasn't going to abandon her. In our life-and-death struggle, we'd bonded. We lay like two shipwrecked survivors, marooned on a life raft, watching the sunrise after a long, dark night at sea. We were each other's raft, perhaps each other's last chance. Maybe together we could be one whole person.

13

Glimmer of Light

After that strange first night together, Donna and I spent all our available time with each other. Wherever I went, she was always at my side, whether leaning against me, hovering just behind me, or with her right shoulder touching my left shoulder. She whimpered or cried every time she had to go home. Her father disapproved of her seeing any boy, but for us, not seeing each other was out of the question. We kept things clandestine.

Donna had two primary needs: to be close to me and to get stoned, in that order. Each time we were together, I learned more about her. Mistrustful by nature, I had trouble at first believing her extreme, unusual stories. But I came to realize they were all true. They explained her tragic air and resigned attitude toward life—so surprising in a fifteen-year-old.

Donna was the most reckless drug user I'd ever met. She'd use any drug, any combination of drugs, and any amount of drugs, with no reflection or hesitation. She was definitely a meth addict. She'd concluded nothing was going to work and there was nothing she could do about it, so we might as well just be together and get stoned. I never knew how much of her bizarre behavior was due to meth addiction and how much was due to her traumatic home life. At times, I wondered if she was schizophrenic.

Yet there was an innocence in her depth of heart. She loved me like no one ever had before. She seemed to think if she attached herself to me and fulfilled my needs, she'd finally be safe. It occasionally made me uncomfortable. But I liked how she anticipated my needs, sometimes before I knew them. Taking care of her gave me strength. If I was worth nothing else, at least I could protect someone I loved.

Extremely dysfunctional in some ways, Donna was highly functional in others. The oldest of six children, she'd been a surrogate mother to her five siblings, as well as the family's primary housekeeper since she was a young girl. Every day she cleaned the house, did the laundry, washed the dishes, and took care of her brothers and sisters. She'd borne this heavy workload for years, along with her father's emotional and physical abuse. Remarkably, she excelled academically, maintaining a straight-A average. Speed helped her maintain her focus and her grades, but at a great cost to her physical and mental health.

After we got together, I didn't see much of my friends. I tried hanging out with them and Donna a few times, but it didn't work. Donna was terribly shy and awkward in a group. She'd get very quiet and tilt her head forward so her hair hid her face. You could just make out her eyes and mouth. It wasn't an effort to be coy but an attempt to disappear. And her strangeness came out unpredictably. She'd take off-the-wall jokes and put-ons literally, asking follow-up questions that made her seem incredibly naïve. My friends didn't understand her or our relationship. They thought my being with her was taking on way too much.

They were probably right. Fiercely jealous, Donna could erupt in fits of anger and hysteria or collapse emotionally with little or no provocation. My walking out of the room, making an offhand remark, or talking to someone else for too long could trigger intense feelings of rejection and her greatest fear, abandonment. I'd have to help her stabilize or she'd panic or even hallucinate. I'd hold her for a while, sometimes hours, until she felt safe and reassured. Comforting Donna this way felt natural. I wondered if this was what my mother went through for me.

Donna and I more or less dropped out of sight. But we were getting to know each other and liked being alone together. There was a lot going on and a lot to figure out. Eric, her sociopathic boyfriend, would soon be heading this way on his motorcycle from boot camp. She wasn't safe at home or with this guy Eric. I needed a plan to keep her safe but hadn't come up with one.

Two weeks before Eric was due to arrive, Donna called and told me her father was moving to Texas in a week. They'd been here less than six months. We couldn't bear being separated. Then I got an idea: maybe Donna could live with us. Previously, my parents had temporarily taken in troubled kids to live with us. They'd all been boys, but maybe we could work something out.

The established rule in our family was that by eighteen we either enrolled in college or moved out of the house. Since college wasn't an option for me, I had less than three years of room, board, and parental support while I figured out how to support myself in the world. My mother hoped I'd get a high school diploma, but that seemed unlikely.

My mother and I were close, despite a lingering strain between us after my suicide attempt. She treated me like a young adult. Her emotional reserve with me was how she protected herself. She didn't know about my drug dealing or my more dangerous Central Y adventures, but we could talk about almost anything else.

So I sat down at the kitchen table with her and told her all about Donna: her speed addiction, her strange behavior, her father's abuse, and her criminal boyfriend who got her hooked on speed and gave her two miscarriages. I didn't mention that he'd prostituted her and was coming to get her in less than a week. My mother, dependable and frank as I hoped she'd be, listened attentively, maintaining her professional poise. When I was finished, she told me that Donna needed treatment for her addiction and that I should be prepared because Donna might be schizophrenic and need to be in a psychiatric hospital.

When I told her Donna's family was moving to Texas and asked if she could stay with us, she said absolutely not. I pointed out that she'd brought other troubled kids into our home without our agreement. Now Donna, whom I cared about deeply, was in real peril. I was desperate. I believed Donna's life was at stake. If something bad happened to her both my mother and I would carry it for the rest of our lives. That affected my mother, who suggested an alternate possibility. If Donna's father had insurance coverage, she could get her into a thirty-day treatment program in a psychiatric hospital. If she got clean and her parents agreed, maybe she could stay with my aunt (my mother's sister), who lived a few miles away. My mother was willing to talk about it with them and her sister.

She also said she'd be doing it against her better judgment. She appreciated that I cared deeply about Donna and wanted to help her, but she had serious concerns about Donna's psychological condition, and my trying to save Donna troubled her. She thought our relationship was unhealthy and probably wasn't good for either of us. But leaving Donna addicted to speed with a physically abusive father and boyfriend was the worst option, so she said she'd try to help Donna but couldn't promise anything.

I called Donna, told her about the conversation and the options my mother had proposed, and asked if she'd be willing to meet all the conditions my mother had set. She said yes, as long as we'd be together after she got out. I told her my mother would call her parents and not to mention any of this to them until my mother had talked to them.

I trusted my mother's plan. She was good at this sort of thing; it was what she did for a living. While she probably felt trapped and obligated by my involvement in the situation, it was in her nature to help others. She'd helped many local parents and kids resolve family conflicts. Neighbors and friends had always come to talk with her about their troubles and to get advice. She was willing to help almost anyone who needed it. I'd always admired that about her.

Two mornings after our talk, I came out of my room to find a man sitting at the kitchen table talking to my mom. I immediately recognized him, though I'd only seen him from a distance, yelling at Donna at her front door. I ducked back into my room and closed the door. *Oh shit,* I thought. *It's happening.* The plan was in motion. I just hoped I'd done the right thing and that he didn't go home and take it out on Donna. I put my ear to the soundproof door; I couldn't hear anything. A couple of hours later I opened it a crack and peeked through. My mother was sitting alone at the table. I went out to see her.

"How did it go?"

"We'll see," she said noncommittally.

She seemed neither confident nor pessimistic. She wouldn't tell me the details of their conversation; they were confidential. I'd have to wait for Donna to tell me what her father said. She called that evening to tell me her parents were still going to Texas, but they said if she went into treatment, she could live with my aunt, and they'd pay a minimal fee.

I figured they were only too happy to be rid of their problem child and relieved of the expense of one daughter from their already-strained budget. Then I realized they'd be losing a maid and a nanny, as well as a daughter. Maybe, as screwed up as her parents were, they cared about Donna in their twisted way. Maybe the physical and verbal abuse was partly her father's sick, frustrated efforts to control and straighten out a wayward daughter. Anyway, he was letting Donna go, and that was all that mattered. Somehow my mother had gotten through to him. I wondered if she'd threatened to expose his behavior, letting him know he could lose Donna and worse. She was savvy and could be very tough.

Donna was anxious about quitting speed in a mental hospital and about abandoning her siblings but thrilled about escaping her father and staying in Chicago with me. Over the next few days, plans solidified. At the end of the week, Donna would enter Riveredge, a well-known psychiatric institute. Riveredge didn't treat drug addiction or provide addicts with psychological counseling to address its roots, though. It was the Stone Age of recovery. At the time, addiction wasn't considered a disease, but a moral failure, a weakness of character. Addicts were judged, shamed, and ostracized. Twelve-step meetings were for alcoholics only. Addicts who wanted and could afford help entered psychiatric institutions, supervised warehouse situations where they would be unable to use drugs for the duration of their stay. After being released, technically clean, they were on their own again. The Betty Ford Center would later establish a new model and more humane approach to treat addiction.

My mother helped facilitate Donna's acceptance into Riveredge. Her father's insurance would pay for her stay there. After that, his financial obligations toward Donna would consist of bare minimum monthly payments for room and board to my aunt, who wouldn't be profiting from her altruism and had also agreed to become Donna's legal guardian.

Meanwhile, the situation with Donna's boyfriend took a new turn. I'd been urging her to call Eric to break up with him over the phone. When she did, he took it badly. He told his sergeant his fiancée had broken up with him and asked for emergency leave to go see her. When his sergeant refused, Eric, as he told Donna over the phone, "kicked his face in" and went AWOL. He was on his way here and would arrive within forty-eight hours, on the day Donna would enter Riveredge. He said he wanted to talk to Donna face to face. I told Donna I wanted to be there, but she and her father said it was a bad idea. They were probably right.

On the morning of the day Donna was to enter Riveredge, Eric called to tell her he was a couple of hundred miles away and would arrive that afternoon. I planned to head over to help her load her stuff into her father's car. He'd give me a ride home, take Donna to meet Eric, and then take her to Riveredge. Her father wanted to meet me in person, before he moved his family to Texas. I was nervous about meeting him and about Donna meeting Eric, but I was relieved that things were turning in our favor.

When I got there, I saw a cop parked across the street. Cops always made me nervous. I rang the front doorbell. Her father opened it. He greeted me by name and politely invited me in. I could tell he didn't like me. He looked much younger than my parents. He was handsome, strong and fit, and naturally charming. He looked like a dynamic, successful businessman, not a brutal wife beater and child abuser. Donna said he'd been a star high school quarterback, her mother had been head cheerleader, and they'd been voted king and queen at their senior prom.

Donna's father looked over my head, smiled, and waved through the open door behind me. I turned around to see the cop in the patrol car wave back. I felt really paranoid. Donna said her father called the cops on Eric and would finally get him busted and jailed for possession. Had he called the cops on me? Was he trying to get me busted? But the cop was probably there for Eric, not me.

"Please wait in the living room," he said. "We'll be a few minutes." Then he went out the front door and across the street to talk to the cop. I went and sat on the couch. A few minutes later, he walked past me in the living room and headed upstairs. When he reached the second floor, I heard him say, "I asked the officer to come back in an hour."

I sat uncomfortably looking around the room. It looked like a typical, well-kept suburban tract house. Labeled boxes were stacked in a corner, but the living room was clean and the furniture was nice. A minute later, Donna's mother came downstairs. She smiled, greeted me politely, and asked if I wanted anything to drink. I politely declined. She also looked surprisingly young and quite beautiful. I could see where Donna got her looks.

Her mother went back upstairs. Moments later, I heard kids' laughter and loud footsteps. Donna's younger brothers and sisters came careening down the stairs. They stopped at the bottom and stood staring at me and giggling. They had lined up by height, as if trained. There were three boys and two girls between six and twelve years old, all clean-cut and good-looking. The only one who didn't make sense in this visually perfect American family, with their tidy tract home, was Donna, the emaciated speed freak with needle marks on her ankles and dark circles under her eyes. It was hard to reconcile what I was seeing with Donna's dark description of alcoholism and emotional and physical abuse. I wondered if Donna might have exaggerated, until I remembered the bruises on her back and arm. Appearances could be deceiving. In this case, they had to be a lie. Donna herself was evidence of a darker reality behind this glossy exterior.

Now her father came down the stairs carrying two suitcases. Donna followed him, carrying a large duffel bag full of the belongings she'd be taking with her.

"Let's go! We have to hurry!" her father called out.

I wasn't sure who he was talking to. I opened the front door, and they walked past me and headed to the car. The kids gathered in the doorway, watching, and Donna's mother appeared behind them.

"It was nice meeting you," I told Donna's mother. "You have a very beautiful home and kids."

I wanted to make a good impression, for whatever it was worth. Donna's mother gave me a blank smile, and the kids just stared at me. I probably looked like Frank Zappa to them. I headed for the car. Donna's father loaded the suitcases and duffel bag into the trunk, slammed it shut, and got into the driver's seat. I got into the back passenger side. Donna sat to my left, behind her father. Neither of us wanted to sit in the front seat with him. It was awkward, but things were already so weird it didn't seem to matter.

We drove to my house in silence. Donna's father pulled into my driveway, parked in front of the garage, and turned around to face Donna. Suddenly, everything changed. An angry, red-faced, frightening maniac replaced the charming, handsome father. He launched into an angry rant about how she'd better not take any drugs from now on and how if he found out she was, he'd come back from Texas, kick her ass, slap her silly, and beat her to a bloody pulp. In less than a minute, he'd worked himself into a frenzy. His words, his tone of voice, even his body language were all threatening. He seemed to be winding up to explode. Donna stared at him in helpless terror. I hoped he'd just chew her out and the storm would pass. Finally, he seemed to finish, and we sat in silence.

"Donna, we should get going," I tried to sound casual.

She shot me a quick glance, gave a slight, pitiful shake of her head, and then her eyes darted back to her father. I felt a sudden chill in the car. I knew I'd fucked up. I didn't know how badly. He looked at me like I'd insulted him.

"You're not going anywhere until I'm done talking!" he started in on me.

He yelled that he didn't trust me and that I was trouble. He twisted halfway around in his seat and raised his right arm in a threatening backhand position. Donna instinctively put her hands in front of her face and started crying, "No, Daddy, no!"

The first blow, a well-practiced backhand, knocked Donna's hands out of the way and smacked her across the side of her head. A brutal flurry followed. Each blow, connecting with a sickening thud, was punctuated with a vicious grunt from him and a gasp or whimper from Donna. He battered her knees and legs, and when she lifted her legs and curled in a ball, he leaned in and swung for her ribs and shoulder. Donna covered herself as best she could while he kept swinging and yelling, "Shut up, Donna! Shut the hell up!"

I didn't know what to do. I was madder than I'd ever been in my life. I would have jumped on him or put my body between them if I'd thought it might help. But I knew if I interfered now, he'd change his mind and take her with him to Texas. Whatever he was doing now, he'd do worse when he got her alone. So I sat with my guts churning, while he wailed away on my frail ninety-eight-pound girlfriend. I kept thinking, *She's his daughter. Just hold on a little longer. Then you'll have her, and you can keep her safe.*

Finally, he stopped, breathing hard, his face red and contorted. It seemed over. Donna was curled on the seat in a fetal position. She peeked out at him between her hands. Then he shifted around and started walloping her upper shoulders, back, and arms on the other side of her body while she jerked, cringed, and twisted around in a futile effort to avoid the blows. Again came the sickening thud of his fist against Donna, mixed with her whimpers and moans.

Thud! Thud! Thud! It seemed to go on forever. It was agonizing to watch and to hold back, to do nothing, waiting for him to finish, hoping it would all be over soon. Then Donna could stay here, he'd go to Texas, and he'd never be able to hit her again.

Donna didn't look at me once.

Finally, he stopped again, completely out of breath. Then he turned to me with a look of pure hate. I thought he was going to start in on me. I'd sit there and take it if that was the price of Donna's freedom.

"If you ever hurt Donna," he snarled, "I swear to God I'll come back and make sure you can never hurt her again."

What a lunatic! He'd just pounded his daughter like a punching bag, and now he was telling me not to hurt her. I didn't know what to say. I just nodded and kept my mouth shut.

"*Now* you can go," he said.

I stared at him, stupefied, my mouth hanging open, then opened the door, and got out. I didn't dare speak to Donna. I was afraid he'd start in on her again. He knew it. So did she. Her beating was also a message to me. I shut the door, and he backed out of the driveway and drove off down the street.

We weren't out of this yet. There was still the meeting with Eric. Standing in the driveway, I vowed no man would ever beat Donna again as long as I was around. My inability to protect her from that last beating sickened me and haunted me for years.

I didn't hear from Donna for several days. The hospital didn't allow new patients any communication from outside for two weeks except by mail, and all mail was read by hospital staff. Donna wrote to me, and her letter said things had gone okay with Eric. Two weeks later, she called me, and we talked on the phone. She said she'd given Eric his ring back, told him that she wasn't going to marry him and that she was going into a hospital to get clean from speed and then move out of the state where he wouldn't find her. After the conversation, he took off on his motorcycle, and she never heard from him again. I suspected that her father had arranged for Eric to be arrested after he left. A few days after Donna entered Riveredge, her family loaded their things into a moving van and headed for Texas. As much as I hated her father, I was impressed with the way he'd dealt with Eric.

Knowing Donna was safe in a hospital, getting clean at last, I relaxed a little. I started feeling a sense of exhilaration. Helping Donna escape from her abusive father was a major life accomplishment. We were tied together now. I knew how scared she must be. Now, Donna was depending on me completely, as well as my family. I also knew my mother was uncomfortable with the arrangement and concerned about both Donna and me.

I felt a nagging sense of unease. Reality was setting in. I wondered if Donna could stay clean when she got out and if I could handle the responsibility I'd taken on. Our future now depended on me. I'd have to find a way to make money so we could get our own place when I turned eighteen. I now had a purpose. I felt totally committed to stand by Donna and to take care of her. I was more fired up and determined than I'd ever been in my life. At fifteen, for the first time ever, I was looking toward a future that might be worth living. I was on the path to becoming a man.

14

Day of the Dead

It was the strangest, saddest day of my life. I was sixteen, attending Central Y, and making little academic progress, but otherwise things were good. I'd gotten my driver's license. Donna was off speed, out of rehab, and doing much better, living with my aunt, less than a mile away at the far end of the co-op. Though still clingy and fragile, with delusional moments, she was mostly clearheaded and very functional. We were hanging out a lot, happy to be together again.

We frequently got high together, only smoking weed and hash. It seemed like a good idea. It helped her stay off speed, which was addictive, wired you for days, starved your body, fried your nervous system, brought you crashing down, and made you crazy and paranoid over time. Weed, hash, and hallucinogens like acid, mescaline, peyote, and psilocybin weren't addictive. They mellowed you out, made you more real, and opened your mind and heart to a greater reality. That's what we believed. But the honeymoon period of the drug revolution would soon be over, crashing into its darker side to reveal an ugly, hellish face.

Late one November morning, Donna, Neil, and I went to visit my co-op friend Marsha, who lived a couple of blocks over the hill from my house. Donna and Neil really liked each other. Now twelve, Neil was still the same sweet kid he'd always been. He loved hanging out with us, and we loved being with him. But the past couple of months I'd begun to cut him out of my life, and we both felt bad about it.

I loved him as much as ever. But my life increasingly revolved around smoking dope and dealing drugs, and I didn't want Neil, who looked up to me as a role model, following in my footsteps and getting caught up in my world. He always wanted to be with me. Whenever I left the house, he'd plead with me to let him come. But I was usually going places and doing things I didn't want him to be involved in. He knew what I was doing. We'd always been so close, so he couldn't understand why I was suddenly shutting him out of my life.

After hanging out with us for a while on this particular afternoon, Neil went to see a friend of his named Jan, my friend Don's younger brother. Later Donna and I headed back home. We came over the hill and started down toward my house.

"David, look at all the people down there," said Donna.

A crowd of fifteen or twenty people gathered in the street below, a couple of blocks away. I knew my friends Toby, Don, and a few other co-op kids were shooting a movie about the Chicago riots that day for a class project with an 8 mm movie camera.

"They're probably watching Toby and Don shoot their movie," I said.

"It doesn't look like they're making a movie to me," said Donna.

Suddenly I felt uneasy. "Let's see what's going on."

I took Donna's hand, and we ran down the hill and cut across a couple of my neighbors' front yards. As we got closer, we started walking again. I was feeling really anxious now. I knew everyone there. They were all co-op people—neighbors, parents, and friends. They looked stricken. Some were crying. They we re crowded around some-one lying on the ground, shaking violently. It looked like Don, having convulsions. At first, I couldn't believe it was him. Then I recognized his father standing over him. Toby and the other kids who'd been part of the movie were all there.

He'll be okay, I thought. *His father is here. We're all here. Someone will help him.*

But his father looked distraught, even frantic. No one seemed to know what to do.

"He's not breathing," I heard his father say.

I heard snatches of conversation around me, something about a knife and part of a pen to stick in Don's throat. Donna was totally freaked out. There was nothing we could do to help. I took her hand, and we started toward my house. We were both in shock.

When we got home, my parents weren't there. We went into my room. I put on some music, and we sat on the couch. A few minutes later, I heard someone come in. I went out to find Neil and Jan on their way upstairs to Neil's room. Neil said Jan's mom told them to come stay here while they took Don to the hospital. I didn't know how much Jan knew about Don or what I should do. I decided not to say anything about it. I wished my parents were home.

"Do you guys want something to eat?" I didn't know what else to say.

Neil turned to Jan, and they both shrugged.

"Sure," Jan said.

Jan and Neil went upstairs. I wondered what had happened to Don, and if he was going to be okay. It was around one o'clock. I opened a can of soup, put it in a pot on the stove, and poured in a can of water.

Just as the soup was ready, my parents returned from a co-op board meeting. They told me Don was lying on top of a car while shooting a riot scene when the driver swerved. Don fell off, landing on his tailbone, and a clear liquid, later determined to be spinal fluid, came out of his nose and mouth. He went into convulsions, and his breathing stopped.

Dad hardly said a word. He looked exhausted and kept rubbing his hand over his forehead.

"I'm not feeling well," he said. "I'm going upstairs to lie down a while."

My mother decided to make some sandwiches to go with the soup. She told Donna to go back to my aunt's house for lunch. Donna was still freaked out. I told her I had to stay with Neil and Jan, so she left.

I went into my room and sat on the couch, feeling as bad as I'd ever felt in my life. After a while, my mother called us all to a late lunch. I went in and sat at the table. Jan and Neil came down. Dad didn't come. We assumed he was taking a nap. A few minutes later, I heard his shrill whistle upstairs. Dad rarely whistled. When he did, it meant come right away. I knew something was wrong.

I dropped my fork on the floor, ran out of the kitchen, and headed upstairs to my parents' bedroom. Dad sat on the edge of the bed trying to button up a long-sleeve flannel shirt. His face looked strangely dark, and he was having trouble with the buttons. He looked up at me. I could see he was scared.

"David," he said, "I need you to take me to the hospital."

His voice was weak and shallow. I'd never seen him like this before. He suddenly turned pale, his face expressionless. But struggle was in his eyes. I felt scared and sad. I went and stood in front of him.

"Dad, what's wrong?"

"I'm cold. Help me with my shirt."

I bent down and started buttoning his shirt from the bottom up. Everything was in slow motion, yet in extreme focus, like a movie close-up. I watched my fingers buttoning his shirt; its soft, cream-colored material with rust-colored stripes absorbed my gaze, becoming an endless pattern. I finished one button and started on the next.

Suddenly Dad jolted upright and grabbed my head with his palms. Holding my face six inches from his, he looked into my eyes. I heard my mother come into the room behind me. I was lost in my father's eyes. I thought I heard him say, "This is it!"

My mother ran back downstairs to call an ambulance. My dad pressed his hands tighter to my head, his face flushed bright red, and he fell back slowly, still holding my head, pulling me down on top of him. I slid off of him and looked into his bright red face.

"Oh, Dad, Dad!…" I heard myself say.

He was still looking at me. I looked back at him and fell into his gaze. It was like he was holding me with his eyes. I felt him struggling for life at the same time that he was incredibly present with me. I felt our connection. Then something began to fade from his eyes. I tried to hold him with me, but he slipped away. In a matter of moments, his eyes became vacant. They were still looking at me, but he wasn't in them anymore. I looked in his eyes but couldn't find him there. I could feel that he was gone. Instinctively, I looked down at his body and then around the room, as if I might see where he'd gone. I wondered, if I'd been stronger, maybe I could have kept him with us. Deep down I knew he was gone, but I couldn't admit it to myself. I didn't have time to process it.

My mother came rushing into the room and threw herself on the bed beside him. She cradled his head in her arms and began sobbing hysterically, kissing him all over his face, saying, "No, Pat, don't go! . . . No! . . . Please, Pat . . . don't go! . . ."

My mother usually dealt calmly with difficult situations, but she couldn't deal with this. My father's face was now a dark purplish color, but she didn't seem to notice. She kept kissing him, begging him not to leave. He wasn't moving, and his eyes had the same glassy look. His color was getting darker, approaching the color of death.

I felt frightened and helpless. I couldn't believe Dad was dead, so I believed he was dying instead. A few minutes later Neil and Jan came into the room. My mother told us to slap the soles of his feet and the palms of his hands. I didn't know what good it would do, but we started doing it. This was before knowledge about CPR had become widespread. Mom was crying and slapping one of Dad's palms. I was slapping the bottom of his right foot, listening for the ambulance.

I was afraid the EMTS would have trouble finding our house. The roads in and around the co-op were confusing. People coming to see us for the first time often had trouble finding us. After a couple of minutes I went outside. I heard a siren approaching the co-op. As it got closer, I could tell it was on the wrong street, on the dead-end side of the neighborhood—exactly what I feared would happen. The EMTs were lost, only a few hundred yards from our house as the crow flies but more than a mile away by the streets. I heard the siren moving farther away. They were going back around to a main street to try to find their way here. I knew they could easily get lost again.

I ran back into the house, grabbed the car keys, got into my dad's car, and drove like a madman through the co-op to the crossroads the EMTs would have to come through. Finally, the ambulance appeared.

I couldn't believe how slow it was going. I waved and yelled at them to follow me, then took off. They were going so slow I had to keep slowing down to let them catch up. I was furious! I knew every second counted, but they kept the same slow pace all the way to the house.

Two medics with a stretcher followed me upstairs to my parents' bedroom. One of them examined my father, felt his heart and throat, and checked his pulse. Dad's face was now a dark shade of gray. He wasn't moving and didn't seem to be breathing, but the medic looked at my distraught mother and said, "He's still alive." The hopeful look on her swollen, tear-stained face was more than I could bear. Despite my father's appearance, we were all clinging to hope. Finally, they put my father on a stretcher, took him downstairs, put him in the back of the ambulance, and drove off with the siren blaring.

My mother followed them in her car. I stayed behind with Neil and Jan. A few minutes later, Mike, one of our neighbors around Emerson's age, came over to see what had happened. When I told him, he asked me if Emerson knew. I shook my head. Emerson was away at college.

"You have to call him," Mike said.

"Yeah, I know."

"Do you have his phone number?"

"I don't know. It's somewhere around here."

"Where would it be?"

Mike was trying to help. I pointed to a pile of papers on the table near the phone. He rummaged through them and finally found the number of Emerson's dormitory. He dialed it and had a couple of brief conversations with different people trying to track down Emerson. Finally, Emerson got on the phone. Mike told him Dad had had a heart attack. Then Emerson asked to talk to me.

"Hey, David, what's going on? Is it true?" He was in a state of disbelief.

"Yeah."

"Dad's dead?"

"I don't know, but it's bad."

"What happened?"

"I think it was a heart attack. He just turned purple and … you have to come home now." I was crying.

"Oh my God!" Emerson burst out crying too.

"Emerson, you've got to come home. We have a lot to do, and I don't think Mom's doing too good."

"I'm getting on the next flight," said Emerson through his tears. "I'll get myself to the house. Don't worry about picking me up."

It was getting dark out. Neil, Jan, and I went to the TV room. They sat down on the couch. I turned on the TV and sat down next to them. I remember the flickering light on their blank faces.

The Bill Cosby Show was on. Cosby played a high school teacher and football coach. I'd always found the show comforting. In this episode, a woman was having a baby in a house during a rainstorm. Cosby's character was there. It was raining so hard they couldn't go out, so he had to deliver the baby. The woman screamed as he tried to comfort her throughout the labor. The moment the baby was born onscreen, something cracked in me. The contrast between new life being born into the world, the mood of joy and wonder portrayed on the TV show, and my father lying still on the bed with vacant eyes and a gray face, the anguish on my mother's face—all of this broke through my denial and hopefulness. At that moment, I knew with absolute certainty Dad was dead. He had died while we were looking into each other's eyes. That's why I couldn't find him in his gaze after it faded. I didn't say anything to Neil. I just sat numbly staring at the screen.

I can't remember exactly what happened after that. Jan left. Later Mom came home from the hospital. She told Neil and me that Dad had a massive heart attack, was dead before the ambulance arrived, and didn't suffer long. She said Don was dead too. My friend Marsha came over. Donna too. I remember all of us standing in Neil's room crying together and holding one another.

In the following days and weeks, I realized how powerful my dad's presence had been in our lives, as well as in our co-op world. So many people came to tell us how much Dad had meant to them, how much he'd helped them, how much they valued and loved him. The vacuum created by his absence revealed the impact of his energy and presence, which we'd relied on and taken for granted. Now that he was gone, we realized how profoundly his presence—his spirit—had colored and sustained our lives.

But where had his spirit gone? Could it simply disappear or be extinguished? I couldn't fathom this. I felt a strange certainty that his spirit still existed somewhere, in some form. When a being full of spirit and power collided with death, it had to continue, to go somewhere. Dad's spirit itself had energy. And I'd heard energy can't just disappear.

I remembered how Dad always made us laugh. Like the time he and Mom began arguing in the kitchen. He wanted to buy an electric knife, and she thought it was a waste of money. So he tried to kiss her, and she said, "No, I'm mad, and I don't want an electric knife, and I don't want to kiss you." And he said, "Come on, let me kiss you." And then they were off, with Dad chasing her around the house.

Emerson and Neil and I were sitting at the kitchen table, cheering and shouting, "Kiss her! Kiss her!" He finally caught her, they embraced, and he was giving her little pecks on her face, saying, "Okay, but I get to kiss you." Moments later she gave a little gasp. "Okay," she said, flashing a smile, and gave him a little peck on his lips.

I remembered when Mom wanted Dad to punish us. He'd scold us and then turn to Mom and say, "All right, we're going to have to throw them away." Then he'd pick us up, take us out to the garage and drop us in the fifty-five-gallon paper trash bin. We knew that wasn't really a punishment. We'd rock back and forth in the bin until it fell over, then climb out, and go back to the table to finish dinner with a little smile, wanting to do better.

I remembered the time all four of us ganged up on him. We picked him up and dragged him from the kitchen into the garage, with his butt dragging on the floor. He was laughing so hard he could hardly catch his breath. Somehow we managed to lift him up and drop him butt first into the paper trash bin.

I began to realize my father had been a great man—a better man than I could ever hope to be. He brought a special light and heartfelt humor wherever he went. Almost everyone he knew loved him and his laughter. Now I saw his humor was his way of letting me know how much he loved me. But I hadn't told him I loved him for several years. Now, too late, I realized how much I loved him. This struck me hard and would haunt me for years.

I used to think when a loved one died, survivors might question how much that person loved them. But now this never entered my mind. Now all I cared about, what I worried about and hoped for, was that my father understood how much I loved *him*—even though I didn't fully know myself. I feared that with Dad's dying, I might have lost any chance of becoming the kind of person he'd been—the best person I'd ever known.

15

OD

Dad's death devastated our family. We'd lost not just the primary breadwinner but also the center post, the spiritual backbone, the heart and soul of our family. The nourishing light of his warmth, steady presence, and delightful humor had gone out. Now, a dark, painful, palpable emptiness filled the house and our lives. Each of us fell apart in our own way.

Emerson returned to college a few days after the funeral. I didn't see him much over the next couple of years. Neil was lost and bewildered. I started letting him hang out with me again whenever he wanted to.

Mom fell into a deep depression, started drinking, and quickly became a functional alcoholic. She'd been working three days a week, but now she started full time. A large thermos filled with vermouth and vodka became her companion in the evenings. She'd come home from work, make dinner, and the three of us would eat together. That was very important to her. After dinner, she'd sit in her favorite chair in the family room and disappear, knitting, smoking, drinking, and watching TV until late. She maintained all her responsibilities, managing the family and finances, keeping Emerson in college and us in the house with virtually no support. It was heroic. In light of that, we overlooked her drinking and tried not to put any pressure on her.

Neil and I were left completely unsupervised. I did my best to watch out for him, but I was disappearing into my relationship with Donna, my own drug use, and dealing. Neil spent more time away from the house with his friends or in the basement rec room Dad didn't have a chance to finish.

Only fifty-two when he died, Dad didn't have much life insurance. We kids didn't know it then, but he and Mom had been buying abandoned houses in depressed neighborhoods. Dad hired neighborhood workers to fix them up and sold them to locals who couldn't otherwise afford to buy houses. He helped them get financing and made no profit on the deals. This was just one of my parents' gifts of community service, their way of helping the less fortunate. They'd done this successfully a number of times over the years. When Dad died, Mom got stuck with a house she couldn't renovate and therefore couldn't sell. We owned it, but it did us no good. We also owned a portion of Mom's family's medical clinic, which didn't yield any income either.

Mom's salary barely covered our living expenses. Our financial crunch motivated me to minimize my family expenses and to earn more money. I hoped to find a legal, less dangerous way to make a living than dealing.

A few months after Dad's death, I got a job making waterbeds and frames with a waterbed company. As a sideline, I'd buy some at a discount and sell them. I made decent money, though not as much as in dealing. Because the repetitive motion of the machines I worked on in the factory put me in a trance, I had trouble memorizing the names of parts and the sequences of tasks, and my boss would get on me for not staying focused. The waterbeds were made of inferior materials and leaked, so customers started returning them. It was a fiasco. So I quit and went back to dealing.

With dealing there were no paperwork, memorizing, sequencing, or quality-control issues. I never bought or sold anything I didn't try first. I only bought quality stuff, so no one ever returned merchandise. I understood the numbers, I had the best weed, the best prices, and the most consistent supply, so I always had repeat customers. And I was my own boss—although no one ever tried to hurt me or rip me off for selling waterbeds.

My relationship with Donna was my main focus. When it was good, my life was good. She was off meth, but her personality remained mercurial and impossible to fathom. She had phases when she'd be disoriented, confused, and hear voices. In the aftermath of one of these audio hallucinations, she often became like a different person—enraged for no apparent reason, accusing me of things that never happened, or forgetting things she did. Sometimes, she became shy and withdrawn, wanting no contact with the outside world; other times, she became a wild woman, wanting to get stoned and do dangerous things. The picture that came to me was of a wonderful, kind little girl who one day found that the person she most loved and depended on had decided he didn't like parts of her. When he threw her to the ground in a rage, she broke into distinct pieces.

Psychology at the time seemed simplistic and not all that helpful. People like Donna who had hallucinations were labeled with schizophrenia or dissociative identity disorder, also known as multiple personality disorder. I didn't know if these diagnoses were correct. I knew she got overwhelmed by life and became very confused, that she had a great heart, and that she loved me.

Growing up, Donna wasn't allowed to experience or to express fundamental parts of herself—not even basic feelings such as hunger, weariness, loneliness. Personal desires, such as wanting nice clothes or compliments, also had been unacceptable. I thought that if I cared and loved Donna enough, I might help her put herself back together. I knew her varied aspects and different personalities were all essential pieces of her. If I could appreciate and accept each part of her, and all her needs, she might be able to appreciate herself too. Then, instead of shifting between her extreme personalities, Donna might come together like pieces of a puzzle into a whole and happy version of herself. Nobody else in her life seemed to care about helping. If I didn't try to help her, nobody would.

It was working. Donna grew in confidence and competence. Her brilliance began to shine. She graduated from high school early, got a job, and began to find her way through the social maze of life. The more competent and plugged into the world she became, the more she impressed me. Despite the fear this brought up in me that she'd eventually leave me, I wanted Donna to succeed. All my life, people started out even with me, but then learned, surpassed me, and left me behind. Donna chose to stay with me. She knew my heart.

Over the next two years our lives improved. Then things began to change. I'm not sure what happened. Maybe I'd started to imagine myself with a future and began to invest more of myself in our relationship. I started taking things more personally when Donna got mad or had trouble relating to me. I started having expectations of her. Or maybe her desire always to do more drugs triggered my need to control her drug use, suppressing her wild girl. The more I struggled with those parts of her, the more distinct and powerful they became. I began to glimpse in her a manipulative, amoral quality toward others and the world in general. I worried what other qualities might be there, hidden from my view. But she still included me in her inner world, remaining heartfelt and honest with me.

Dealing was still my only way to make enough money to get by, to prove myself as an independent, can-do guy. Dealing gave me a prestigious rep in the 1960s counterculture. I was buying hash, mescaline, acid, THC, and other drugs that came through Chicago. A couple of times Donna and I gave Mom money to help out, telling her we were both working and saving money

Mom's drinking and my drug use escalated at the same time. We formed an unspoken agreement to ignore each other's addiction. I didn't mention her thermos of vodka and vermouth, and she didn't mention the smell of weed in my room. I remember one night Donna, Neil, and I were hanging out in my room listening to music. I was sitting at my desk with a kilo of marijuana broken open in front of me, weighing and bagging ounces on my scale. Beside the scale, a candle burned in a green wine jug. Suddenly, the door opened, and Mom shuffled in, drunk. She looked at us, then at my desk. Her puffy eyes narrowed to slits, and she looked at me. "That's a beautiful candle," she said. "It's late. Neil needs to go to bed." Then she turned and walked unsteadily out of the room, closing the door behind her.

Mom insisted that anyone who came into her house be introduced to her. It was how she tried to maintain some kind of control at home when our lives were spiraling out of control. A few times, bikers in leather jackets came over to buy a few kilos of weed. I'd invite them in and lead them single file through the house toward my room. Mom, sitting in her chair as they filed by, would stop them politely, introduce herself, and look each one in the eye. These hard-core bikers treated her respectfully and seemed to like her.

Meanwhile, Donna was still living at my aunt's house. I was sneaking into her room a lot at night to sleep with her. We were stoned most of the time. We did pretty much whatever we wanted, whenever we wanted, as long as we stayed in school.

Donna had periodic episodes where she'd fly into fits of jealousy over innocent encounters. Once we were in a motorboat in the middle of a Minnesota lake when she started screaming about my interaction with a store clerk while buying groceries. She jumped on me from behind, grabbed me by the hair, and began wrenching my head around. I lost my grip on the steering wheel, and we fell down in the hull, as the boat began veering in tight circles. I struggled to get hold of her until she finally relaxed in my arms, crying. When she calmed down I got up and steered us back to the dock.

Afterward, Donna often had no memory of these incidents. Smoking weed seemed to help her; then I could gently coax her to remember. She'd begin to accept, in gradual stages, what she'd done. She might remember an episode in pieces or suddenly and all at once. At such times, she seemed very young and open, like a little girl. These were some of our most intimate moments together.

We knew we were screwed up. Whenever things improved enough to lead me to start thinking a good future seemed possible, they'd turn again in the wrong direction. But the world itself was screwed up. King Richard Daley's Blue Knights brutally cracked down on Chicago's antiwar protests. Mississippi police brutalized blacks and civil-rights protesters. The United States was bombing Vietnamese villages, supposedly to defend us from communism. My generation didn't believe warnings about the dangers of drugs because they came from compromised authorities whose lies, exaggerations, and heavy-handed tactics discredited any truth their point of view might contain. And we wanted the truth, not the half-truths used to manipulate and control us, supposedly for our own good. Compared to the world's insanity, my personal compromises and shortcomings seemed minor.

It was easy to rationalize my excesses in a world full of bullshit. Yet I knew my life was heading in a bad direction, and I wasn't doing anything to change its course for one very simple reason: I didn't know what to do. I felt powerless to change my life and hopeless about my future and the future of the world. People would say to me, "You should learn to read and graduate high school." *Yeah, thanks, I never thought of that.* It was worse when they'd say, "There must be something you can do." These useless platitudes, offered by uninformed people uncomfortable with the reality of my predicament, reflected their denial. The superficiality seemed almost cruel. Why must there be something I could do? I'd tried and exhausted all the options I knew of. These were not stupid people. It seemed to me that when they couldn't find answers to problems, they resorted to platitudes reflecting their unwillingness to accept the truth. The possibility that there might *not* be anything I could do was too disturbing for them to accept, and so it was easier to assume I wasn't trying hard enough.

This only intensified my sense of hopelessness. It made sense for Donna and me to stay stoned until I could find answers that worked for both of us. Everyone was rationalizing their choices and behaviors. Donna and I were no different that way. Perhaps we were more aware of it. I didn't know what I suffered more: what I knew and others apparently didn't, or what I didn't know and they apparently did. So we continued self-medicating our pain and hopelessness, moving deeper into a life of denial, danger, and disintegration.

One night Donna and I and our friends Nan and Todd went to buy five pounds of weed from a dealer named Jim, a tall, skinny guy who lived with his wife, Suzy. I'd bought weed from Jim before and knew he had a gun, but he was dealing dope in large quantities, so it made sense. He and I had never had any problems. Jim had just gotten a large shipment of Colombian weed and we'd come to score.

I parked in front of Jim's house, and we all went to the front door. I knocked, and immediately all the lights in the house went off.

We heard the sound of hushed voices inside. It was weird. Todd and I looked at each other. Then the front door opened a crack, and the porch light revealed Jim's haggard face peering out, paranoia in his eyes. He didn't seem to recognize me. He was clearly strung out on speed, stretched to the limit and ready to snap.

"What do you want?" he asked suspiciously in a hoarse whisper.

"Hey, Jim, it's me, David. We want to buy some weed."

He opened the door, waved us inside, then shut the door behind us, and turned the lights back on. That's when I saw the gun in his hand, pointed in our direction.

"Where the fuck is Suzy? What have you done with Suzy?" he asked in the same weird voice.

He waved the gun, gesturing randomly as he spoke. He wasn't trying to threaten us; in fact, he seemed almost oblivious to the gun in his hand. I decided the best thing was to ignore the gun and act as if everything was cool. I ignored his paranoid questions about Suzy. "Good to see you, Jim. Did you get the weed? We need some weight."

He perked up. "How much?"

"Five pounds?"

He looked at me suspiciously and asked, "Where's Suzy?"

"Hey, man, we haven't seen her."

Suddenly he started to cry. He stood sobbing with his back to the door—still waving the gun in our direction. I tried to steer the conversation back to the deal.

"So what about the weed? You got five pounds? How much per pound?"

He looked at me blankly. "Yeah, sure," he said. "I'll get it. It's a hundred and ten a pound."

He walked past us, through the living room, and into the back of the house. Just before he turned the corner, he looked back at us, lifting the gun that was dangling at his side. "Don't any of you move," he said. Then he disappeared. I heard him rustling around in another room. At one point he yelled, "Don't you fucking move!"

Donna, Nan, Todd, and I looked at each other and didn't say a word. We knew even a whisper might trigger Jim's paranoia. I waved the girls to go, and they quietly snuck out the door.

A couple of minutes later, Jim came back around the corner with a big burlap sack. He set it down on the coffee table. He seemed unaware that half our group had disappeared. He opened the sack and showed Todd and me two kilos of Colombia's finest, wrapped in dark paper, and a loose bag I assumed contained the last of the five pounds. I wasn't about to challenge him on it. Jim put one hand out for the money, still holding the gun on us with the other hand.

"Is this shit any good?" I asked casually, hoping he wouldn't notice the girls were gone or bring up Suzy again, who'd probably split on him and his amphetamine psychosis.

"Definitely," said Jim. "It's real good shit.

"Cool."

I pulled a wad of bills from my pocket and slowly counted out five-hundred-and-fifty dollars on the table beside the open gunny-sack. Jim nodded, apparently satisfied.

"Thanks, Jim," I said. "Good doing business with you."

Todd and I stood there.

Looking into Jim's crazed eyes, trying to sound as relaxed as possible, I said, "You need to clean up."

"Yeah, get the fuck out of here," he said, still pointing the gun at us.

"We'll see you later," I said.

I picked up the sack of weed and followed Todd outside, closing the door behind me. Donna and Nan were in the car with the trunk open. Donna sat behind the wheel with the engine running.

"Shit," I said to Todd. "I just bought five pounds of weed without tasting it or weighing it."

I threw the sack in the trunk and got into the car. Donna took off like a rocket. She was a really good driver even when she was stoned. We were a good team. I knew I could rely on her if we got into a serious scrape. Some friends jokingly called us Bonnie and Clyde. If we were threatened and Donna had a gun, I was pretty sure she'd use it.

Dealing wasn't always like this. I'd met a lot of cool people I really liked through dealing. I also met my share of lowlifes, paranoid crazies, emotional cripples, and criminals—the kind of people I wanted nothing to do with. But I got used to it. One guy bragged to me about going to jail for killing a cop who tried to bust him. Pretty sure he was telling the truth, I stopped dealing with him. If he got busted for killing a cop and wasn't in prison, he had to be a narc. He was. He later turned in an acquaintance of mine, who then tried, unsuccessfully, to set me up for a bust. It made me more cautious. Unlike a lot of other dealers, I seemed to have a sixth sense for danger, which kept me from getting busted.

At first I didn't notice I was gradually changing into someone I never thought I'd become, doing things I'd never thought I'd do. I thought I was separate from my business and better than the people I dealt with to make money. I'd look at some of them and think, *I'll never be like that guy.* But only a few degrees, a series of choices and crossed lines, separated me from them. You can't help becoming like the people you hang out with. Gradually, I crossed one line after another.

I started doing things I regretted afterward. Once, a friend stole some money from the safe in my room. I told him to pay up or suffer the consequences. He was scared, but he kept stalling and telling me he didn't have the money. Finally, I went over to his house with two friends and banged on his door. His mother answered. She knew me and had always liked me. Now she was scared of me. She handed me a check for three hundred dollars, about half of what her son had stolen.

"It's all I have," she said. "Please take it, and don't hurt him."

She was a young widow with six kids and had fallen on hard times. I knew the three hundred was probably all she had. But it wasn't enough for me. I couldn't let him get away with it. I'd trusted him, and he'd ripped me off. I took the check, went inside, and took the phone off the hook. One friend stayed downstairs to keep an eye on the mother. My other friend and I went upstairs and found the thief in his room. We didn't hurt him too much. I just pushed him around. He was terrified and apologized, but he didn't have the money. On the way out, I took his amplifier. His mother stood fearfully by the door, watching us leave.

I felt really bad about the incident, but I still took her money, justifying it to myself. He'd stolen from me. He'd betrayed me. He deserved it. He made me do what I'd done. Eventually my conscience broke through, and I couldn't justify it. I'd scared someone's mother, who was always nice to me, taken all her money, and pushed her son around in her house. I knew then I was heading in a bad direction. I was becoming the kind of person I despised. I had to find a way out of this. I had to find another way to survive. But I didn't know what else to do.

For years I'd felt a sense of impending doom, a certainty that sooner or later something bad would happen. Dad's death and the gradual unraveling of our family intensified this feeling. Things were getting worse. My future held no hope or joy. There was no solution, no escape. My accelerating drug use gave me no relief; it only made me feel more hopeless and estranged from life. My relationship with Donna no longer provided the sanctuary it once had. She was also unraveling. The wild part of her that craved more and more dope increasingly dominated her. My influence on her diminished, and she became less available and harder to deal with. We sank into our own private hells, taking each other down. I couldn't imagine living this way indefinitely. It wouldn't turn out well. But I couldn't stop. Mom had warned me about this from the start.

The turning point came at the end of one of our drug binges— a week in which Donna and I consumed over one hundred hits of synthetic mescaline. Each day required larger doses to get off. That last day we took a megadose. An hour later, when we didn't seem to be getting off, Donna suggested we buy some acid. I called a dealer I knew who said he had some sixteen-way acid. I'd never heard of such a thing. I figured he was exaggerating. I didn't want any, but Donna did. Against my better judgment, we went over and bought two hits. I only let her take a third. I didn't take any.

We were tempting fate. We'd been in a bad place before the run. After a week of tripping, we both felt like crap, and everything seemed grim, horrible, and hopeless. We ended up hiding out in Donna's room at my aunt's house, lying naked in bed. The mescaline finally kicked in. I was as high as I'd ever been, glad I hadn't taken the acid, but worried about Donna, who had. What if it was as strong as the guy said? She was more wasted than I'd ever seen anyone. She couldn't talk. She finally curled up in a fetal position and withdrew completely. I had a really bad feeling, but I was tripping so intensely I didn't trust my judgment. Maybe I was just being paranoid, freaking myself into a bad trip by focusing on worst-case scenarios.

As I lay there, eyes closed, a nonstop flood of chaotic, scary, mescaline-induced thoughts and visions pouring through my head, I swore this was the last time I'd ever put myself in this situation. Every few minutes I'd open my eyes to examine Donna and to listen to her breathing. She lay completely immobile, almost lifeless, her breath shallow and her skin a weird grayish color. But maybe I was hallucinating. I couldn't tell. I tried talking to her, but she didn't respond. She seemed aware of me. At one point, I put my ear to her mouth to listen for her breathing, then against her chest to listen for her heartbeat. But my own heart was pounding so loudly in my ears I couldn't hear anything else. I told myself not to panic. I was just tripping. Donna would be okay. People didn't die from taking LSD, unless they jumped out a window or something.

We lay there for hours, with Donna not moving, not responding to words or touch. My anxiety grew. The loud ticking of the wall clock began to drive me nuts. Gradually, the intensity of the mescaline began to fade, and I was able to think more coherently. I could see the time by the light of the lamp near the bed: 4:00 a.m. I leaned my face close to Donna's and whispered to her to wake up. I was sweating profusely, and my mouth was dry as sandpaper. I felt like a rock sinking to the bottom of a dark well. Putting my mouth to her ear, I started speaking her name and talking to her in a hoarse, desperate whisper. I didn't want to wake my aunt. She didn't know I was there, and I didn't want to deal with her in the state Donna and I were in.

"Donna. Donna," I whispered. "You have to wake up. Just tell me you're okay, and I'll let you go back to sleep."

She didn't respond. Was she dead? I lifted her up and shook her roughly, fiercely whispering her name, begging her to wake up. Then her eyes fluttered; she gave a little moan. Thank God!

"Donna, can you hear me? Are you okay?"

Her eyes opened, barely a slit, and she mumbled, "Blood—there's blood in the streets..."

Her eyes shut again, and she reverted to a catatonic state. At least she was alive. I decided to let her sleep it off. I lay beside her, holding her in my arms, relieved but still scared. She always felt better when I held her like this. I rocked her gently. I realized I was rocking her as much for my benefit as for hers. At one point, I began saying out loud, "Please, please, Donna, live. I promise I'll change. I'll do something different. I'll find a better way to take care of you. I'm sorry for everything...I know we have to change. Just please, Donna, live."

Finally, the morning light began to peek through the curtains. The mescaline was wearing off, and my head was starting to clear. I didn't know what I was going to do. But I knew I had to make a change.

16

Desperate Hope

I left Donna that morning, burnt out and shaken to the core, convinced she'd come close either to dying or retreating into a catatonic psychosis. I couldn't imagine how I'd have lived had one of those things happened. I'd had enough. I went home and flushed the rest of the acid down the toilet. I knew I had to change, but I didn't know what to do, how to become a different and better person. The limitations that had set the course of my life and defined my identity still seemed insurmountable.

I was seventeen. Donna and I had been together over three years. Her desires and needs had come to define much of my life. Her thirst for drugs was now all consuming—and unmanageable by me. Getting high every day since I was fourteen had numbed me to the gnawing desperation I felt about my future, and the desperation I felt about my future allowed me to rationalize my spiraling drug use and the chaos of my illicit life. But that last bad trip and almost losing Donna were warning signs I couldn't ignore.

I felt again the raw desperation and hopelessness that had made me reach for drugs. Yet I saw no solution, no options, besides suicide. The specter of my future institutionalization seemed more real than ever. The numbness and oblivion in drugs, until now preferable to conscious anxiety and pain, weren't helping. I felt a new sense of urgency. Something had to change. I had to get my life together. I had to graduate from high school. I had to find a life worth the struggle and a self I could live with.

I'd been hearing about Transactional Analysis, a remarkable new therapy pioneered by Dr. Eric Berne and presented in his best-selling book *Games People Play*. Transaction Analysis, or TA, was a big deal at the time, touted as a radical and life-transforming therapeutic method. Other authors had also written best-selling books based on Berne's work. In the late 1950s, Berne began organizing weekly educational meetings for psychotherapists, the San Francisco Social Psychiatry Seminars. I sensed that TA might help me and Donna.

Donna began reading *Games People Play* to me. She also read another best-selling book on TA to me, *I'm OK, You're OK* by Thomas Harris. I got very excited. TA was simple yet radical. Traditional Freudian therapy helped patients acquire a theoretical understanding of their inner drives, motivations, and dysfunctions. But the growing consensus, including the critique from TA, was that this didn't translate into healthy behavioral changes and transformed lives. TA focused on the drives, motivations, dysfunctions, and roles we play out in our relationships and lives.

Transactional Analysis divides the personality into three ego states: Parent, Adult, and Child. These states operate on what Berne called *scripts*, formed through key relationship dynamics, or *transactions*, in childhood that become fixed patterns in adulthood. The Child's character and the Adult the Child grows up to be are significantly formed by messages or scripts determined by the Parent. Healthy transactions result in healthy behaviors and ego states, while unhealthy transactions form unhealthy behaviors and ego states.

Berne claimed that understanding dysfunctional roles and scripts, making healthy behavioral changes, and learning to function in practical ways alleviated and even cured many emotional and psychological problems. He created a contract that set an agenda of specific changes and results a patient desires, which the patient and the therapist signed at the outset of therapy, and he promised a bottom-line, practical result Freudian psychotherapy did not.

Noticing my enthusiasm for TA, my mother gave me a pamphlet about a woman named Jacqui Schiff, a disciple of Berne. Schiff had created a radical program for treating schizophrenics. Donna read me the pamphlet for us; it was very interesting. So I got a copy of a book Schiff wrote with Betty Day, *All My Children*. Donna read that to me too. The book told how Schiff and her former husband, Moe, both psychiatric nurses frustrated by the inadequate care for schizo-phrenic patients in the mental hospital where they worked, resigned from their jobs and began taking schizophrenic patients into their home, inducing in them schizophrenic regression, and then repar-enting them using the developmental stages of childhood in Berne's theories. This even included an infancy stage, where they bottle-fed and diapered adult schizophrenics.

I'd experienced poignant moments with Donna when I felt the pieces of her come together and she became open, childlike, and lov-ing. Perhaps Jacqui Schiff could help Donna become more integrated. I'd done my best to protect her from the negative conversations and messages about herself that went on in her head. But I was in over my head, and Schiff was a professional.

Schiff's regression approach was radical and controversial. Psychiatry viewed schizophrenic regression as mere pathology, with no therapeutic value. To encourage or induce regression seemed gro-tesque, even harmful, like intentionally triggering a psychosis. Yet Schiff reported remarkable successes, even some cures, using her reparenting process. In 1969, she claimed to have cured fourteen patients. Berne invited Schiff to the San Francisco Social Psychiatry Seminars. He enthusiastically introduced her, saying, "She takes peo-ple into her house that are very confused and unconfuses them, which confuses some people in the profession because it isn't supposed to work."* The *New York Times* published a feature about her that year too; Schiff was mothering eighteen "children" whose real ages ranged from nine to twenty-nine.†

A number of Schiff's patients apparently "grew up" and out of their schizophrenic disorders and regained healthy, functional lives. Some became capable facilitators of Schiff's method and began lead-ing their own "families" of schizophrenics through the reparenting

---

* "Theory as Ideology: Reparenting and Thought Reform," *Transactional Analysis Journal* 24, no. 1 (January 1994).

† "An Approach to Schizophrenia That Is Rooted in Family Love," *New York Times*, April 28, 1969.

process. I was excited by all of this. Modifying Jacqui Schiff's methods to address nonschizophrenics might offer Donna and me a new possibility for change.

When my mother learned that Jacqui Schiff would be presenting her theories at a meeting for psychiatric professionals in Chicago, she arranged for Donna and me to see her. We all drove into the city to the hotel where Jacqui was speaking. The event was in a medium-sized room; about thirty people showed up. Jacqui Schiff seemed unimpressive as she walked to the podium. In her forties, she was short, plump, and professionally dressed. Her voice was soft, almost childlike, and she had an oddly blunt, almost mechanical, style of speaking. She spoke in clinical terms, without emotion or feeling, and it was quickly apparent that she possessed tremendous confidence, authority, and charisma. By the end of the evening, I was completely under her spell.

Jacqui explained the details of her theories and methods in compelling terms. Her goal was to help severely dysfunctional people— schizophrenics—become functional and rebuild healthy personalities. She spoke matter-of-factly about the current "family" of thirty-five schizophrenics she was reparenting, assisted by several recovered schizophrenics who'd completed her reparenting program.

Jacqui believed that schizophrenics need to confront the source of their psychosis in order to change. She described a process of regressing schizophrenics back to their Child ego state, mothering them through each developmental stage and rebuilding their personalities. She variously called her method *reparenting, attachment therapy*, and *healing the inner child*. She said when schizophrenics are put in the right circumstance, they naturally regress, as if they instinctively know they need to reprogram parts of themselves. She also said most schizophrenics prefer to stay in their psychosis and had to be confronted boldly or they'd continue to choose their familiar schizophrenic strategies of escape.

Jacqui's method was to induce a breakdown in her patients by confronting them with a highly structured environment and intense pressure to function beyond their capacity. This triggered all the dysfunctional defense mechanisms and faulty programming the patients used to avoid feeling and confronting the emotional traumas—such as severe neglect and emotional, physical, or sexual abuse—that underlay their schizophrenia. Once regression was induced, patients could be guided back to places where crucial decisions and patterns had occurred that led to their schizophrenia. From there, they could be guided to make new choices, write new scripts, and develop new behaviors that would enable them to function effectively in the real world under the normal pressures of life. Schiff used various methods to do this, including talk therapy, self-affirmations, self-forgiveness, anger management, self-discipline, the continued demand for practical functioning, and firm consequences for irresponsibility and acting out.

After the crisis phase, she said the process became very nurturing. Jacqui saw the ability to function effectively and responsibly in the real world as the litmus test of recovery. And while her method was radical and controversial, it apparently made recovery from an otherwise incurable illness possible for some.

Hearing Jacqui Schiff speak, I sensed a brilliant and forceful personality at work, using highly unorthodox methods, and apparently succeeding where others had failed. This could be exactly what I was looking for. She seemed to have no judgments about emotionally and psychologically disturbed people. She described them as nonfunctional. Some well-known psychiatric professionals attended her presentation that night and aggressively challenged her methods during the question-and-answer session. But she confidently dismantled their arguments with analytical brilliance. In the end, most of the audience seemed persuaded, and even the skeptics seemed impressed by her.

After Schiff spoke, two former schizophrenics, Eric and Aaron, who'd gone through her reparenting process, came onstage and briefly told their stories. They were both articulate, apparently high-functioning individuals, who handled themselves well onstage—and they were taking other schizophrenics through the same process Jacqui Schiff had taken them through.

I was shaking by the end of the evening, almost euphoric. Jacqui's talk filled me with hope. Her method seemed perfect for Donna and might also hold a solution for my inability to organize or prioritize information in a linear fashion, which prevented me from functioning in the world the way others did. If she could help severe schizophrenics who'd been relegated to the wards of psychiatric hospitals for ten years or more , maybe she could help Donna, and even me.

After the talk, I went up to Schiff. I spoke excitedly to her, as my story gushed out of me. She listened intently and then delivered insights into my situation no one else had come close to. In her assessment, I had likely gone to school too early, before I'd fully mastered speech and before I was developmentally prepared, which had intensified my developmental and learning problems. I was unable to deal with the normal curriculum because I was struggling in an environment that was over my head. This left huge gaps in my education and hampered my ability to learn and progress. She also pinpointed areas of in my learning process that were the most problematic and underdeveloped. She seemed to be a possible solution to my problems, but she wasn't promising to take me on. She spoke in a hypothetical way about how she would proceed if she did. She described the circumstances she thought would serve me and allow me, finally, to develop and learn.

When I asked her about helping Donna, she said it didn't sound as if Donna was a danger to herself or to others and that Donna would have to want her help.

For days after the presentation, I was excited about Jacqui Schiff's work. I talked to my mother about the possibility of Schiff working with Donna and me. My mother was also very impressed with Schiff and had gotten her phone number. She called her one afternoon, and they began a series of conversations about me and the possibility of me living with Schiff and going through a program she would develop specifically for my needs. I wasn't involved in any of these conversations, but my mother reported to me after each one.

As excited and hopeful as I was, I had some doubts. Yet I had no alternatives. Donna was unwilling even to go to therapy, much less try something like this. In the past, therapists had criticized our mutual dependencies, so Donna had no interest in this. No matter how much

I reassured her, she saw it as a threat to our relationship.

My mother was divided. On one hand, she thought having me go to Jacqui Schiff's was a great idea. But there was a catch. When Jacqui reparented someone, she became that person's mother in a significant way. My own mother might be removed from that role in my life. A psychic bond would be created in the reparenting process that could supersede my relationship with my real mother. Sometimes this had to happen for the reparenting process to be effective. In theory, even though I wouldn't be regressed, Jacqui would be attempting to tear apart the "inner parent" within me in order to rebuild it.

In Jacqui's view, my inner parent, which reflected my mother, represented the part in me that wasn't working. In the TA system, parents were a primary source of children's dysfunctional scripts, with all the fears, judgments, strategies, and rules contained in them. So a detachment from my mother might have to occur in order for me to form a healthy attachment to Jacqui. She wanted my mom and me to be prepared for that possibility.

This disturbed my mother, who was reluctant for me to go through the reparenting process. The bond my mother and I had established, especially in those first few years when she was connected to me almost around the clock, was very deep. My mother also had doubts about the process and worried that it might end up doing more harm than good. She expressed her all her concerns to Jacqui. Finally, after much consideration, my mother consented, and Jacqui Schiff agreed to take me on.

Jacqui said she normally wouldn't select someone like me for her program because I wasn't schizophrenic. But she was intrigued by the challenge I represented and curious to see if her specialized program could benefit someone with severe learning disabilities. We would pay Jacqui a minimal fee with my Social Security income from my dad's death, and my working in the house as an assistant would pay the balance. I didn't know that Jacqui would also become my legal guardian. I wouldn't be part of the "family," but I'd eat, sleep, and live at the house as part of the job of helping the others. It seemed perfect: I'd be getting a job, help with my learning, and help for Donna later on if it all worked out. When my mother spoke to Jacqui about Donna, Jacqui said that over time Donna might come around and that we could revisit it then.

Jacqui was in the process of hiring professionals for a new school called Cathexis. She was creating this school based on her understanding of the stages of child development and the inner-child work in Transactional Analysis. I would attend this school while I was with her. I was to go back and review the developmental stages and relearn the basics I'd missed at each stage. Jacqui said she would be able to fill in the gaps and bring me all the way through to functional maturity at my current age. She also said I'd be able to graduate high school from her school with a GED. Jacqui cautioned me that some things I needed to relearn might seem stupid but that they'd help build new patterns in me. I'd have to relearn simple things in order to learn more complex things. We'd identify the weakest areas, where the basics hadn't been properly integrated, work on those, and then move forward from there. These were huge promises.

I was convinced this was the answer. My mind raced ahead, planning my future. The first thing Jacqui's program would do was get me off drugs. The intensive rigor and structure of her program would be like a boot camp. I'd be busy all day learning to function at a very high level under constant pressure. I'd also learn about psychology, a subject I was drawn to. Maybe I could go on to help others like me, people with learning disabilities, the way some of Jacqui's schizophrenic graduates helped other schizophrenics through the process they'd benefited from. Maybe I could turn this into some sort of counseling career. Jacqui Schiff might have the solution to many of my problems.

My mother wasn't convinced this would work for me, but she realized it was the only option on my horizon. She was very supportive as the time drew near for me to go and to live with Jacqui and her family in Northern California. I think she convinced herself this might be what we were looking for. We both needed hope. We needed something big and full of promise, and Jacqui Schiff seemed to fit the bill. And I believed that if this worked for me, Donna would eventually come around.

17

The House

I flew from Chicago to San Francisco with one suitcase packed with a few clothes and toiletries. It was 1971. We were allowed few personal possessions and no medications or anything that could be used as a weapon. A "family" member named Jake met me at the airport and drove me to the small town of Alamo, about forty-five minutes away. We entered a suburban neighborhood and pulled into the driveway of one of the many large homes with half-acre yards. The house didn't seem so big when I remembered I'd be sharing it with thirty-five other people, most of them schizophrenics. The ground floor had a big living room, a family room, a kitchen, and a dining room with a huge table. Upstairs was the men's dormitory—six large bedrooms stacked with bunk beds—and a small bedroom at the end of a hall, where Jacqui slept. A large building behind the main home housed Jacqui's office, a meeting room, a kitchenette, and several more bedrooms, where the women slept. I never knew exactly how many of us lived on the property at any one time.

On my first day, Jacqui came into the main room like a marine drill sergeant. She barely acknowledged me and started yelling at one of the kids who was waving his arms in the air, telling him to stop acting crazy. All family members were called "kids" regardless of their age. Jacqui told another kid to sit up straight, shouted various orders to several others, then turned and left the room.

I was hungry, but they'd finished lunch so I didn't get to eat until dinnertime. But the family members on dinner detail didn't make enough food, so everybody left the table hungry. I went to bed late, totally exhausted, hungry, and ready for sleep, but Rudy, one of the "older" schizophrenics, who was in charge of my room, saw that I could function at a higher level than other family members, concluded I was older too, and gave me an assignment.

"Older" referred not to anyone's birth age but to emotional age. Whether you were older was determined by your ability to function responsibly and effectively and to be accountable to both the household and Jacqui. When someone older was in charge, you had to obey him or her. Period. Arguing or resisting was "acting out" and resulted in serious consequences.

So, before I got into bed, Rudy put me in charge of Simon, one of my roommates. I had to get Simon to do his bedtime routine— wash his face, brush his teeth, take off his clothes, put on his pajamas, get in bed, and stay there. But schizophrenics need to feel safe, so they test you—and they could be crafty. Seeing I was new and didn't know what the hell I was doing, Simon passively resisted by talking strangely and being as difficult as possible without getting into trouble. Passive resistance was common behavior here. I didn't know what to do with Simon or how hard to push him. I was tired, hungry, frustrated, and worried about getting in trouble with Jacqui.

It was midnight before I got to bed. I lay there thinking, *This is fucked up*, over and over, like a mantra, as I fell asleep. I didn't have an alarm clock, and the next morning nobody woke me up. So I missed breakfast. I was given a warning and told that not having an alarm clock was no excuse for not getting up on time. When I asked for an alarm clock, I was told they didn't have one for me. I could see there was no winning in this place.

* * *

From the start, it was go-go-go, from morning until night— cleaning, serving, functioning, and responding in the moment to whatever the occasion required. Most Sundays, another guy and I escorted ten to fifteen of the best-behaved family members into the family VW van and the family station wagon and took them on day trips. We went to the beach, the San Francisco Zoo, Golden Gate Park, and any other place we could think of within reasonable driving range. It was grueling and required incredible vigilance. You had to be on top of things and nip the slightest misbehavior in the bud.

Managing unmedicated schizophrenics required establishing personal power and maintaining constant vigilance. Much communication was done with eye contact and body language. I'd had a lot of practice observing unpredictable people, from Emerson to sociopathic characters at Central Y. I knew how to read the slightest signs of hostility and threat—a gleam in the eye, a subtle facial expression, a sudden movement, a shift in posture, or a tone of voice. I knew the importance of expressing confidence and authority through body language and tone of voice. My job required constant awareness of the room, correcting behaviors, and trying to look in charge instead of looking like the anxious, at-times-terrified person I was inside. I continually engaged the "kids" verbally, talking to them, giving them directions, pushing them to function, establishing dominance, or trying to comfort or calm them. So much of it depended on gaining their confidence and establishing a bond. Sometimes I could be friendly, but I always had to be firm. I couldn't be their friend.

Most people here were unpredictable, and some could be dangerous. Soon after my arrival, two of Jacqui's assistants taught me how to physically restrain someone, a necessary skill every functional family member had to learn. The standard method required four people: after two grabbed the person's arms and another two grabbed the legs, they pulled the arms behind the person's back and moved him or her into a corner. If the person still resisted, the feet were lifted off the floor and the arms were forced back as far as they could go. It was painful but effective. If a person struggled too hard in that position, a shoulder could pop out of the socket. On occasion, you might have to intentionally dislocate a shoulder to subdue someone.

If anyone needed to be restrained, every functional family member in the vicinity knew what to do and had to do it quickly or be punished for negligence. The rule was that everyone in the room was responsible for what went on in the room, and everyone would be punished for anything wrong that happened on his or her watch. We were all brothers and sisters and responsible for one another. If you were in charge at night, you slept lightly, with your back to the wall.

Any kind of rustling noise and you got up immediately. Many family members were handcuffed to their beds at night. If they had to get up to go to the bathroom, the person in charge of the room had to go with them, which meant you lost sleep.

During my second week, a new schizophrenic named Timothy joined the family. Before he arrived, Jacqui took a small group of us aside and told us that a paranoid schizophrenic in a very agitated state would be arriving shortly, that he had attacked several members of his own family, including his parents, and that he was potentially danger-ous. Jacqui told me she didn't use drugs to manage behavior because it prevented schizophrenics from learning from their experience, so Timothy wouldn't be medicated when he arrived. We'd be dealing with a full-blown paranoid schizophrenic acting out.

Jacqui said paranoid schizophrenics had two irrational states of mind, scared and belligerent or scared and submissive. Our job was to get Timothy into a submissive state. Otherwise, he'd see us as being weak, and he'd be dangerous to anyone he saw as weak, especially to any person in a position of authority. Jacqui said paranoid schizo-phrenics know they're out of control, and this makes them feel unsafe. So Timothy would be testing us to see if we could control him. He'd feel a lot safer once he knew we could handle him at his worst.

When Timothy arrived from the hospital, four of the strongest family members brought him back to Jacqui's office, where we were waiting. Timothy was twenty-five, around six feet tall, about a hun-dred and ninety pounds, with wavy brown hair. Jacqui got right in his face and started provoking him until he exploded and tried to take a swing at her. The guys were ready. Six of us piled on Timothy, grabbing his arms and legs. We got him into the restraint position and forced him onto a leather couch. I'd been in a lot of fights, but I'd never been involved in anything like this. Timothy screamed and fought with unbelievable strength, but we pinned him down tight.

Now Jacqui really started in on him, calling him a wimp, ask-ing him who he thought was in charge here. "This isn't like anyplace you've been before!" she yelled in his face. He yelled back at her, and she slapped him hard on the face. "Shut up!" she said, "Is that all you've got?" He yelled at her again, and, *boom*, one of the guys socked him in the jaw and another slugged him in the stomach. More blows followed. Timothy was being pulverized, but he kept fighting back. Soon everyone was hitting him except for me. One of the guys glared at me and snarled, "David!" So I hit Timothy a few times. I didn't know what I was doing. The others seemed to know when, where, and how hard to hit him—and when to stop. They'd all done this before. The whole time Jacqui stood there overseeing the operation, talking to Timothy and giving us directions. After a while, Timothy gave up and stopped struggling.

"You're good now, right? You're not going to pull anything?" asked Jacqui.

That just set him off, and the whole process started over again. Finally, we broke Timothy like a wild horse. He went completely limp and lay still, breathing hard with tears streaming down his face. When we let go of him, he was completely compliant. He just lay there while Jacqui talked to him. "You're safe here. We won't let you frighten or hurt anyone. We can and will stop you if you try. We can and will make you behave. You see we can handle you. You're safe." Timothy seemed to take this in, and calmed down. Jacqui apparently knew what she was doing.

The incident freaked me out. I wondered if something like this could happen to me if I got out of line or into an argument with the wrong person. I swore to myself I wouldn't be involved in an incident like this again. But a few days later, Timothy acted up and threatened some of the other kids. Jacqui ordered us to carry him into the bathroom and stick him in the tub. Five or six of us carried him to the bathroom, but we couldn't all fit inside. The four biggest guys brought him in and pinned him down in the empty tub. I stood in the hall, watching through the door. He screamed and fought the whole time. Jacqui yelled to the younger kids to bring buckets of ice from the freezer. Then she came in and turned on the cold water in the tub while the four guys held Timothy down. The younger kids started bringing in bags of ice, emptying them onto Timothy, at Jacqui's orders, as water filled the tub. He started screaming and fighting harder, but he couldn't get up. Soon he was covered with ice and submerged in frigid water.

"We'll let you out when you stop fighting!" Jacqui kept shouting.

But Timothy kept fighting, even after he started shaking and turning blue. They kept dunking him down, holding him under, letting him up to breathe every so often. I thought he wasn't getting enough air, but what did I know? Jacqui seemed absolutely confident and was in control of the process. After a while, Timothy stopped struggling and became passive. At Jacqui's command, they lifted him out of the tub and started drying him off with towels. He stayed quiet, so we all went back to our usual places. It was one of many bizarre events I would find myself involved in at Jacqui Schiff's home.

Jacqui's three birth children lived with us in the house and went to public school each day. A handful of family members—high-functioning schizophrenics "cured" through Jacqui's process—attended the local college. One of the family members didn't live in the house but came in the morning and left in the evening. Hired assistants did the shopping and other household errands.

Jacqui was gone much of the time. Two groups of people were in charge of the household under Jacqui: family members who'd gone through regression and come out the other side of their schizophrenia and hired staff, who were psych majors who got some pay and college credit. There was always a designated "person in charge," who made sure everything ran smoothly when Jacqui wasn't around. The PIC could be either a staff member or a resident she considered responsible. The family members in charge were the most highly functional people I'd ever seen. They seemed totally together, not crazy at all. They were mostly men, but the women also commanded respect and had strong, confident voices.

Everyone started at the bottom. You worked your way up by demonstrating your ability to function under pressure and to handle responsibility. The "healthier" you became, the more responsibility and freedom you were given. At the bottom to middle ranges, you had little or no freedom but plenty of demands and responsibilities to meet; you were always under watch and had no privacy. At the middle to upper ranges, you had more responsibility, pressure, and stress, but with permission, you could go to the store, the movies, and even on dates.

Turnover among hired staff was high. Most of them couldn't hold a candle to older or recovered family members in terms of functioning, handling the pressure of restraining others, and dishing out consequences. When any family member acted out and needed restraining, the call went out. Older kids within hearing range came running, and the troublemaker was taken down. Hired staff often lacked the stomach for this and often quit if they had to do it more than a few times.

Within two weeks, I was a high functioner. At times, I was made PIC of the house. It was grueling. At any given time, one or more family members could act out. One family member acting out in response to another one was called a satellite. If a few satellites went off together, an entire room could escalate into total chaos. The pressure was indescribable. This often resulted in someone getting hurt, causing periodic trips to the hospital.

I soon realized I'd been brought to Jacqui's house under false pretenses. I was told I'd only be there for a few weeks and not as a family member. I'd just work there while I went through an evaluation process and set up a curriculum to get my high school diploma. But once I arrived, I was put in the same basket with the rest of them and treated like everyone else. I was angry about this, but Jacqui told me she was now my legal guardian, and I had to do whatever she said.

After the initial shock wore off, I realized this was my only real option, so I might as well give it my best shot. I was used to being in situations designed for people with needs different from my own. For this to work, I had to be open and try new things. I had to discern what was useful and incorporate it into my life, and recognize what wasn't helpful to me and be strong enough to throw it away, no matter how useful it seemed for others. I'd at least get clean from drugs here. I knew I couldn't do that on my own. But I was on my own in another big way, given no parameters, no orientation, no formal schedule, and no emotional support. This made me extremely anxious.

For the first couple of weeks, I kept asking to talk to Jacqui. I wanted to find out why our original agreement had changed and to ask her for some sort of schedule or program to follow. Finally, Jacqui agreed to talk to me. The conversation only lasted a few minutes. She listened briefly to my complaints, then interrupted me and told me that I was under observation and that I just needed more time to adapt to the routine. Then she left the room. After that conversation, Jacqui increased the pressure on me by giving me more chores and responsibilities. For the next few days, she had me cooking dinner every night for as many as thirty-seven people. She ordered me to create a family vegetable garden in the backyard. Then she came out one afternoon and tore it apart in a rage, accusing me of doing a terrible job on purpose by planting too many carrots and not enough corn. The last thing I wanted to do was piss Jacqui off. I realized how hard she could make my life, and I needed her help. She said she was in the process of putting the school together. I just hoped it would start soon.

Jacqui was the most baffling personality I'd ever encountered. She was alternately angry and indifferent, brilliant and obtuse, and her attempt to control everyone around her inevitably resulted in chaos. I couldn't tell whether she didn't know what she was doing and nothing was under control or whether everything was part of her cunning intention to frustrate, disorient, and trigger everyone. I was nursing grave doubts about her and feeling increasingly anxious about having put myself so completely in her power.

We weren't allowed to identify others as crazy or insane. We only referred to their behavior. We didn't say they were crazy, only that they acted crazy. Jacqui bragged about taking the most hopeless schizophrenic patients from hospitals glad to be rid of them so that she could prove her methods by curing them. The more bizarre the schizophrenics, the smarter and more willful they also seemed to be. Jacqui picked them smart and active. She said these qualities increased their chances of being cured. Their resistance and acting out gave her something to work with. But if it gave them a better chance of recovery, it also made them more difficult to deal with.

One girl, Rachel, a quiet, sweet-natured, nineteen-year-old, who was the daughter of a famous couple, walked, talked, and behaved like an old lady. One day Rachel ran away. For two weeks, she eluded police and family members who went out daily searching the neighborhood for her. One afternoon, a man called the house saying he'd seen a girl matching Rachel's description acting very strangely. He lived a few miles away. As PIC that day, I took the call. Jacqui was gone, so I left Rudy in charge and took the van to look for Rachel. I drove to the address and found Rachel standing on the sidewalk, looking extremely disoriented and grubby, her face and scalp red and peeling from sunburn. I got out and told her she had to come back to the house, but she didn't want to go. I couldn't leave her there, so I grabbed her and started dragging her toward the van. Just as I feared, she started screaming at the top of her lungs and fighting me as hard as she could. It looked like I was kidnapping her. A man stuck his head out of a second-story window and yelled, "Let her go! I called the police! Leave her alone!"

I couldn't let her go, and I wasn't about to argue. I stopped and held Rachel's arm until the cop car came racing up the street, blue lights flashing. It pulled to a stop behind me and an officer got out. "What's going on?" he shouted.

"He's kidnapping that girl!" the man in the window shouted.

Rachel stood there looking crazed, and the cop realized what was going on.

"You're from that house, aren't you?" he asked me.

"Yeah."

"Go ahead and get her into the van." He looked at Rachel and told her firmly, with full cop authority, "You have to get in the van and go with him."

She got into the van without any resistance. I tied her hands to the seat and drove her back to the house. We learned that she'd been sleeping outside and hooking to support herself. Jacqui saw this as a sign of improvement because it showed a boldness and initiative previously lacking in Rachel's character.

Some of the nonparanoid schizophrenics in the house could be a handful. Rob was twenty-three years old, extremely intelligent, and psychologically sophisticated. He understood the Parent-Adult-Child concept. Rob was also completely delusional. He had a habit of waving his arms around when he talked. When he was agitated, like when I scolded him for not doing his chores, Rob would wave his arms wildly in a threatening manner. I didn't like it, it wasn't acceptable, and we discouraged him from doing it. Crazy, aberrant behavior wasn't tolerated in the house. Persisting in such behavior after being told to stop was official grounds for punishment. That could mean being told to stand in a corner, being restrained, whipped, given an ice bath, or any other punishment Jacqui deemed necessary. Rob took the whole TA Parent-Adult-Child thing literally. When we had a normal conversation, he talked to me as my Adult self and called me David. But when I scolded him, he addressed my Parent self and referred to me as either Mr. Patten or Mrs. Patten. Whenever Rob started acting out, I'd say in a firm voice, "Rob, stop acting crazy." He'd say, waving his arms, "Okay, Mrs. Patten."

Jacqui said her job wasn't to be loving but to make demands, push people to their limits, and apply necessary controls that forced them to confront the roots of their illness and grow beyond it. She was a fearsome presence. She insisted on total loyalty and obedience to her, her methods, and her work, and demanded absolute control. She could see right through people. She'd walk into a room, size it up in a flash, and know in moments everyone's game, strategy, psychological state, and how to deal with them. When she entered a room, everyone, even full-blown schizophrenics, straightened up and gave her their attention. When she yelled, everyone was afraid. She also knew how to cause tremendous stress with a few quiet words. Jacqui had an energizing, almost intoxicating effect on people.

According to Jacqui's theory, every year in the life of a schizophrenic required about a month of regression at that age. In practice, regression was more random and flexible, varying from person to person. Each person in regression got time alone with Jacqui. Depending on someone's phase of regression, she might feed them with a bottle

(I even bottle-fed some family members), let them crawl or teethe on things, play children's games, or read picture books. These were also the rare occasions she demonstrated anything that looked like love.

Full regression took the "kids" back to infancy. Some kids only had to go back to a particular stage in their lives, perhaps when a decisive trauma occurred, to address and heal the damage. They might need to be that age for only a day or two in order to come out of it restored and functional. Some came out of regression noticeably improved. I saw and felt the change in them. Something remarkable had clearly happened to them in the process. I wondered if part of Jacqui's success was due to her charismatic personality, which inspired a great deal of faith in her. In a way, she was a kind of hypnotist or faith healer.

The general insanity of the environment, the relentless demands to function, and the serious consequences for nonconformity and resistance all created immense pressure. Jacqui wanted us to be overwhelmed and anxious and was always looking to get someone in trouble. This created a hypervigilance that Jacqui felt made us more observant and try harder. Everyone got into trouble at one point or another for minor infractions. Jacqui frequently made patients stand in corners. She considered "corner contracts" a form of "passivity confrontation."

At times, Jacqui and her assistants focused on different people, making sure they repeatedly got into trouble. This sometimes triggered regression but also created a great deal of fear and anxiety in the house. Not wanting to become a target, I stayed vigilant and tried harder. Jacqui was so powerful and bigger than life that when she broke patients, it triggered in them a kind of submissive adoration of her. Then they seemed to crave being regressed and mothered by her. It was more than just the power she wielded or that the alternative to submission was punishment and rejection. It was partly a mysterious effect of her personality. Even I was affected. I didn't like her or trust her, but I still craved her approval.

Living under more stress than I'd ever experienced, I exerted myself more than I ever had in my life. I didn't want to be there, but I had no other options and no life of meaningful possibilities to return to. This was boot camp, my last chance to get somewhere in life, and I wasn't going to waste it. In the crucible of Jacqui's madhouse, I began to tap into inner resources I didn't know I had. As I learned to do my assigned tasks and function under intense pressure, my self-esteem and confidence grew. I also earned the respect of others, including Jacqui, who then increased my responsibilities.

While I came to see the demand for high functioning as good for me and everyone else in the household, I never saw the component of terror as good for anyone. Despite its negative effects, I did see that terror made people stretch to be their most genius selves. It definitely made me function at supernormal capacity. Though such methods often worked, I wondered at what cost.

The high-functioning schizophrenics who had successfully completed Jacqui's reparenting process didn't seem mentally ill, but they did seem oddly mechanical and emotionally detached. At first, I thought it was a leftover part of their schizophrenia. Later I found myself becoming similarly mechanical and detached. I realized I was shutting down emotionally to avoid feeling the intensity of the stressful environment, while maintaining constant vigilance to avoid getting in trouble. This happened to everyone. Our common goal wasn't recovering but not getting into trouble.

Jacqui's inner circle of high-functioning graduates was her evidence that her chaotic and dangerous methods produced results. She held these graduates in special regard and gave them special status and privileges. We obeyed them as if they were Jacqui. They were less scary than Jacqui, yet potentially more dangerous. It was the danger of acting by proxy, trying to duplicate the judgment and authority of a leader whose limits were unclear.

The combination of uncertainty, bizarre intensity, and craziness of the environment and its people with my growing doubts about Jacqui gradually took a toll on me. I was tense and hypervigilant all day and didn't sleep well at night. Everything was a struggle—getting enough sleep, enough to eat, a turn in the shower, and getting through each very long stressful day. I clung to hope, while nursing fears that this wouldn't help me, that I wouldn't get my high school diploma, that nothing I'd been promised would pan out. I thought about running away, but where would I go? I was living in a small California town, two thousand miles from home, with no cash and no friends, under the legal guardianship of a powerful woman who meted out physical punishment and restraint like a prison warden.

I had no clarity and didn't trust my assessment of things any more than I trusted Jacqui. My personal track record was one of chronic struggle, bad choices, and failure. I was never really sure if Jacqui was right or wrong. Her supreme self-confidence and absolute certainty about her methods made me doubt my perceptions and myself. It seemed Jacqui could always sway anyone to her point of view.

Charismatic people had always fascinated me. Many seemed to have a freedom, intensity, dynamic drive, and sense of purpose ordinary people lacked. They were not constrained by self-doubt, a conscience, social inhibitions, or the feelings and opinions of others. Such compelling personalities seemed to transmit an exhilarating energy that drew others to them yet kept them separate and made them different and special. Many charismatic people I'd encountered were criminals, political radicals, or sociopaths. You couldn't take your eyes off them. I saw this quality in some of my biggest dealers, in a few of the major Central Y players, and in Yellow Shirt, the Blackstone Ranger who tried to thrown me down the stairwell. And I saw it in Jacqui Schiff. She wasn't willfully cruel, just ruthless in her purpose and indifferent to the feelings of others. She frequently hurt people in the course of going about her work. We were all subjects in her surreal little kingdom.

Like everyone there, I was getting about four hours of sleep a night and functioning from the minute I woke in the morning until the minute I went to bed at night. My job on any given day could include single-handedly wrestling a guy nearly a foot taller than I was into a corner and making him stay there; changing a diaper on a large man with a three-day growth of beard, who'd regressed to the level of a two-year-old; or calming a roomful of frightened and hysterical schizophrenics. I was cooking meals for thirty-five people when I'd

never before cooked a full meal. I couldn't read a cookbook and keep
an eye on my paranoid schizophrenic kitchen assistant, Timothy, who
was tied to me with a rope and wasn't supposed to be around knives.
Timothy could read fluently, so I had to rely on him for the cooking
instructions. But he liked to mess with me by changing the recipe
ingredients or amounts without telling me, which on more than one
occasion ruined a meal and got me into trouble.

One evening, a large group of us were sitting in the living room
watching TV when we heard the sound of shattering glass in the
bathroom down the hall. A bunch of us older kids immediately
jumped up and ran to see what had happened. A girl named Francine,
one of the "cured," mature schizophrenics stood in front of the sink
surrounded by pieces of shattered mirror. She was holding a shard of
broken mirror in one hand. Her wrist was slit open, and there was
blood all over the floor. I'd only just met her, as she now lived on her
own and had a real job in the world. She'd just come for a visit. I let
some of the older kids she knew deal with this situation.

Francine fought them off using the shard as a weapon. Her
arms flailed wildly and blood flew everywhere. By the time they got
the shard away from her, she'd cut herself in several more places on
her arm. They wrapped her bloody arm in a towel, and Jacqui and a
couple of her assistants took Francine to the hospital. I went into
the bathroom to clean up the mess. Blood and broken glass were
everywhere, on the floor, on the walls, and in the toilet, the sink, and
the bathtub. It took me almost two hours to clean it all up.

Later, when Jacqui returned with Francine, I could tell Jacqui was
shaken. I'd never seen her that way before. I guessed that having one
of her "cured" kids attempt suicide got to her. She immediately started
yelling at people, giving orders and appearing confident. Oddly, that
seemed to calm everyone down. I didn't know Francine very well or
what had triggered her suicide attempt, but it still upset all of us for a
few days. It definitely shook my remaining confidence in Jacqui.

* * *

Unexpected delays prevented the opening of Jacqui's new school for weeks after my arrival. I was incredibly frustrated. I'd come here thinking Jacqui was going to help me relearn things I'd missed in my early developmental stages, learn to read, and get my GED. But so far, none of that had happened. I was basically an unpaid, highly functioning assistant—a captive, subject to family rules. I'd gotten some benefit in terms of discipline and improved functioning, but I'd have gotten as much by joining the army. It was starting to look like I'd never get my diploma.

Finally, Jacqui's school started up in a small two-bedroom house she'd rented in Danville, a few miles from the main house. I was the only student from the house attending the school. Five other kids from the surrounding community who had been kicked out of public school for various reasons, attended with me; none were schizophrenic. Jacqui received money from their parents and the public school system.

There were three teachers: Dee Dee, a counselor, who was a very nice woman trained by Jacqui; and Robert and Jane, a ministerial couple, paid assistants trained by Jacqui who were getting credit toward their psychology degrees by working in the home. Though considered part of the family, I'd learn they had their own misgivings about Jacqui's methods.

After the first month, I finally started at Jacqui's Cathexis School. For six days a week, twelve hours a day, I studied the California GED study guide for the high school equivalency test. I was excited to begin the curriculum Jacqui had promised and relieved to be away from the pressure of the main house. The teachers were encouraging at first, assuring me I'd be able to pass the test and get a diploma. But the encouragement faded as I struggled with the disabilities that had always held me back.

I really liked the encounter groups we had, guided by Dee Dee. I'd been instructed by several family members not to talk with the teachers or students about Jacqui's house. They wouldn't understand,

and it could cause a lot of trouble. But in the encounter groups I discovered I had a knack for counseling kids. I had a lot of experience and insight, and the other students seemed to trust me and look to me for guidance. For one of the rare times in my life I felt competent in the world, like I was really helping people and doing some good. The teachers confirmed this to me privately and encouraged me to consider counseling as a potential career.

A couple of months after starting school, Jacqui found a dormitory-style building a few miles away and moved most of the guys there, including me. We called it "the cabin" or "the boys' dorm." Now, every morning I had to get everybody awake and washed, make sure they cleaned the cabin, and manage any crisis that arose. Rudy and I would drive the guys to the main house for the day, and then I'd go to Cathexis for twelve hours of school. In the evening, Rudy and I would pick the guys up at the main house, drive them back to the cabin to do evening chores and get cleaned up. We'd manage more crises and chaos and get them into bed. I usually got to bed between midnight and 2:00 a.m.

✳   ✳   ✳

After six months in Jacqui's program, I felt so alone. I missed Mom and Neil and still missed Dad. But I missed Donna most of all, especially at night when it was quiet. I missed her laughter, her face, her body lying next to mine, and her arms around my neck. I'd never left her alone before and didn't know how she was doing. I was constantly surrounded by other people but had no one I could talk to, no one I trusted, no sense of love or closeness with anyone, especially Jacqui. It wasn't a family in any sense of the word. I kept hoping it would all be worth it. Sometimes I wished I were home again, but then I'd remember how awful it was for me there. I didn't want to sell dope anymore. I didn't want to end up in prison or on the street.

When things got really bad, I'd think about Eric and Aaron, the two men who'd spoken at the first presentation I'd attended with Donna and my mother back in Chicago. Eric had a real job and his own apartment in the outside world. Aaron ran his own family in another house, using Jacqui's methods on other schizophrenics. I'd met them both, and they didn't seem crazy at all. This gave me the trace of reassurance I needed to keep going. But the main reasons I stayed with Jacqui were the promise of a GED, and my view of the place as my only chance for a future. I though if I could succeed here, I could succeed anywhere. And if I failed here, it was the end of the line.

18

Madness Treating Madness

Finally, Jacqui allowed me to talk to Donna on the phone every week or two. But I still couldn't talk to talk to my mom. One day at school, I snuck out and called her from a payphone. I told her Jacqui and the home were nothing like what we were led to believe. Mom said she was glad to hear from me, but she'd promised not to take calls from me and not to call her again.

The schoolhouse at Cathexis was very different from the main house; it was more relaxed and casual. It had two bedrooms without beds but was otherwise comfortably furnished. I liked it there. We had a daily group session, sitting on the couches and stuffed chairs in the living room. One afternoon when the kitchen phone rang during a session, I rushed to answer it because I was expecting a phone call from Donna. I'd told the other students and our teachers about Donna in our sessions. I stretched the long phone cord to the nearby bedroom and closed the door for privacy.

I'd come out here not realizing how long I'd actually be here. Now I'd been here far longer than Donna and I ever imagined I'd be. Our conversation was very disturbing. Donna was a mess. She'd gone through an ounce of MDA over the past few weeks and was crashing hard. I flipped out and started screaming at her. MDA was a new heavy drug that trashed the body—a harsh predecessor to MDMA, or Ecstasy—which combined the effects of speed, cocaine, and LSD.

When I hung up and returned to the group, I was visibly upset and told them what was going on. I worried that Donna was spiraling into addiction and the resulting mental dissolution. Word got back to Jacqui, and the next day she came to see me. She suggested that

Donna come out to be evaluated to see if she should get into the program. I was thrilled with the idea. This would get Donna away from her drug connections, and we'd be together again. I missed Donna terribly. I hid my excitement from Jacqui, who might leverage this against me later.

I knew Donna wouldn't want to be part of Jacqui's household. She'd just turned eighteen and didn't need her parents' consent or Jacqui's legal guardianship. I told Jacqui I'd encourage Donna to come on the condition that she wouldn't become a family member subject to the rules, pressures, and consequences the rest of us lived under. Donna just needed enough support and supervision to get clean. Jacqui and I negotiated an arrangement, subject to Donna's consent. She'd work eight hours each day as a housecleaner in the main house in exchange for counseling with Jacqui, lunch each day, and her own room at the house of a third party, perhaps with the parents of one of the schizophrenic kids undergoing treatment.

When I called Donna that afternoon and told her the plan, she was totally into it. Jacqui arranged for Donna to sleep in a spare room in the Hartwells' house. Their schizophrenic son, John, had a special arrangement with Jacqui. He spent every day at the main house as a family member and went home each night to sleep. The Hartwells agreed to give Donna a room plus breakfast and dinner at no charge in gratitude for Jacqui's taking their son into her program. They lived half a mile from the Cathexis School.

When Emerson learned Donna was coming, he decided to come too. He knew from mom that my situation at Jacqui's wasn't good. He'd already been planning to visit a friend in South San Francisco, a Romanian poet named Andrei Codrescu he'd met at the University of Michigan. Emerson had written a collection of poems that Andrei was going to help him publish. Emerson contacted Jacqui beforehand, who invited him to assist her part-time, buying groceries and running occasional errands. He'd receive no training, would interact only with Jacqui or her staff, and would have no responsibility or direct contact with family members. This arrangement was made behind the scenes without my involvement.

When Donna finally arrived, I was so happy to see her after our six-month separation. Each day she'd hitchhike from the Hartwells to Jacqui's house, put in her morning hours of cleaning, and then hitchhike to the schoolhouse in time for lunch. After lunch, we'd walk to the Hartwells, who both worked. With the house empty, Donna and I could hang out in her room and be intimate. Then she'd hitchhike back to the main house and I'd walk back to school.

Emerson arrived two weeks after Donna. I wasn't allowed to see or to talk with him. After seeing the house and the "kids" and meeting Jacqui, he quickly assessed the situation I was in. He told Donna it was bad and I needed to get out of there. But I wanted to stick it out and get a high school diploma.

Donna and I were surprised by how accepting and open people in California seemed to be about marijuana. The kids at Jacqui's school all talked openly in our groups and with the teachers about getting high. They said smoking weed was a common public school pastime. I hadn't gotten high since arriving in California. I didn't think weed was bad, and I figured Donna would need to get high to stay off hard drugs. I knew by now she couldn't do without drugs completely, though I hoped working with Jacqui would change that. In the meantime, Donna did score some weed. The teachers at school had to know. How could they not smell it on me and the other students? I'm pretty sure Jacqui also knew. But no one seemed to think it was a big deal.

Our new routine ran smoothly for a while. I was more relaxed with Donna around. Not living in the main house, where all the real insanity was happening, also helped. But after a few months, I knew Donna wasn't going to get any help. She had a few conversations with Jacqui but never any formal counseling. Things took an unexpected turn when the Hartwells found a stash of weed in Donna's room. It set a strange chain of events in motion.

Very upset, the Hartwells called Jacqui. Jacqui talked them out of kicking Donna out, but someone had to be punished. Since Jacqui had no authority over Donna, that someone was me. I don't think Jacqui was really mad at Donna for smoking pot or even getting caught. But she had to diffuse the Hartwells' anger and saw a way to push me to my next edge. I knew I was in trouble when Jacqui called and told me to come to the house the next day.

When I arrived, Jacqui told me Donna had put her in a difficult spot and it was my fault since Donna was my girlfriend. She said if I was going to break the rules I had to take the heat. I felt like was in trouble not for doing the deed, but for getting caught. She said I had to be punished and sent me to the living room. I sat there with a group of the least functional family members, reflecting on my situation. I hadn't gotten into any real trouble since I'd arrived and had shouldered a lot of responsibility, so I figured I'd get off relatively easy.

A while later, Jacqui came in with two of the big guys, Rudy and Narrow. She told me to come with them to her bedroom, where I was going to be whipped. Then she ordered one of the family members to get the willow branch, a big branch with a whipping tip as thick as my forefinger. I pretended to go quietly until we got to the stairs; then I broke away and ran for the front door. Before I reached it, Rudy tackled me from behind, and I went down hard. Both Rudy and Narrow pounced on me, and a couple of others joined in. Now four of them held me down, twisting my arms back and bending my elbows until my shoulder was close to popping out of the socket. I gave up; further resistance would only get me a dislocated shoulder and an extra beating.

They lifted me to my feet with my arms twisted back in the control position, then walked me down the hall and up the stairs. Once in Jacqui's room, they took off my shirt. Jacqui had them pull her dresser out a couple of feet, tilt it back against the wall, and then stretch me across it while they held my arms and legs. Then they pulled down my pants and tied my wrists to the dresser with my back exposed.

Jacqui gave one guy the branch—I couldn't tell who—and told him to whip me as hard as he could. The whipping began. It hurt like hell. The beater wailed on me with the branch while Jacqui yelled "Harder!" I tried not to make a sound, but the impact of each lash forced the air out of me in an involuntary grunt. The sound of the whip whistling through the air and the thud as it sliced into my back were so loud I was sure everyone downstairs could hear.

I didn't know when it would stop. I just took it. With each blow, the whip cut into my back, and I saw myself running away and never coming back. Finally, Jacqui told them to stop. I felt blood dripping down my backside. I don't remember things clearly after that. Someone washed my back with a damp cloth. I felt like raw meat. They untied me and stood me up naked in front of Jacqui. She told me to pull up my pants and underwear. Then someone gave me a clean T-shirt, and I put it on. I did my best to wash my backside before going to sleep that night, but my T-shirt and sheets were bloody when I got up the next morning.

I didn't go to school until the next day, and I was so ashamed I didn't tell anyone about the beating. I was now demoted, with no authority in the house. The older kids at the house and the teachers at school were watching me closely, on Jacqui's orders. That was how it went when you really fucked up.

Donna came over at lunchtime, and we went on the back porch to talk privately. I told her what had happened. When she pulled my T-shirt up and saw the bloody, swollen welts covering my entire back and butt, she totally freaked out. I'd never seen Donna feel so guilty about anything before. It ripped her apart knowing I'd gotten whipped because of her. At that point, she became completely committed to my escape. But if I escaped, where would we go?

The matter of escape was as problematic as our relationship. Donna and I needed each other to function and served each other in so many ways. The combination of my attentiveness to Donna and the demands my disability made on her stabilized her in some way, forcing her to become more functional. I was an anchor that somehow allowed Dona to keep her delusions at bay; at times she counted on my reality as her own. But I didn't have the clarity or purity to be her reality because I needed her and because I couldn't keep her off dope or protect her from herself. All this put great pressure on me.

Given a certain level of demand and structure, most people, even schizophrenics, tend to stabilize and strengthen. Yet Donna and I knew the demands we placed on each other might also become the catalyst for the end of our relationship. Another big concern was my education. Where else could I get the kind of tutoring I needed to earn a diploma? Even the military wouldn't take me without a diploma. But in the end, we both knew we had to escape.

That night Donna went to see Emerson. The next day she told me she and Emerson had a plan for me to escape that night. She gave me Emerson's phone number on a scrap of paper. I wasn't sure I could pull it off, certainly not at night. Family members in charge in each room slept with virtually one eye open. I'd have to seize an opportunity in the moment. Once they discovered I was gone, they'd have a team of family members out on the streets, and Rudy and Narrow in the van scouring the neighborhood for me. If they didn't find me within an hour, they'd call the police. Once I ran, Donna and I would have no way to communicate. Emerson would be our mutual contact. He was staying at Andrei Codrescu's house; Andrei was in on the plan too.*

I wanted to leave ASAP, yet I felt an overwhelming disappointment at not having gotten any of what Jacqui had promised. I'd come with such high hopes and would leave, more or less, the same as I came, with no diploma, no healthy reprogramming, no improved learning or marketable work skills, and no new plan for my future. I'd improved my ability to function under incredible pressure and stress but at a great emotional and psychological cost. The realization was sinking in that I'd gone through all this craziness for nothing. My escape wouldn't be a move forward but a flight backward, perhaps to my old life of insanity, drug deals, paranoia, and the struggle to survive. But I had no choice, and at least I'd have Donna. I decided to do it.

The next day at school I acted like I just wanted to get back to work on my GED. At one point, I snuck into one of the empty rooms and opened a window. A little while later, I asked the teacher if I could study in that room. He said okay, but I had to leave the door open. I went in with my GED book, climbed out of the window, and

---

*Andrei Codrescu later wrote a wonderful fictionalized account of my escape from Jacqui Schiff's entitled "TP: A Case for Sanity," which appears in his memoir *In America's Shoes* (City Light Books, 1983).

took off running across the front lawn and down the street. I figured I had maybe twenty minutes before they noticed I was gone.

Soon I was standing on the main road with my thumb out and my heart pounding. I kept looking back to see if they were coming after me. The first few cars passed me by. Finally an elderly man picked me up and gave me a ride to downtown Danville, a few miles away. I found a payphone outside a small market and called the number Donna had given me. Emerson answered. I was never so glad to hear his voice. He said he'd call Donna at the main house and call me right back. I hung up and stood in the phone booth. Twenty minutes passed like an eternity. I'd been gone over an hour. They were probably out searching for me by now. I kept scanning the parking lot and the street for cops or the family van. Finally, the phone rang. I picked it up.

"Goddammit, Emerson, that took way long!" There was a pause on the other end of the line. "David, there's a problem," Emerson said.

I felt my heart beating hard and fast, and a chill passed through me as if all the blood were draining from my face, down through my body toward my feet.

"Shit! What kind of problem?"

"Jacqui has Donna."

"What do you mean, she has Donna? Donna's not part of Jacqui's family. She can't hold her there."

"I know! I told her that. But she says she's holding Donna until you come back to the house."

"She can't do that, can she? That's false imprisonment or kidnapping or something. That's a federal offense."

"I know," Emerson said. "But she's not letting her go."

I realized he was right. Jacqui didn't care about such things. Jacqui did whatever she wanted. I knew there was no way she'd let Donna go. I licked my lips. My mouth was parched, and my hand was shaking.

"Shit. I have to go back."

"I know it's fucked up, David," Emerson said. "Sorry it happened this way."

The reality of it was sinking in. I fought back tears of disappointment.

"Oh, man, I bet they beat the shit out of me for this."

"What do you want me to do?"

"Nothing for now. We'll have to try this again later. I'll call you when I can. It may not be for a while."

I hung up, walked back to the main street, and stuck my thumb out. I caught a couple of rides and made it back to the house. I walked slowly up the driveway, savoring my last moments of freedom. I was going back to prison. Before I reached the door, Rudy and Narrow came out to meet me. They escorted me around the back of the house.

"Where's Donna?" I asked.

"She's going out the front door right now," said Rudy sternly, "and she's never welcome here again." *Well, at least she's safe from you assholes*, I thought.

"Mom wants to see you," Rudy said, meaning Jacqui.

Rudy led me to a recently constructed outbuilding, Jacqui's new office. I didn't get the feeling I was about to be whipped, but I was very nervous. I'd never pulled a stunt like this before. Rudy knocked on the door.

"Come in!" Jacqui's high, childlike voice called from inside.

Rudy opened the door and nodded for me to enter, then turned and left. Jacqui sat alone behind her desk. It was hard to reconcile her dumpy housewife look with the power and authority she wielded so completely. At her invitation, I cautiously sat down on one of the couches.

"Would you like a drink? Maybe some soda or water?" she asked, her tone almost friendly.

I didn't know what to think. She'd never been this nice to me before. Knowing Jacqui, some psychological strategy lay behind it.

"No, thank you," I finally said.

She got out of her chair and started doing office stuff, like I wasn't there. She tidied up her desk a bit, went over to her filing cabinets, rummaged around for a minute, then rearranged some papers and other things stacked on the wall shelves. It was odd. I couldn't tell if she was killing time, gathering her thoughts, or trying to make me nervous. Finally, she returned to her desk, sat down, and looked right at me. Her steady gaze showed no feeling.

"David," she said, "why did you come here?"

I figured I had nothing to lose at this point, so I might as well be completely honest. I wouldn't know how to manipulate her anyway; she was way out of my league.

"I really wanted to get the GED you said I'd be able to get. And I wanted to get some help understanding myself. I wanted to learn how to learn better or at least understand why I have trouble learning."

"Is that really it?"

"Yes. I also wanted to know why I'm always depressed. And why I can't feel happy the way other people say they feel. I don't ever remember really wanting to be alive. I've been happy a few times. I get excited about getting things or doing things sometimes. But it never lasts, and there's always this feeling of hopelessness deep down, like I'm doomed. I don't see a future for myself. I was hoping coming here would change that somehow. But it hasn't."

"I have you in my school studying to get your GED."

"I've been working with that book, and I don't see ever getting through it. What about all the other stuff you were going to work on with me? Even if I get my GED, what kind of job can I get? I'll probably have to live in a flophouse and get by on menial work. You knew I was coming here because I was desperate. You said you were going to be able to help me. But you haven't. This hasn't worked out at all. And I don't know what else to do."

"You know what I'm about here, David. We're devoted to helping people truly change—the ways they want and need to."

"That's great, but I don't see it. I'm afraid of you, and so is everyone else. So if you're supposed to be our mother, how does that help? Nothing has changed for me, and I've been here nine months."

"I've told you all before, my job isn't to be loving or to teach anyone else how to love. All I can do is help people change and learn how to live responsibly. And if they have to be afraid of me to get there, then so be it. I show my love by helping them get better, not by being nice. Look, David, I know Donna and your brother have been trying to get you to leave. Before you decide whether or not to try to leave again, you need to consider the people who want you to leave and their motives."

"What do you mean?"

"Donna is a very sweet girl, David, but is she good for you? Does she have your best interest at heart or her own? You have to look inside yourself to answer that."

"What do you mean? Both of them are out for themselves?"

As always, she'd somehow thrown me off balance and into confusion. I didn't understand what she was telling me. I thought she was trying to make me mistrust Donna and Emerson and trust her instead. She fixed me with a cool, penetrating stare.

"I'm talking about people lying to you and manipulating you to get what they want."

"You mean Donna? I think I could tell if she was doing that."

"No, David, I don't think you could," she spoke with absolute certainty. "With someone like Donna, no one can ever tell for sure. Even lie detectors can't tell if she's lying or telling the truth. She doesn't even know herself. She may or may not be schizophrenic, but she definitely has a character disorder. People with character disorders don't know the difference between right and wrong. They have no ability to empathize. They're capable of just about anything when there's enough at stake or even to get what they want." Jacqui paused.

I stared at her in disbelief.

"I'm not saying Donna's malicious," she continued. "I don't think she is. But because of how she grew up, she hasn't developed a conscience or a sense of morality—a guiding sense of right and wrong. She's a sociopath. She wouldn't hurt someone for no reason, but she will use people to get what she wants or thinks she needs. That includes you."

Jacqui paused, giving me a chance to respond, but I had nothing to say. Jacqui was missing something. Donna could be crazy at times, her personality was fragmented, and she was driven by deep fears and an incredible neediness. But I knew I really loved Donna, and she really loved me. I couldn't say this to Jacqui. Trying to explain it would only make me look naïve or stupid. And I didn't want to look stupid to Jacqui.

"You know I'm right," Jacqui continued. "Donna desperately needs you, and she'll do anything to keep you, even if it destroys you. This kind of relationship is one of the worst things for a person as paranoid as you are."

I could understand Jacqui saying Donna would do almost anything, but this last statement shocked me with a kind of physical impact. I didn't trust Jacqui, but when she made psychological observations I couldn't just shrug them off. She had penetrating insight into people and their motivations. I'd seen it many times before. And she had a way of making you doubt yourself and lose all confidence.

"What do you mean?" I asked, reluctantly. "I thought paranoids were delusional. Do you think I'm delusional?"

"No, of course not. You're not clinically paranoid," she said. "But think of the definition of *paranoid* as becoming what you're afraid of. That's you. You live in fear of what you might become, and that's what you do become. It's something we all do, but for the last few years it's been the dominant pattern of your life. You practice paranoia without knowing it. In times of crisis, you let your fear determine your response. Every time you tried to be as tough or as scary as the people you were afraid of, you were practicing paranoia."

Her argument was compelling and seemed so accurate that I couldn't deny it. But she dissected and pathologized everyone.

"Well, then I'd better stop doing that," was all I could say.

"That's easier said than done, David. Bad habits are much harder to break and take longer to unlearn than to learn."

I pondered her words, trying to understand their true meaning. Was I really paranoid? Was I doomed to live out this pattern she was describing? I didn't know how to even begin to change—that was why I'd come here. She was supposed to help me. Now she seemed to be telling me I couldn't do it. Or maybe I was being paranoid right now. I couldn't tell.

"Emerson is your brother, and I know you love him," Jacqui said. She was starting on Emerson now. "But you know he has trouble taking other people and their feelings into account. He's a narcissist. He can act sympathetic, but he's all about himself. He's incapable of empathy. He lives as if he's the only person who matters. His needs, his opinions, his feelings are more important than anyone else's. He thinks he's right and everyone else in the world is wrong."

"But everyone's like that," I said weakly.

In a way she was right, but she was also exactly the kind of person she was describing Emerson to be. I couldn't say that to her. If you argued with Jacqui, you only dug a deeper hole for her to bury you in. The problem with Jacqui was that she was always right in some essential way.

This was a lot to take in all at once. I'd never thought about Donna the way Jacqui described her, but I realized she might be as right about Donna as she was about Emerson and me. I had to consider it. Was Donna manipulating me? Was I supporting her delusions by taking care of her? Had Donna been lying to me, and I just couldn't tell? Or was Jacqui triggering my paranoia, directing it at Donna to separate us, so she could control me? That fit my picture of Jacqui. She really was everything she was accusing Emerson and Donna of being. But she was also brilliant and powerful. I was so confused.

"So should all people with character disorders be put in prison?" I asked.

"No, not at all. They're not necessarily criminals; they're just incapable of distinguishing and functioning stably within conventional social norms—what's appropriate and inappropriate, right and wrong. Nonmalignant character disorders function best in highly structured environments. They do well in prison, either as inmates or as guards. They do well in the military, in the police force, and in other strict environments that give them clear rules and guidelines of right and wrong. My father had a character disorder, and he was a police sergeant who did very well."

"Can someone have a healthy relationship with people who have character disorders?"

"Well, yes, with some character disorders, if they're generally well-balanced, productive people. I also have a character disorder."

I couldn't believe my ears! That she'd admitted this to me. *I fucking knew it!* I thought. *I should trust myself. I can always tell with certain people.* Carefully, I asked, "How is your environment highly structured?"

"Well, I have an outside psychiatrist who oversees me and regularly reviews my work with me. This way I can continue my work within appropriate limits, under qualified supervision."

A guy with curly hair came to see her sometimes. I thought he was just a friend. He never looked around. They just went into her office and talked. Some of us speculated that they might be lovers.

"The point is that neither Donna nor Emerson has any kind of structure or accountability for their behavior, especially where you're concerned. And I don't think they're capable of having your best interests at heart. I can say that I do, because I don't need anything from you. I only want to help you, and I know how. I think you know it's true. This place is your best chance, David. You're not going to be punished for now. But I'm putting you under twenty-four-hour, one-on-one supervision for the foreseeable future. Do you have any questions?"

Yeah, thousands, I thought, *mostly about you.* By now I didn't trust anything she was saying. Maybe she believed she could help me. But I didn't.

"I don't know." I shrugged.

"David, if you really want to get better, you need to seriously consider what we've talked about."

"I will."

What else could I say? I didn't know what to do or what to think. After half an hour alone with Jacqui, I left her office with my mind spinning, half believing everything she said, doubting myself, and feeling paranoid about Emerson and Donna. Was I really paranoid? Was she trying to *make* me paranoid? She clearly wanted me to mistrust Donna and Emerson and to trust her. But she'd taken Donna hostage and was holding me prisoner, and they were trying to help me escape.

I was shaking when I got back into the house. My mind was racing, my body felt uncoordinated, and I couldn't think straight. The only thing I had to hold onto in this world, the only thing that meant anything to me right now, was my love for Donna. I'd always thought Donna needed me more than I needed her, but maybe it was the other way around.

I went into the family room and sat down on a couch with some other kids. I'd lost all my privileges and was back at the bottom of the pile. Rudy was in charge and keeping an eye on me. I'd been responsible for many of them for months now.

I was now committed to escaping. Donna and I would be on our own. I needed to assess what I'd learned here.

I looked around the room at the schizophrenic family I'd been responsible for, stressed out by, and frustrated with. They were all pains in the ass, but there was something about each one of them that I loved. I'd glimpsed the human beings trapped behind the madness and felt an empathetic connection to them. Under the pressure of managing them, it was hard to feel that. But I felt it now. I felt as if I'd learned to understand them.

Their minds were out of control, spewing distorted thoughts, lying to them, leading them into wild fantasies they mistook for reality. It wasn't their fault. Their schizophrenia seemed to me like a random misfire going off in their heads, an explosion shattering the mind's continuity of reality, scattering fragments of bizarre thoughts, ideas, and images, like shrapnel in all directions. To create an order out of the unmanageable chaos of their inner lives, to make some kind of sense out of what seemed insanity to everyone else, they further dissociated from a whole level of reality that included their thoughts and perceptions, and they even perceived their thoughts as voices coming from outside them. Their strange behaviors were misguided survival strategies, futile efforts to find meaning and stability in a maelstrom, failed attempts to patch the fragments together into a whole that made sense. But a broken mind cannot fix a broken mind, and the whole they constructed, meaningful only to them, appeared insane to the rest of the world.

I wondered who they'd have been if their minds didn't misfire. I wondered who Donna and I would have become if we hadn't been broken in our own ways. Maybe it was no accident I had ended up here in this "family." I had a lot in common with these people. We were all lost in our own orbits, out of place in the world. Our only hope was Jacqui, and she was mad and broken in her own way.

I realized Jacqui hadn't stopped their delusions at all. She constantly confronted her schizophrenics with painful consequences for their abnormal thinking and behavior, forcing them to want to see a reality different from their own perceptions. She reduced them to abject humility and desperation, until they finally became willing to question rather than cling to their own skewed perceptions. Some did become better able to distinguish between their delusions and reality and began to trust their capacity to judge what was real and what was not. But that process required a terrible ordeal, being broken when one was already broken.

What would it be like to be told, and then be forced to accept, that what I saw, heard, and believed to be true, was unreal, a mere delusion? What would it be like to try to ignore what my mind and senses seem to be telling me and try to adopt under extreme duress someone else's version of reality as my own? It seemed to me that we all naturally cling to the special truth of our own beliefs and perceptions. And the degree of our attachment to our delusions reflects our fear that they might not be true; to this degree, we are driven by fear, and suffer. For this reason, it was imperative to me that my thoughts be true and correct. If they weren't, if I doubted my own perceptions, I'm not sure I could step out of the house with any confidence.

But Jacqui's method was to shatter the schizophrenics' faith in their beliefs and perceptions and to force them to adopt new ones alien to their consciousness. While I hated Jacqui's methods, I saw how it seemed necessary to her to force this crisis on those who were apparently lost in unreality. Because the more they believed in their delusional thoughts and perceptions and acted on that basis, the more they suffered.

And yet, they were only different from "normal" people by degrees. As far as I could tell, we all suffered, to one degree or another, from skewed and inaccurate thoughts and perceptions, and actions taken on their basis. How else could you explain all the crazy things supposedly normal people did and the crazy world that was the result, a world I was unable to fit into? To the degree that any of us saw and thought clearly, we could act appropriately and minimize our suffering. But I hardly knew anyone who seemed to do this consistently. And here I was in an environment designed to shatter and rebuild broken people, including me, controlled by a woman who seemed both lucid and mad, whom I absolutely did not trust.

Why had Jacqui created this environment and made herself a dictator in a family of lunatics? Was she trying to heal herself by healing us? Was she trying to control her own madness by managing ours? Did she need to force others to see reality in order to stay in touch with reality herself? Maybe she needed all of us as much as we needed her. Maybe this was just an exaggerated piece of a world in which everyone was mad and broken to some degree. Maybe we all needed each other in dysfunctional ways to get by in life—and in that way help and hinder each other.

Jacqui tried to force the schizophrenic mind to question its perceptions, discern its delusional components, and choose reality instead. I'd tried to do something similar for Donna using love instead of force. We'd worked hard to establish necessary trust. But Donna needed me to be constantly with her, and instead of her resource for greater freedom, I became a crutch preventing her from developing the confidence and discernment she needed to rely on her own abilities and perceptions. She'd been so broken by life that she was willing to trust me more than herself. The utter innocence and necessity in that depth of trust broke my heart. It was why I could forgive her profoundly difficult missteps. And now we had to leave together with only each other for support. The only hope for us now was for Donna to take responsibility for her own reality and for me to learn to function effectively in the world with all my handicaps. And that would require of us an ordeal perhaps as difficult and painful as any Jacqui might ever put us through. But first, Donna and I had to escape, because my gut told me Jacqui was far more dangerous to us than we were to each other.

For months before the whipping incident, I'd had a bad feeling that someone was going to be seriously hurt or killed one day. And I didn't want to be there when it happened. I was scared. I didn't belong here. But I didn't know how or when I could try to escape again. If I got caught, my punishment would be something worse than a whipping.

I lay in bed that night churning with anxiety. How long would I be here? Where was Donna? Was she with Emerson? Was she wandering out there by herself? I hoped she was okay. She had an uncanny knack for finding bad company. She had Emerson's number. I hoped he was helping her. Lying there worrying, unable to fall asleep, I knew I couldn't stay here one more day. I decided to sleep lightly, if I could sleep at all, and get up before dawn. I knew I couldn't hitch a ride out before then. I drifted off and woke up several times; each time it was still dark. Finally, I woke, and this time there was light and a few birds singing.

I freaked out for a minute. Rudy had taken my watch along with my clothes so that I couldn't run away. I had no idea what time it was. I lay there for a minute, listening quietly. Everyone was asleep. I hoped I had an hour or so before they woke up. That would give me enough time.

Rudy lay facing me on the floor beside my bed, directly in front of the door to the backyard. I grabbed the scrap of paper with Emerson's phone number I'd hidden under my pillow. Then, quietly, I got out of bed and stood over Rudy naked, staring at the space between his head and the door, wondering if I could open the door and slip out without bumping his head and waking him. I looked for my clothes, but I couldn't see them.

I tiptoed to the laundry basket fifteen feet away. Rudy hadn't thought of the laundry. I looked inside and found a pair of my pants, but nothing more. They'd have to do. I grabbed them but didn't put them on. I had to slip through a narrow gap and every centimeter counted. I tiptoed back to the door, gently turned the handle, and slowly pulled it open, stopping each time it made the slightest sound. The open door was about an inch away from the back of Rudy's head. It looked just wide enough for me to slip through. I took one last breath and silently exhaled, pressing my chest and stomach in as far as I could. Then, as carefully as I'd ever done anything in my life, I stepped sideways into the gap and slid through. The doorknob pressed against my stomach, and then I was on the other side. Slowly, gently, I pulled the door toward me, almost but not quite closing it.

I stood outside in the dawn light, stark naked. I quickly slipped the pants on and put Emerson's phone number in my hip pocket. Then I crept around the side of the house through the dewy grass and came out in the front yard. When I hit the sidewalk, I took off running. I could feel the house receding behind me, like a heavy weight being lifted off my back. A newspaper boy rode past on his bike and stared at me. I realized how strange I must look, running barefoot down the street with no shirt on. I didn't care. I just wanted to get as far away from that house as fast as I could. I ran for several blocks, my feet pounding the sidewalk, breathing in huge gulps of air. I felt alive, hopeful, and scared.

As I ran, I scanned the sides of the road for places to hide if I needed to, glancing back a few times over my shoulder. I passed a couple of guys in suits getting into their cars to go to work. They looked so normal. They glanced curiously at me as I ran by, but they didn't seem alarmed. I tried to look casual, as if I were out for a morning run.

I heard the rushing sound of cars on the freeway up ahead. I was only a couple of blocks from the underpass that led to the freeway on-ramp. Soon I was jogging onto the on-ramp, gasping for breath. Facing the approaching cars, I stood on the asphalt shoulder. As soon as a car turned onto the on-ramp, I stuck out my thumb.

Within a few minutes, a guy in a Volvo picked me up. He didn't comment on my clothes or ask questions. He didn't say much, except that he was only going a few exits, to Walnut Creek. When we got there, he pulled over to the shoulder of the exit and let me out. I ran back to the freeway on-ramp and stood waiting for the next car to come by. I stood with my thumb out, feeling like a neon sign. No one stopped to give me a ride. The longer I stood there, the more anxious

I felt. I was sure they were after me by now and worried they might drive by and spot me. I kept seeing cars that looked like the family cars, but none of them were.

I'd been standing there for about fifteen minutes when I saw a green van approaching in the distance, driving in the middle lane. It looked like the family van, but I couldn't be sure. I hunched down and kept my thumb out; all my attention was on that van. As it came closer, I saw Rudy. He was looking right at me. He tried changing lanes and almost hit a car in his blind spot. The angry driver honked, and Rudy swerved back again, narrowly avoiding a collision. Our eyes locked across the lanes as he passed by. I saw his intense expression in a perfect snapshot.

I figured he'd get off at the next Walnut Creek exit and take city streets back to this entrance. He'd be back around in less than ten minutes. I was desperate. Several more cars passed me on the ramp. I began looking around for a place I could run to or hide. I started running on the asphalt, the stones digging painfully into my feet. Then I noticed that one of the cars was slowing down. It came to a stop, and I ran to it. A woman was driving with a man in the passenger seat. He rolled down the window a few inches.

"I'm sorry—we didn't mean to make you think we were giving you a ride," he said.

I thought it was unusually nice of them to pull over to apologize and explain the misunderstanding. I felt like a salesman about to close a deal. Opening the door, I asked, "Where are you going?" I tried to sound friendly and nonchalant.

"We're just going two more exits up," the man said.

"That's perfect!" Without missing a beat, I was in the back seat. It was either that or wait for Rudy to come get me. They both looked startled.

"Well, where are you going?" the guy asked nervously.

"Berkeley, but you can drop me off wherever you get off. It's not a problem. Let's just get going."

They glanced at each other. I couldn't tell if they were annoyed or afraid. I couldn't afford to care; this was my only chance. I slid down low in the seat, hoping Rudy hadn't reached us yet. Then the lady pulled onto the freeway.

"Well, I guess we could drop you off at the first exit headed for Berkeley," she said reluctantly.

"That's great. Thank you very, very much for the ride."

Nobody said a word for the next few minutes. They slowed down and pulled off at the exit. As they pulled over to the side of the road to let me off, I said, "I can't tell you how much I appreciate the ride. Thank you. I hate to ask you this, but do you have a dime to spare? I need to make a phone call."

"I think so," the guy said. He reached into his pocket, pulled out a few coins, and handed me a dime. "Good luck," he said.

The woman glanced back at me and nodded. I could tell they meant it. They knew I was in some kind of fix.

"Thanks; I need it," I said and got out.

I ran down the exit ramp and across a road to the on-ramp. I looked back and saw them wave as they drove off. Then I realized they probably saw the red welts on my back as I turned and ran. I wondered what they were thinking. This on-ramp was much safer. The pillars of the underpass completely blocked me from view of freeway traffic. Rudy wouldn't be able to see me even if he did drive by. A few minutes later, a guy in a station wagon stopped and picked me up. In the back was a dog in a cage. It looked like the guy and his dog lived in the car. I think he wanted money but quickly realized I didn't have any. He dropped me off in Berkeley.

I found a payphone and called Emerson. Luckily he was there.

"Is Donna okay?" was the first thing I asked him.

He said she was safe and that he'd found a place for her to stay with Jacqui's former house manager and her boyfriend. Emerson didn't have a car, but he said he'd send some friends to pick me up.

"Have them bring me a shirt and zoris," I said. *Zoris* was the Japanese word for flip-flops we'd always used in the co-op.

I hung up and sat down near the payphone to wait. I felt nervous being in public with nothing on but a pair of pants and Jacqui's assistants still looking for me. About an hour later, a car pulled up to the payphone. A man and a woman in their twenties sat in the front, with Donna in the back. That was the first moment I felt I'd actually escaped.

I got up and went to the car. Then I recognized the woman in the front passenger seat. She'd been Jacqui's house manager. Emerson had met her during his brief time buying groceries for the household. She'd quit a couple of months back. I looked at her uneasily, and we shared an awkward greeting. Later, I learned that she strongly disagreed with Jacqui's methods and had agreed to help Donna and me at Emerson's request. I got into the back seat with Donna—it was so good to see her!

"Are you all right?" I asked her, meaning *Are we safe with them?*

"Yeah, they're cool," she said. "They're helping us."

The man said hi to me and handed me an oversized sweatshirt and a pair of flip-flops. I immediately put on the sweatshirt, and then Donna and I hugged and didn't let go of each other. It was about ten o'clock, and we were all getting hungry. Donna had the chutzpah to ask them if they could get us some weed. I couldn't believe it. I could tell it made them uncomfortable, but they said they could probably score some after we had lunch.

They did manage to score some weed after lunch, and we went back to their place and got high. Donna and I spent the night there. Emerson called the next morning after talking with Mom. Jacqui had called the night before and told her about my escape. She told Mom a sixteen-year-old girl at the house who'd grown attached to Donna and me had also run away. Jacqui was convinced the girl was with us, and she'd reported it to the police. Since Donna and I were now both eighteen, the authorities considered the matter a kidnapping of a minor. According to Jacqui, an all-points bulletin for Donna and me would go into effect at midnight if we didn't return. It was just the kind of thing Jacqui would do to get Donna and me to turn ourselves in. Donna and I needed to get out of the state by midnight.

The rest of the day was a frantic rush, as we tried to get enough money for two airline tickets to Chicago. Mom refused to help at first; she thought I should have stayed at Jacqui's. But when Emerson told her I'd been tied naked to a dresser and whipped bloody with a willow branch, she relented and wired money for the tickets. Donna and I caught a red-eye flight out of San Francisco International Airport to Chicago, just in time to beat the police APB.

A few months after that, one of the kids under Jacqui's care died. It was John Hartwell. Apparently, John had been acting out, so the family members in charge subdued him, tied him up, gagged him, and put him in the bathtub the way they'd done with Timothy. But instead of filling the tub with ice and water, someone decided to turn on the hot water instead. They held him down while the tub filled up with scalding water. They pulled him out when they noticed his skin peeling off, but it was too late. By the time they got John to the hospital, he was burned over his entire body. He died a few days later.

The authorities stepped in, and there was an investigation. The house was shut down, and people started getting prosecuted. Some of the schizophrenics were sent back to hospitals; others were turned out onto the street. Still others were temporarily taken in by neighbors who'd come to know them. A few later committed suicide.

I never saw Jacqui again. She left the country and ended up in Bangalore, India, where she continued her unorthodox work with schizophrenics. She returned to America in 1985, in poor health, and died in California in 2002 of multiple sclerosis.

19

Turning Around

My mother picked us up at O'Hare International Airport. Her face was drawn, and she looked grim. She moved the way she did at the hospital after my suicide attempt. As we hugged, I could sense her anguish. It was obvious she loved me, but I could feel the heartbreak I was for her. Once again, my relationship with her significantly changed.

We walked in awkward silence to her car in the short-term parking area. Before turning on the ignition, she looked over at Donna and me and said, "I love you both dearly. But you're eighteen now, and so my obligation to provide for you is over. If you come home with me, I want you out by the first of the month. I need a drop-dead I can count on for you to leave."

"We'll try," I told her, "but that's less than two weeks from now. We may need a month to get things together."

"I know you're still smoking pot," she said. *Jacqui must have told her.* "You'll have to keep all of your drugs in the bathroom next to the toilet."

For quick disposal in a bust, I thought. I agreed. That she was willing to let me have weed in the house told me she didn't feel she could stop me anyway and was disconnecting from me in a significant new way.

To move out and be on my own in a month, I'd have to do some serious dealing. I knew leaving Jacqui's meant I'd have to go back to dealing drugs. Being over eighteen now, I wouldn't be going to Charlietown if I got busted; I'd go to prison. To make the money I needed, I'd have to get out of selling retail and exclusively deal wholesale—pounds at a time—while controlling the number and quality of my contacts. That meant I'd have more dope than I could flush down the toilet in a bust. I'd keep an ounce of weed in the downstairs toilet for show and bury the rest in a camouflaged waterproof pit in a vacant lot behind our house. I hated lying to my mother, but I didn't feel like I had any choice.

Donna and I moved into my room, where I found my old balance-beam scale and got busy locating our old drug contacts. It wasn't easy. Some were in jail, others had disappeared, a few friends had gone away to college, and even more had died from drug-related causes. When I did locate a number of contacts still doing business, another problem arose. I'd disappeared for nine months without a word, and suddenly I was back. That was highly suspicious in the drug world. It wasn't uncommon for dealers to get busted and turn narc. They'd disappear and reappear to buy dope from former contacts, turn them in, and then and testify against them.

I told my contacts I'd gone to California but decided to move back home. They were wary. That was when Donna told me about Steve, a guy she'd met in the mental hospital where she'd gone to get clean. She wasn't sure why he'd been there. I didn't remember if she'd mentioned him before or not. So Donna called Steve, who told her he had pounds of good weed to sell. She explained our situation, and he agreed to sell to us. He also had a batch of Black Beauties, potent truck-driver speed. I didn't like the idea of selling speed, but it was part of the deal. I was willing to do just about anything for some fast cash.

We were off and running. The private phone in Neil's room was my business line. I immediately called all my old clients and told them I was back in town, about to score some really good pot, but needed the money upfront. I'd always been a reliable source; I was hoping they'd trust me. A bunch of people said okay and fronted me their money. Donna and I got in the Chevy Vega she'd recently inherited from her dead grandmother and drove around to pick up the money. Then we drove to Steve's house with enough cash to buy two pounds and a hundred Black Beauties. Steve fronted us another third of a pound. We went home and broke down each pound of weed into one-

ounce baggies. I shorted each ounce, telling myself it was a one-time
thing, and we made deliveries to all my clients.

But I kept wondering about Steve. Why hadn't Donna told me
about him before? Why was he fronting us a third of a pound? He
seemed nice enough, but it wasn't like he had money to spare. He was
nineteen and living in his parents' basement with his pregnant wife.
Why was he doing Donna favors? I asked Donna, and she assured me
there was nothing between them. Jacqui had said I was paranoid, but
she'd also said Donna was an amoral, undetectable liar with a character disorder. That echoed in my head now. Still, we needed the money,
and I couldn't afford to turn down help because of a combination of
paranoia and principles.

Less than a week later, Donna and I had enough cash for a
deposit on an apartment in nearby Brandywine. We continued dealing and saving money and soon moved into our new place. We'd made
it. We'd moved out by the deadline my mother had set. It had been
awkward with my mom; we were all glad to part. I took most of the
things from my room—my chair, couch, desk, stereo, and records. We
got other essential household items from friends and Goodwill.

It was all very exciting. We were in our own place, living as a
couple. I continued dealing weed, while Donna got a job as a waitress
at a high-end steak house. A few months later, she became a cocktail waitress at the bar of the same restaurant and started making
even better money. We were fully supporting ourselves. We opened a
checking account. In some ways, Donna was the brains of our part-
nership—the functional one who could read and manage the bills.
I was the engine, the driving force—the one who could make deals
and manage the budget. We both needed and completed each other.
Together, we almost added up to one person, functioning in the face
of all life's practical, emotional, and energetic demands.

Words like *dyslexic*, *schizophrenic*, and *character disorder* had
always haunted us. *Symbiotic* was another word experts and professionals had applied to us. They said we were bad for each other, that
we had an unhealthy relationship because we needed and depended
on each other. But wasn't that true to some degree of every relation-

ship? What did they think our life should look like? Because we had extreme disabilities, we also had strong dependencies. What did they expect? I thought we were making necessary, relatively healthy compromises to survive.

Most of the time our relationship was mutual and strong. Donna was lucid, and we could talk about everything, including the best way to help her with her delusional episodes. We were real partners in this. But trying to be everything for each other had proved impossible. Leaving Donna alone while I went to Jacqui's had also damaged our relationship. She resented being left alone, and her trust in me started to break down. If I did it once, I could do it again. At my end, Jacqui had injected gnawing questions about Donna's motives.

Shortly after we moved, my mother learned of a new school for "exceptional children," meaning kids with autism and learning disabilities, those who couldn't function in public schools. The curriculum was customized for each student, and the teachers were specially trained. The school's staff thought they could help me with my reading ability, memorization, and attention deficit problems, my biggest liability in day-to-day functioning. They expressed reservations about me being older than the other kids, but they decided to give me a chance. I didn't mind being in class with kids much younger than me if I could get a high school diploma. I was far below the eighth-grade level academically, and reading was more important than ever to me now that I had to support myself in the world.

The school was sixty miles away. I took a short yellow bus there and back each day with a bunch of kids ranging from first-graders through eighth-graders. It was humiliating, but not unfamiliar, and certainly better than living in a crazy house full of schizophrenics. I'd given up my personal preferences and need to look good so many times already, with the hope that something could help me. I worked hard and made progress, while I continued to deal weed at night and on weekends. But it all fell apart after a few months because someone broke into the school medicine cabinet and stole all the meds. I didn't do it, but everyone assumed I did. So they kicked me out.

* * *

My friends, who witnessed Donna's wild emotional swings and personality changes, had thought she was manipulating me. I'd always resisted their point of view because I felt they didn't understand how confused she got. I seemed to be the only one who saw her struggling to incorporate the distinct personalities living inside her.

But after Jacqui's, I began to wonder if I was enabling Donna's extreme behavior. Feeling the need to guard against her dependency on me, I decided to try to use what I'd learned from Jacqui's about dealing with schizophrenics. If I put a greater demand on Donna to distinguish reality from delusion and to take responsibility for her emotional state, she might have a breakthrough. This would free me from that responsibility, and we would have a healthier relationship. I loved Donna and wanted to be her boyfriend, not her caretaker or therapist. I knew she had to learn to discern reality on her own, just as I needed to learn to function in the practical world on my own.

I was already less willing to see her confusion and her inability to remember hitting me during her rages as a part of an illness she couldn't control. Now I wanted her to take responsibility, and I even questioned her honesty. I saw people sicker than Donna manage to do this at Jacqui's. But my new demands were devastating to Donna, intensifying the cycle of mistrust between us and undermining much of the progress she had made. Her fears took over, and she became less able to control her outbursts. The more I fought against it, the worse things got. It seemed we were fighting a losing battle for her sanity. We both knew if things didn't change, we were headed for disaster.

Donna's fears of abandonment had often triggered fits of unreasonable jealousy. Now my insistence that her fits had to stop made her more suspicious and jealous than ever. I'd always been confident in my ability to handle her physically, but that was changing. One morning I woke up with her on my back, screaming at me, hitting me on the head and pulling my hair, accusing me of not wanting to be with her and desiring other women. Her episodes of confusion and angry, paranoid outbursts grew more frequent.

One night when she was reheating a spaghetti dinner in a cast-iron skillet, she started accusing me of having looked at a girl walking down the street. If it was true, I was unaware of it. I sat at the table in front of an empty plate, feeling frustrated and overwhelmed. I knew something was coming. She'd had a migraine a few hours before, and that often preceded one of her episodes. We'd smoked a joint, but it wasn't helping. In the past, I'd normally hold her and rock her to try to calm her down and stave off a full-blown delusional episode with voices. But now I was determined to get her to take responsibility.

"I love you," I told her. "I may have looked at a girl, but I wasn't 'looking' at a girl. Everything's okay. Don't lose yourself in this fear. It's not true."

"I saw you looking at her!" screamed Donna.

"Donna, cut it out!" I said forcefully. "You're being paranoid. Get it together."

Donna suddenly got very quiet. She seemed to be trying to control herself. When she walked over with the skillet, I thought she was going to ladle some spaghetti onto my plate. Instead, she dumped the hot food onto my lap. I jumped up with a yelp and burned my fingers trying to brush the hot mess off my lap. Then I felt a hard crack across my nose and forehead. Donna had hit me with the skillet. She dropped it on the floor and began punching me.

Instinctively, I grabbed her, pinned her arms at her sides, pushed her back against the wall, and lifted her off the floor, the technique I'd learned at Jacqui's. Now she had no leverage to hurt me or to get away. I held her there while she screamed in my face. I flashed back to the woman in the psychiatric hospital who used to beat up her husband and how I'd thought the guy must have been weak and stupid to be in a relationship with such a woman. Now I understood. I had to get out of there. I dropped Donna and ran for the front door. She ran after me, screaming, "No! Don't leave me! David, don't leave me!"

She grabbed me before I could open the door. I whirled around and shoved her back as hard as I could. She fell on the floor, and I ran out of the apartment, down the hallway, and out of the building. I hit the street and kept on running. I heard Donna screaming behind me, coming after me. Then the screaming stopped.

Soon after I heard a car coming up behind me. I glanced back and saw Donna's Chevy Vega rapidly approaching. I ran off the road onto the sidewalk. Then I heard the loud thump of tires going over the curb. I looked back again. She was right behind me on the sidewalk. I veered right and scrambled up a six-foot chain-link fence in front of an empty lot. Donna veered after me and slammed into the fence. The impact knocked me off the fence, and I fell onto the hood of the Chevy. She put the car in reverse and started backing up. I scrambled off the hood with a whole new level of motivation, climbed to the top of the fence, and jumped down to the other side. I heard the Chevy's engine gun, and I took off running as fast as I could. The Chevy plowed into the fence again, but I didn't look back.

I walked around the neighborhood for a while, rethinking everything I was doing. I knew Donna would have to come to a crisis before she really changed. I'd seen it over and over at Jacqui's. But I couldn't keep us safe in the meantime. I couldn't be her boyfriend and a parental figure. I didn't know what to do. I gave her an hour to calm down and went back to the apartment, hoping she'd have returned to normal so we could talk it over.

The incident scared us both. We talked most of the night and came to an agreement: no more violent outbursts or else I was leaving. The violence stopped after that, but our relationship continued to degenerate. We argued, got stoned, had sex, and grew increasingly mistrustful and estranged from each other.

Not long after the Chevy incident, Donna suggested that we needed to live in a house instead of an apartment, for greater privacy and security. Now that we were dealing wholesale, we had to be more careful than ever. It was only a matter of time before the noise from our fights and the smoke from our dope wafting through the walls of our apartment would get us in trouble, either busted or evicted. Donna said we could save money by getting a house with Steve and his wife, Marianna. It says a lot about my confused state at the time that I even considered the idea, let alone agreed to it.

We looked around and found a nice four-bedroom house. Our share of the rent was less than we'd been paying for our one-bedroom apartment. Almost immediately, I knew it was a mistake. I'd been wondering lately if Donna was having an affair, something that had never occurred to me before. If she was, I thought it might be with someone at the restaurant where she was cocktail-waitressing or it might be Steve. I also began to wonder if something else was causing Donna's episodes. Was she doing speed? Some other drug? The thought that she might get back on speed terrified me. It would make our relationship impossible and eventually destroy her.

We'd been living in the house for a month when Marianna moved out. Donna and I weren't there at the time and didn't know why she left. A few days later, Marianna called the house, and I answered. She told me Steve had beaten her and kicked her out. She also told me he'd been in the psychiatric hospital because he'd threatened his father with a knife, and that he'd given Donna speed when she was in the hospital to get clean. I blew up. I couldn't believe Donna hadn't told me. To my knowledge, she'd never lied to me before, even through omission. But lying to me about speed could destroy the trust that made our relationship possible. Her omission about Steve and the speed he'd given her in the hospital made me question their involvement and whether I could believe what she'd say about it. Her keeping this secret with Steve also made me incredibly jealous.

Mulling it over in my head made it worse. It was bad enough that Steve had played me for a sucker, but for Donna to have conspired with him hurt me deeply. Furious, I confronted her. She claimed she'd told me and said there was nothing between her and Steve. I didn't believe her. Things were so painful between us I almost didn't care. I insisted we both leave the house immediately. I didn't want her living with someone who gave her speed. But she didn't want to leave.

I didn't understand how terrified Donna was that I'd leave her again. From her point of view, Steve was the only person in her life besides me who seemed to care for her. Reaching out to Steve was a survival mechanism. I started yelling, insisting we had to move out.

She ran into our bedroom and locked the door. The argument ended when I put my fist through the door, injured my hand, and walked out. I was done.

I decided I'd go back later to get my stuff. I was relieved to get away. Then it hit me. If I couldn't make it work with Donna, who would have me? Tears streamed down my face. I'd been the best person I knew how to be, caring and thoughtful, yet Donna still didn't want to be with me. Now I wondered how I'd function without her. How would I pay bills? Who would help me remember things? Who else but Donna would ever want to be with someone like me? Feelings of doom descended on me.

I decided to go to my mom's house. I knew she wouldn't want me there, but I had no place else to go. I was hoping Donna might have called to tell me she'd changed her mind. When I got home, Mom was asleep. On the weekends, she was still in the habit of staying up late drinking and getting up around noon. I crashed on my old bed in my old room and slept for most of the day. When my mother got up, I told her that Donna and I had broken up and asked if I could stay at home for a few days to get things together. At first she refused but finally relented under two conditions: no weed and Donna couldn't come over.

That evening, I returned to the rented house to pick up my dope and my clothes. When I got there, all the lights were off. Donna and Steve were either out or had gone to sleep early. I was disappointed. I'd hoped to talk to Donna. I still had my key. As I opened the front door, I heard Steve yelp, "What're *you* doing here?"

"You're not supposed to be here," Donna echoed.

It was too dark to see, but from their voices I could tell they were on the living room couch. Eric Clapton was singing "Layla," a song about a guy who is in love with his best friend's girl. The smell of weed filled the room. I felt sick. I didn't say a word.

I walked past them, through the living room, and upstairs to the bedroom. I flipped on the light and saw a beautiful long dress I'd recently bought for Donna lying across the bed. I'd always believed there was a place in Donna's heart that was true, faithful, and always open to me. Finding her on the couch in the dark with Steve and seeing the dress was unbearable. How could she be with him after all we'd been to each other? We were more than just a couple in love; we were comrades in a war of survival. I couldn't take it. I had to get out of there.

I put my several pounds of weed into a duffel bag, stuffed some clothes in with it, and added my toiletries. I'd have to make another trip to pick up the rest. Fighting back tears, I gave the room a last look and turned out the light. I went down the stairs, through the living room, and out the front door without saying a word or looking in their direction. Donna didn't say anything either. After more than four years together, she let me leave without a word. I was devastated.

I needed cash right away, so on the way home I stopped at a friend's house and negotiated a deal to sell him the rest of my weed The next day I took my mother's extra car in for a tune-up. I hoped she'd let me have it for a reasonable price.

That night Donna called to tell me she'd left Steve's house, was at a payphone, and needed to talk. I told her I'd meet her outside my mother's house, but she couldn't come in. I waited for her out front, wondering what she wanted to talk about. I was feeling a little more confident. She was coming to me. I noticed that when I thought she was leaving me, I felt hopeless, but now that she was coming to me, I felt strong enough to break up.

Finally she arrived, and I met her in the driveway. "What do you want?" I asked her.

"I just want to talk. I need to explain," she said.

Her coming to me was just what I needed. Maybe I could finally be free of her. I couldn't think of anything she could say to excuse herself from what I'd seen or to change how I felt.

"I don't have any feelings for Steve—"

"Bullshit," I interrupted.

She insisted, but I didn't believe her. I told her I wasn't interested in getting back together and that I wasn't going through this again. She dropped her head in tears. Then she looked up at me, still weeping, and tried to put her arms around me.

"I'm sorry; please forgive me," she pleaded. "I'll wait as long as I have to. I'll do whatever I have to do. I know how screwed up I am. I know I really blew it. You aren't like anyone else I've ever known. You've always been honest and good to me and been there for me no matter how full of shit I am or how crazy I get. I don't know what I'd do without you. I could never be with Steve. I could never love him or feel safe with him. I didn't realize it before, but you were right. He's a bad person."

I reminded myself that she was a liar, but I couldn't help asking, "Why can't you feel safe with him?"

"He's a jerk," she said. Then she started to cry. "He made me have sex with him."

Rage welled up in me.

"I'll fucking kill him! I'll fucking kill him! He's a fucking dead man! I'll rip his fucking heart out! God damn that asshole!" I was beside myself. Then doubt crept in. Jacqui said Donna would say anything, tell any lie, to get her way and survive. And Donna needed me to survive. "Donna, you need to tell me the truth. If he really did rape you, I may really kill him. I need the absolute truth. Did he really rape you?"

She shrugged and said, "I don't know."

"What do you mean you don't know? Was it rape or not?"

"Yeah."

"Are you sure?"

"Yeah."

"What did he do? Did he push you down? Did he hold you down?"

"No."

"Did he threaten you? Did he hurt you?"

"No. He got in my bed. I said no, but he climbed on top of me and pulled up my nightgown. I said no again, but he had sex with me anyway."

"So he forced you to have sex with him when you didn't want him to?"

"Yes."

She was hesitant as she spoke, cowering, as if I might hurt her—something I'd never do. I understood fight or flight, but I didn't understand what the fear of rape and dominance could cause a woman to do.

"Well, I guess that's it. I'll take care of it," I said.

I didn't know what I was going to do; it was a bewildering mess. I'd been suspicious of Steve's motives for a while, but Donna had said I was being paranoid. Now I knew I was right. But I was conflicted. Donna knew I thought she'd slept with Steve and her only chance of me taking her back was if he'd forced her. Now she was back with the ultimate victim story, looking for me to take care of her again, just when I was feeling strong enough to let her go.

Also, I'd fronted Steve two pounds of weed, which I'd done before, but now he was stalling in paying me back. I knew he'd been observing how I operated, who my contacts were, and the problems Donna and I were having. I suspected he wanted to move in on both fronts, Donna and my business. He wanted it all.

We both knew the rules. The world we operated in was territorial and predatory. You had to watch your back at all times, and above all, you had to protect your street credibility. Your life depended on it. Things could escalate and get violent quickly if people thought they could pull one over on you. Steve was highly competitive and hungry to prove himself. I saw his frustration once when I avoided a confrontation in a deal that went haywire, which Steve saw as a sign of weakness on my part. His move on my business was a challenge I couldn't afford to let slide. His move on Donna required a violent response, and he knew it. I had to do something.

I told Donna she had to leave before Mom got up or Mom would kick me out. I didn't know where Donna would go, but I had other things to deal with now that she'd handed me a bigger problem. I was back to taking care of her again, and the stakes were as high as they'd ever been. An hour ago I was ready to leave her, and now I was about to go after a guy over her. How did this happen?

After Donna left, my mind raced, trying to sort things out. What really happened between Steve and Donna? What should I do?

Everything was fucked up. If Steve had raped Donna, I wanted to kill him. I wanted to kill him anyway. But what if he hadn't raped her? I had to find out what really happened. I felt bad not believing Donna, in case she was telling the truth. I decided to go see Steve. Maybe I'd be able to tell by the look on his face when he saw me. As I considered which knife to take, I asked myself, *Why am I doing this? Is it because of the dope or because of Donna?* It didn't matter. Whether for the weed or for the rape, I still had to do something.

I got up the next morning, drove to Steve's house, and went through the side door into the kitchen. Steve, his brother, and two friends stood around the kitchen table, piled high with no doubt stolen steaks wrapped in butcher paper. *A bunch of fucking thieves*, I thought to myself. Steve looked up as I came in. He was shocked to see me. It wasn't necessarily the look of a rapist—maybe just the look of a guy suddenly confronted by the guy whose girl he fucked. I wanted him off guard. I didn't start by asking about Donna.

"I need the money you owe me for the two pounds I fronted you," I said.

"Bullshit!" he said. "You both left me with this house to pay for. I don't owe you anything. In fact, you owe me money for your and Donna's share."

"I owe you money, Steve? After you raped Donna?"

"Bullshit! I didn't rape her! She was as into it as I was!"

I looked in his face. He seemed startled but defiant, as if he believed what he was saying. But I wasn't about to give him the benefit of the doubt. This might be my best chance. I needed to provoke him and get him to come after me. If he did, I'd hurt him. Bad. Maybe I'd kill him. It would be self-defense. I checked inside myself for the rage I needed to do what I needed to do. I looked at him with total contempt. He was a sewer rat.

"You're a fucking liar, Steve. You rapist piece of shit."

"I didn't rape her! She's lying! I don't know why, but she's lying!"

"Okay, then, was she passive during sex, or did she do anything to make you think she was into it?"

That stopped him in his tracks. "Yeah," he hesitated, "she put her arms around me and kept telling me how much she loved me."

It stung me to hear this, but it didn't sound right to me.

"That isn't how she does things. That proves it. You're an asshole rapist, and you know it." I stared at him for what seemed like a long time, but he didn't come after me. He stayed right where he was.

Then I heard myself say, in a whisper, just loud enough for everyone to hear,

"Come on, do it, motherfucker. This is your best chance. You know I'll be coming for you."

"You better watch your back, asshole!" Steve yelled at me. "I'll burn down your mother's house!"

That was just the kind of thing Steve would say. And he'd do it. The idea of getting a gun flashed through my mind. It was him or me—that's how it felt in the moment.

"I'm going to kill you, Steve," I said. He moved just a little. He looked at me but didn't say a word. If I couldn't settle this now, somehow, I'd always have to watch my back. I growled in disgust, "You chickenshit! You worthless peace of shit!"

I had to get him to come at me. He just stood there like a gunslinger with his arms at his side, but no weapon. He looked like he wanted to kill me as much as I wanted to kill him, but he wouldn't move. I wanted him to make a move, so I could retaliate. I turned my back and slowly walked out the door, mumbling, "You backstabbing little wuss! You fucking coward! You'll take advantage of Donna, but with me you're too scared to even move."

He still didn't move. I left the house. There was no way to find out what really happened between him and Donna. I'd probably never know, but I was furious because either way Steve had fucked the girl I loved. My gut told me the truth probably lay somewhere between the two. Maybe she gave Steve mixed signals. The first night I met Donna, she'd given me mixed signals. She'd undressed, gotten in bed with me, and then said, "No, don't." A lot of guys might have thought she was being coy. If I'd ignored her feeble protests that first night, she probably would have given in and had sex with me. Would it have been rape? Maybe. Maybe Steve thought she was being coy. Maybe Donna didn't say no convincingly and back it up. Maybe she'd slept with him because she wanted to and then regretted it when she wanted to come back to me. Maybe I was a sucker for wanting to believe her. *Fuck!*

I wondered how much of this was my fault. Maybe I'd been pushing her too hard to take responsibility for her behavior. Then my mind flashed back to the slinky dress on the bed. I guess it didn't go the way she'd hoped. Maybe I should leave her to suffer her own consequences. She'd gotten herself into this. She'd kicked me out and stayed with a creep who'd given her speed in rehab, who'd beaten up and kicked out his pregnant wife, and then moved in on Donna when our relationship was falling apart.

The thought that Donna might lie about being raped so I'd take her back, knowing I might commit murder on her word, shocked me. But the bottom line was that I couldn't leave her on her own. She was much stronger and clearer than when I met her, but not strong or clear enough to survive on her own in the world. Without me, when she reached for help, she'd always pick out wolves that would devour her. When I arranged for her to leave her family three years ago, I knew I was taking on more than just a girlfriend. My mother told me then that even if our relationship fell apart, we'd still be responsible for her. Now she was alone again, scared, and looking for me to take care of her. How could I not help the person I still cared about the most? I couldn't leave her, pleading for my help, when I knew the wolves would eat her alive.

Still, I'd lost trust in Donna, and it felt like I'd lost everything. Rage filled me with energy and a sense of purpose, as my mind raced out of control with fantasies of killing Steve. Maybe I'd go see him and provoke him again and not stop until he attacked me. I'd have my knife ready in my pocket. When he came at me, I'd pull it out, flick it open, slide it into his belly, draw it up inside him, and twist. Maybe I'd grab his throat with both hands, squeeze, and watch his face change colors, swell up like my dad's. Either way, I'd look right into his eyes and watch the life drain out of him. I'd give him what he deserved.

I knew I wasn't a sociopath. I didn't prey on weak people or enjoy hurting people. Yet I often found myself in extreme circumstances, doing things I didn't want to do but felt I had to do, things that went against my better nature. Now I was contemplating murder. I felt trapped. I'd threatened to kill Steve, and he'd threatened to burn down my mom's house. We were both capable of carrying out our threats. Something was going to happen; I didn't know when, where, or how. I felt I had to act before he did. He probably felt the same. If I killed Steve, I'd cross a line I'd never crossed before. It would change me. It would damage my soul and move me to the next level of hell. Was this my conscience speaking beneath the volcano of emotions, from the depths of my being? Or was I a coward trying to talk myself out of doing what had to be done?

A fundamental, life-changing argument was going on inside of me. Steve had raped Donna or fucked her and stolen my dope. To me, any of those things required retribution. Part of me believed killing Steve would give me back some control over my life and that not killing him was to be weak, a coward, a victim, to lose control. Yet part of me knew killing Steve would be an ultimate loss of control and the ultimate surrender to fear. My life would now turn on the choice I made.

I had chosen to be in this life and play by these rules. The game was about controlling life by controlling fear. But to live and survive on these terms, I had to become the kind of person I hated and never wanted to be. If that was the price of surviving, it wasn't worth it. I had to find a better game. I had to grow up for real and put away these childish and destructive rules.

I heard a voice deep inside me say, *It's your fear that's in control.* I realized Jacqui was right: with fear, the logic of overcoming fear is to become the thing to be feared. But in trying to conquer fear this way, you become like the thing you're afraid of, and also the thing you hate. What you hate and fear outside becomes a part of who you are inside. When fear is in control, over time you become more like what you fear and hate. This strategy for conquering fear never works; it only allows fear to define and rule your life. And it brings violence to you.

This was a turnaround for me. The behavior I'd seen as strength and control I now saw as weakness and lack of control. My childborn habit of turning fear into rage had gotten me this far but would get me no further. It was no longer a viable solution. It was the problem. To live on a new basis required a fundamental change of my personality and character. I wasn't sure I could change in this way, but I knew I had to.

I still felt tremendous pressure to do this thing I also didn't want to do—kill Steve. Life always seemed to make me do things I didn't want to do. But now I saw I had a choice. I didn't have to become what I feared and hated just because I wasn't in control of my life. No one was in control. The only power I had was to choose on what basis to live, what game to play, and who I wanted to be. I didn't have to live running from my fears or trying to conquer them in this misguided way. I didn't have to live in the insanity of a world based on fear. I could choose something different.

I returned to find Donna waiting for me in the driveway. She pleaded desperately with me to take her back. When we first met, I thought I could save her, and maybe in the process save myself. Mom told me then you can't save people; you can only help them to help themselves. Now I understood. If they're going down, you can't stop them; if you try, they'll take you down with them. I needed time. Not knowing what else to do, I snuck Donna into my bedroom, telling her it didn't mean we were back together.

Overnight something inside me broke. I remembered the real person I was deep inside, who never wanted to kill anyone. Now, I chose to be that person. Whatever Donna or Steve had or hadn't done ultimately didn't matter. What mattered was who I was, what I was willing to do, and what I did, and it had nothing to do with anyone else. I wasn't willing to live anymore as the person I'd become. I wasn't willing to live a life anymore in which murder and suicide were options. I was going to change my whole approach to life. I would have to give up the personality I'd created when I was seven. I knew this would leave me vulnerable and weak in ways I'd previously used anger and violence to avoid.

Donna and I would have to leave Chicago. I couldn't become a new person here, learn to live on a new basis and also keep us safe. Yet deep down, I didn't believe I could survive as I was. I'd seen myself as stupid, broken, and dysfunctional for too long. I'd seen myself through the world's narrow, judgmental eyes. I could never meet its minimum requirements for basic functioning, belonging, and fitting in. Others saw me as lazy, but I wasn't lazy. I worked harder than anyone I knew but never got the results I needed. Society's messages—never give up; be a fighter; where there's a will, there's a way—hadn't served me. I'd look at people and think, *Everyone else seems to know a secret, the secret of who they are and how to live. But I don't know who I am or how to live.* Now I realized it wasn't about becoming more than I was but about accepting *who I am.*

I wondered to what degree the life I was living and the world I was living in were of my own making. Were they a result of what I believed the nature of the world to be? My mind seemed to be an illusionist, appearing to be the source of truth but then leading me in circles. From my mind's point of view, I'd be a fool not to be afraid. I had to decide if the world was simply a bad place or not. If it was just a machine of death, then it didn't matter what I did. I'd made friends with death anyway. But if the world was a place of meaning and my life had a greater purpose than mere survival, then my choices and actions had profound significance. They shaped and defined who I was. If I hurt someone, killed someone, I'd suffer the consequences of those actions.

I used to scare myself with my own thoughts, spinning worst-case scenarios in my mind. My mind would tell me it could figure it all out, but most of my thoughts were born of fear and generated more fear. My mind was a liar. I couldn't stop the thoughts, but I could stop believing them, the way Jacqui taught the schizophrenics to do. When I believed fearful thoughts, I only felt fear, and it crippled me in life. When I thought I had to learn how to read or things wouldn't turn out well for me, that was a thought that seemed true on the surface, but there was no way of knowing if it was true or not. When I believed it, it only undermined me. Even believing everything would be okay in the future was an illusion. When I stopped and looked deeply into any thought, any hope or fear, I could find no substance, no absolute truth, no certain future I could rely on. There was only myself, alive in the moment, with no ultimate knowledge or certainty. It wasn't about believing in one thing more than another; it was about my relationship to myself and to my life. If I was at peace with myself and my life, I was okay in that moment, not regretting the past or clinging to hopes for the future; otherwise, I suffered.

Trying to think and struggle my way through life hadn't worked out for me. I couldn't find any security or truth in my mind or in the future. I had to trust life in a new way and live the best I could now. I came up with a motto for myself: *I'll do my very best in this moment, no more and no less, and let the future take care of itself.* That was the most I could do. How things turned out after that was none of my business and beyond my control. The future was a mystery to me and everyone else.

Releasing the illusion of control was a profound relief. I remembered being in one of the worst situations I'd ever been in, locked up in the mental hospital after attempting suicide at fifteen, with no vision for my future. It's what I'd been afraid of all my life. Yet in that experience, I felt relieved of the burden of my hopeless life, with all its hopes and fears. I felt an ecstatic sense of oneness, of freedom, of peace. I felt profound gratitude for being alive and aware. I felt connected to everything, not threatened by life and death. Perhaps for the first time, I felt present in my own life. I wondered if it was possible to live on this basis. Then life would be tolerable. And that's how I wanted to live now.

From now on, how I lived now was everything. *I'll do my very best in this moment, no more and no less, and let the future take care of itself.* I could no longer afford the luxury of taking things personally, of wasting time feeling bad about what I did or didn't do. My life was an adventure, and I was not in charge. My only responsibility was to do my best in the present moment; let the future take care of itself. A huge weight was lifted from my shoulders.

When I got up that afternoon, Mom was waiting for me. As soon as I opened the front door, she handed me the keys to Dad's abandoned house and told me she'd call the police if I didn't get all of my stuff out immediately. Neither Donna nor I had anywhere else to go. I told Donna she could come with me for now, but she'd have to quit all drugs and it still didn't mean we were back together. I would no longer try to force her to be responsible or to see reality. What the hell did I know about reality anyway?

I knew Donna was stuck, and I'd help her as much as I could. She knew better than I did that she couldn't manage her life independently. So she agreed to my terms. She said she was very sorry and she'd come with me anywhere as long as I'd let her. It broke my heart. I didn't see how I could be her boyfriend anymore, but I loved her and wasn't going to leave her unprotected.

20

Inkling

Donna waited in the car while I packed my clothes, some toiletries, two sleeping bags, and some camping gear into the back seat. Then we headed for the rundown apartment building my dad hadn't lived to fix up. On our way there, we stopped at a store and bought some cleaning supplies, water, hamburger and Hamburger Helper, and a small canister of propane gas for the camp stove.

The building was in one of the worst slums in Chicago. The Black Panthers had been in a famous shootout with the Chicago police a few blocks away. The entrance to the building was in the back. We chose the upper apartment and quickly went upstairs. The door had three locks—a padlock, a deadbolt, and a lock on the knob—and opened into a small kitchen with badly torn linoleum floors and no fixtures of any kind. There was no water or electricity. At least the windows weren't broken and the roof didn't seem to be leaking, so we were protected from the wind and rain.

We stood in the kitchen for a moment taking it in. I wondered if this apartment was a taste of what my life would be like now that I was no longer selling drugs. Whatever life had in store for me now, I couldn't turn back. This was my test. Would I accept life as it came, even if it looked like this, and would life accept me as I am? We cleaned up the apartment the best we could and set up in the living room, laying our sleeping bags on the floor. I set the camping stove up in the kitchen, cracked a window for ventilation, lit the burner, and started heating some water in an aluminum pan to get dinner started. We put the beef and Hamburger Helper into a pan and cooked it. While we were eating, I noticed a piece of fur in my food. I was sure it was rat fur. We both ran out to the back and started spitting over the banister. I felt nauseated every time I thought about it, more repulsed than sick. We went to bed in our sleeping bags without dinner.

We set out the next day to look for work. Donna searched the want ads for jobs. There was a recession, so jobs were hard to find. After a few bad starts, she interviewed for a job at an envelope factory in Addison, working the graveyard shift. We drove there together, and I waited for her in the car. Donna came out about forty minutes later. She'd gotten the job, and they had more openings. So I went in to apply. I didn't tell them I was a high school dropout who couldn't read or write. I figured they'd find out eventually. They had a number of openings, but the only one I qualified for was the same work Donna would be doing with the envelope-folding-and-gluing machine. The manager told me they'd never hired a male for this position before, but I could have it if I wanted it. I was just glad to have a job. For the next two weeks, we worked the graveyard shift. At the end of each shift, we washed ourselves in the factory bathrooms and returned to the abandoned apartment to sleep.

One morning, a few hours after coming home from work, Donna and I were awakened by a loud tapping on the window. I got up and looked out the window to see two angry black women in their forties and three young boys standing in the middle of the street. They looked nervous and threatening—a bad combination. They'd been throwing pebbles at our second-story window to get our attention. They signaled me to open the window. As soon as I did, one woman started yelling, "You can't stay here! Ya hear? You have to leave now! Today!"

"We don't want your kind here dealing drugs to our kids!" shouted the other woman. "We see you leaving at night! We know what you're up to! You'd better get out if you know what's good for you!"

I tried to tell them we weren't selling drugs to their kids, but they would have none of it. I was more afraid of them and the surrounding community than of Steve. Donna was terrified. This unwelcoming committee felt like Chicago telling me to pack up and get the hell out. I was afraid to stay even one more night. Neighborhood vigilantes breaking in while we slept seemed entirely possible.

I decided to leave the next day for California. Between what we were owed at work and what we'd already saved, we had almost a thousand dollars. I'd get my check that night, quit my job, cash the check in the morning, and head for California. When I told Donna, she asked if she could go with me. I said it was up to her, but no drugs.

That morning we picked up our last paychecks, then snuck into my mother's house to get a couple hours sleep. I planned to be gone before she woke up around noon. We got up a few hours later to leave only to find all four tires on our car slashed. It had to be Steve—at least he hadn't burned the house down. I just wanted to get out of there. Chicago had really kicked my ass.

I went back in, woke up Mom, and told her what had happened. Knowing we were trying to leave, she let me use her AAA card to have the car towed to an auto shop. I had enough cash on hand to buy four new tires. I had the mechanic check the gas tank for sugar, a popular form of sabotage that ruined an engine. No sugar was detected. When the car was ready, Donna and I drove to the bank and cashed our checks.

When we returned several hours later, Mom said the police had come looking for me with a warrant for my arrest. She technically hadn't lied when she said I didn't live there anymore. I had no idea what the warrant was for, and I didn't want to find out. The APB on Donna and me for allegedly kidnapping the girl from the Schiff house in California had been dropped months ago. The girl had been found and testified that we'd had nothing to do with her running away.

Just a few months ago we were fleeing California and an APB there. Now we were fleeing Chicago and a warrant to go back to California. Later I'd learn the landlord of the house we'd shared with Steve had filed a complaint against Donna and me after Steve told the landlord we'd damaged the house and defaulted on the rent. The only damage we did to the house was the door I'd put my fist through during my argument with Donna. We had jumped the rent, but I figured the two pounds of weed Steve ripped off and his having sex with my girlfriend more than covered our share.

* * *

Donna and I recorded a dozen records onto tape, bought a tent that fit over the open hatchback of the Chevy Vega, and had sleeping bags and camping gear. We were all set, excited about the road trip ahead and the possibilities for a new life. Maybe I could love and trust Donna again and find some kind of happiness in a quiet life. If we worked really hard at it, maybe we could continue not using drugs.

On the long drive from Chicago to San Francisco, I made a series of firm decisions. I would never hurt anyone ever again, unless it was absolutely necessary to protect myself or someone else. When I got to California, I would not use or sell dope, and I'd stop hanging out with the kind of people I'd grown accustomed to these past few years. I'd find a legal way to make money. I'd get a straight job, maybe picking fruit. I'd live a quiet life. And I'd begin to learn how to live on a spiritual basis. I knew I'd have to struggle, but I'd struggled my whole life. I also knew that by making these decisions the unalterable basis of my life, I might not survive. But it was the only way to regain my self-respect and recover my soul. I committed to live by the motto I'd made for myself: *I'm going to do my best in this moment, no more and no less, and let the future take care of itself.* That would be good enough. I'd repeat that motto to myself thousands of times in the coming years.

Donna and I shared these things on the drive, and by the time we got to California, we were excited about the possibilities for our new life. I didn't know if we'd stay together. I wasn't pinning any hopes on that. I'd been disappointed too many times before, so I wasn't pinning my hopes on survival fantasies that never panned out. I knew there were no guarantees. Even if I did my best, I might never succeed. I might never learn how to learn. I might never get a high school diploma or have a satisfying career. I might always be poor. I might never find workable solutions to the practical dilemmas of my life.

But now I knew all that didn't matter and wasn't the point. The point was deeper than all the things I'd been chasing for so long—survival, acceptance, respect, money, education, and control over my life. The point was to be able to live at peace in my own skin, to be able to face myself in the mirror and to look anyone in the eye. The point was to contribute something to life instead of turning it into a war zone.

There was more to it than that, but I couldn't fully grasp what it was. It lay in the realm of spirituality, on a path I dimly intuited but had not yet traveled. I knew something different was happening inside me now. I'd started this trip running away from my old life. Now, I was stepping into a new life, yet to be discovered, with a clarity I'd never before felt. I couldn't know the future or base my actions on a particular outcome. How things would turn out in the end was not a relevant factor anymore because I realized the future was a mystery and now was all I had. From now on, how I lived was everything.

21

Hope and Fear

We stayed at camping grounds and bought bags of potatoes, our staple while on the road. The occasional fast-food restaurant became our special dinner out. We arrived in California a week later, low on money and ready for a break from the road. Northern California was too expensive, so we headed for Southern California. We arrived in Los Angeles and found a campground near Disneyland. We were almost broke, but we decided to go to Disneyland. As tacky as it was, we pretended it was our new home where we'd live forever. The cheerfulness of the tourists and the generally happy vibe rubbed off on us. We were the happiest we'd been in a long time. It was a dramatic contrast to the life we were fleeing.

We found a small one-room house for seventy-five dollars a month. We'd be living among migrant workers. We never imagined we could get a place that cheap, let alone a clean house with electricity and running water. Things seemed to be going our way. The first night in our new home, Donna looked through the want ads for potential jobs. On the way out to look for work the next day, we found an amazingly clean sofa bed left at the curb next door. Without a word, we looked at each other, got out of the car, and dragged it to our house. Later that day I got hired for a paper route. Every morning we'd pick up the papers, fold them, and load them into the Vega. I drove and threw papers while Donna guided us to the next house. It wasn't much money, but it was enough. Still, I felt I was holding Donna back. How long would she want to be with someone who wasn't pulling his weight and most likely never could?

Since we were working from two until seven in the morning, we signed up for classes at the local junior college. Donna took English and social science classes; I took algebra, geometry, and remedial reading. As long as I was under twenty-one and in school, I qualified for almost two hundred dollars a month from my dad's Social Security because of his military service. Our lives became calm and manageable. We couldn't go out to nice restaurants the way we used to, but we could go to McDonald's or walk to Walgreens for an ice cream every few weeks.

After a grueling first semester, I got my grades. I thought I'd done pretty well in my math classes, but I was afraid to get my hopes up. In the past I'd thought I'd done well on a test or in a class only to find out I'd failed or gotten a D. When our grades came in the mail, Donna opened the letter and read it to me. First she read, "Remedial Reading: Pass."

"Okay," I said, "but I knew I'd pass that because all I had to do was show up."

Then Donna got excited. "David, you got a B in algebra and an A in geometry!"

I was in shock. "Donna, are you sure?"

"Yes, it's true!"

"I've never gotten grades that good before, and this is college!" I looked up at Donna. "You know, I like math. Do you think maybe I could forget about reading and just do math?"

"I don't know, hon. Maybe."

I had some hope. This was the best my life had been for as long as I could remember. Then one day Donna came home with a bag of weed. She told me about an old Hell's Angels guy she'd met in one of her classes. He was cool and had this really good weed at a cheap price, and she just had to get it. *Here we go again*, I thought.

22

The Teaching

I'd lost track of Emerson. We'd grown closer through the Jacqui Schiff nightmare, especially when he helped me escape. He'd been traveling and heard about our return to California. We had no phone, but we got a letter from him saying he'd be stopping by. Sure enough, he did. During his visit he told us about an American spiritual teacher named Franklin Jones, who'd adopted the curious name Bubba Free John. Emerson had read a great deal of spiritual literature, so I valued his opinion. He said this guy was the real deal, the best spiritual teacher in the United States.

Coming from a Western culture, I found the idea of a guru strange. Many of the American countercultural youth were already turning to Eastern spirituality, partly because of the Beatles' public involvement with their guru, Maharishi Mahesh Yogi, a Hindu meditation master. That was how most people in America first heard the word *guru*. I remembered being fascinated by the boy I'd met at summer camp who practiced a mantra. That was my first glimpse of any Eastern spiritual practice.

After Emerson's visit, I began to study Eastern teachings, mainly India's Vedanta tradition and some Buddhism. I couldn't read the books; instead, I listened to audiotapes and went to lectures and discussion groups. These traditions focused on the transformation of the individual through meditation, yoga, and a deep investigation of the nature of the mind. The goal was to realize the true nature of your being and to be liberated from suffering. This was very different from Christianity, whose goals were to be forgiven, to be saved, and to get into heaven.

I found the Eastern teachings difficult to apply and began wanting a living teacher. Although Bubba Free John was an American, he'd been a student of Baba Muktananda, an Indian yogi from the Siddha Yoga tradition. Bubba visited ashrams and holy sites in India during the course of his spiritual journey. He was steeped in the yogic tradition and Vedanta, an esoteric branch of Hinduism. Many spiritual organizations and self-actualization techniques were coming onto the scene at this time.

There were also large communes of young people trying to live collectively, with a set of values different from their parents and "the establishment." Having grown up in the co-op, this way of life appealed to me. More important, the solutions the conventional world offered me weren't working. Psychologists and therapists had failed me, and no expert or authority had ever helped me to find a workable solution. None of them even seemed to be happy.

Years before, the priest I'd talked with had told me there were two parallel paths in the search for happiness and meaning. The first path was a practical path of success in the world. That path was closed to me. The second path was a path of spirituality. He'd said that was the only path to true happiness. That is what Bubba Free John was saying as well. His teaching was about being happy, being free of suffering, seeing through the illusions of the conditional world, and realizing the divine nature of your own being. More than anything, I wanted to find meaning in life, to know what it was to be happy. Bubba Free John seemed to be happy and free, and he was inviting people to take up a true spiritual practice in relationship to him as a realized teacher. This was not a religion about somebody who died two thousand years ago. This was an opportunity for a living relationship with an enlightened being. Or so I hoped.

Bubba Free John had only published one book at that time—his autobiography, *The Knee of Listening*. In his picture on the book cover, he looked young, in his early thirties, with a broad, open face and large, wide-set eyes. He wore a tailored shirt with no collar and held up his hand in a clenched fist. This was his gesture for the activity of the ego, its "self-contraction," the clench of our being that creates the sense of a separate self, which is at the root of all suffering. That separate self-sense was the root of attachment and desire that caused us to continually grasp for external objects, conditions, and relationships, as if they could bring ultimate fulfillment. But all such grasping and all such seeking were just more clenching of the fist and reinforced the sense of separation, the identification with an illusory "I." In understanding this, however, you could begin to unclench, open, surrender, release the contraction, and awaken as the true Self, the Heart. *The Knee of Listening* describes Bubba's experience of enlightenment while sitting in meditation at the Vedanta Temple in Los Angeles in 1970. The book was published in 1972. Bubba's second book, *The Method of the Siddhas*, was due to come out in just a few weeks.

Over the next couple of months, Donna began reading to me from these books. I was immediately taken by Bubba's description of real spiritual practice, which he called "Radical Understanding." His fundamental assertion was that conventional life is suffering and that we cannot find ultimate fulfillment from any experience, not even spiritual experience. But there is a prior condition, untouched by experience, that is not a result of or dependent on any experience. That prior condition is our true nature, a transcendent reality, always and already happy and free. He called it "the Heart"—not the physical heart, or the heart in the emotional, romantic sense, but the heart of reality, of the true self. The Heart exists prior to ego, prior even to our birth, prior to all manifestation. It is the substratum of all existence. According to Bubba, seeking happiness as a goal to be attained at some point in the future was an activity of ego that only took you further away from the already perfect condition of the present moment and your prior transcendental nature.

The more I studied Bubba's teachings, the more impressed I was. He seemed to express my deepest intuitions, something I felt but could never put into words. His teaching was not a New Age spiritual philosophy of magical thinking. It was grounded in the reality that experience is unavoidable suffering. It spoke powerfully to me—someone who had known suffering at every turn, who had failed at every attempt to succeed in life, who felt continually boxed in and caught in a trap with no way out. My failed confrontation with life had finally led me to the conclusion that all I could do was be as present in the moment as I could, do the best I could, and let the future take care of itself.

I'd always assumed that my predicament was caused by my disabilities. But Bubba's teachings showed me that everyone was suffering their own version of the same condition of separation from reality. What was true for me was true for everyone, no matter how successful they appeared to be in life. It was the universal condition. I didn't need to be convinced that life was suffering. But Bubba's teaching took my epiphany, that all I could do was be completely present in the moment, to the ultimate spiritual level.

At that time, Bubba had a spiritual bookstore on Melrose Avenue called Dawn Horse Bookstore. It was a point of entry for anyone interested in his teaching. It also served as the meeting place for his students. Donna was interested in Bubba too, but panicked when I told her I wanted to join his following. I was going to do it whether she came or not. She reluctantly decided to join, and in November of 1973, we formally became students.

Donna and I were nineteen then, among the youngest in the group, which included people with a wide variety of backgrounds—hippies, dope fiends, ex-New York gangsters, middle-aged housewives, even Harvard scholars. All kinds of people were showing up from all over the world. But what struck me the most was that they were all very smart.

To meet Bubba, we first had to fulfill conditions that were the prerequisites for becoming his students. At the time, I thought I'd be taking up a quiet, meditative, contemplative life. For the first few months, we adapted to a vegetarian diet, did hatha yoga every day, read Bubba's teachings, and attended a regular study group at the bookstore. I had problems with it right away. I felt agitated while meditating, sometimes finding myself suddenly jumping up, and a vegetarian diet left me craving sweets. But shortly after we became students, the neat and tidy routine of yoga, meditation, and a vegetarian diet relaxed. Around Christmastime, Bubba threw a party with all of his formal students. Donna and I couldn't attend because we were preliminary students adapting to the regular practices.

The party, we were later told, was an ecstatic celebration. Bubba gave a talk about how spiritual enlightenment had nothing to do with good behavior, a pure diet, or obedience to his teaching. Enlightenment was about throwing yourself into infinity, becoming ecstatic for no reason, and surrendering to the Divine with every fiber of your being. The first party was the beginning of a celebration that would last for eight months. Bubba used these parties as occasions to give marathon talks on "the process" of spiritual realization, to break people out of their conventional thinking and to give them a taste of true liberation. Now his teachings and the content of his books came from the talks he gave at these gatherings.

One of Bubba's main objectives was to create a spiritual community in which students could live his radical teaching together, breaking what he called "the cult of Narcissus." He said the average person is like Narcissus in the Greek myth, eternally distracted by the reflection of his own image and cut off from all relationship. The habit of Narcissus is the activity of ego itself, the root and epitome of all suffering. Narcissus meditating on his own image in a pond represents our unconscious meditation on an illusory self and a complete forgetting of our true self. This separative activity is duplicated in the structures of conventional culture and politics and results in a society that reinforces and traps others in the illusion of separative existence. As Bubba said in one of his talks:

The cult of this world is based on the principle of Narcissus, of sepa-rated and separative existence, and the search for changes of state, for hap-piness. There is not now, nor has there ever been, nor will there ever be an individual being. There is no such thing. All of the cultic ways are strategic searches to satisfy individuals by providing them with various kinds of fulfillment, or inner harmony, or vision, or blissfulness, or salvation, or liberation, or whatever. But the truth is that there is no such one to be ful-filled; literally, there is no such one. The principle of spiritual Community is that there is already no such person, no such separate one, no such dilemma.*

---

*Bubba Free John, *Garbage and the Goddess* (Clearlake: Dawn Horse Press, 1974), p. 5.

The underlying premise, that there is in actuality no separate self, is a radical principle. But this doesn't mean there aren't individual people with individual bodies and personal perspectives and experiences. It means there isn't an independent, self-contained entity living inside each body who is separate from everyone and everything else. The "I" or "me" we believe ourselves to be, who seems separate from everything that is "not I" or "not me," is an illusion we each create unconsciously from moment to moment, as a kind of meditation, like that of Narcissus gazing at his image in the pond. This radical idea is the basis and the realization in many Eastern spiritual traditions, especially Buddhism and Advaita Vedanta. The ego, the separate "me" trapped inside a body, isn't real. Who we are in reality has no independent existence. According to Bubba, the path to realization required a kind of ego death, a death of the illusory self that distorts our natural perception of reality and prevents us from knowing our true nature.

23

Goodbye, Devi

Soon after the parties began, Bubba decided to close down the Los Angeles center and move the whole community to Northern California. In January 1974, the Communion, as it was known, made the down payment on a dilapidated hot-spring resort in Lake County. This sanctuary gave Bubba the privacy he needed to do his work and a place where his students could live out his radical experiment in community. He named the property Persimmon.

After Bubba left for Northern California, Donna and I moved into his vacated house in Laurel Canyon to help load the van with his belongings. His waterbed was the last thing to be packed, so Donna and I slept on it overnight. We'd both slept on waterbeds many times before, but we became nauseous on this one and threw up all night long. The next morning we felt fine. When the other students showed up to finish loading the van, we told to them about our night. They laughed and told us about shakti, powerful energy transmitted by an enlightened spiritual teacher. Apparently, it was common for people to get sick after experiencing it for the first time. I smiled politely, thinking it would be remarkable if such a thing were true, but I didn't believe it.

By the end of February, the first wave of people had gone to San Francisco to find apartments and to look for work. In March, we arrived and moved into an apartment with some other students.

Everyone was focused on Bubba and what was going on at "the land." A core group of people living on the property with Bubba and his household was refurbishing the decrepit buildings. Emerson was there, working as an editor on Bubba's next book.

It had been four months, and Donna and I still hadn't met Bubba. Finally, the day came. We were invited to Persimmon to meet Bubba on Saturday, March 23. Excited out of our minds, we packed the Chevy Vega with as many people as it would hold and headed up to the land to join the party.

It was a two-hour drive from San Francisco to Lake County and the top of Cobb Mountain, where Persimmon was located. It was drizzling when we got there. We walked down from the parking lot to the main dining room, located next to a large kitchen. The old resort had been built around a natural hot spring. The property had an assortment of cabins, a small three-story hotel with individual rooms, a family-style dining room, an outdoor Olympic-sized swimming pool, stables, and an outdoor pavilion, the site of many dances and social events over the decades. There was also a bathhouse with a medium-sized soaking pool and half a dozen individual rooms with sunken tubs. All of it was in disrepair; many of the buildings were condemned.

As we walked down the drive, we heard music and laughter coming from the dining room. Fifty or sixty students were there, waiting for Bubba, who lived in a small house a short distance from the dining room, close to the main buildings at the center of the property. The dining room was filled with a random collection of old couches and chairs. Right away I noticed a single upholstered divan sitting on a small dais, slightly elevated off the floor. I figured it must be for Bubba.

I'd seen many pictures of Bubba but wondered what he'd look like in person. He entered about an hour later, his laughter announcing his arrival. He wasn't very tall, maybe five feet nine, but his large head, big round belly, and his presence made him seem much larger than his physical size. He wore a plaid shirt, and a knit beanie on his head.

Everything about him seemed round and whole. He never stopped laughing and joking. He was fascinating, but I also had my antennae out, not wanting to be blindly swept up in something I'd regret later. I'd met charismatic people before, and they all seemed to posses the ability to act with complete freedom and disregard for the rules of society and feelings of others. They made you feel special and invited you into a world more glamorous than your own. The next thing you knew you were doing or allowing something you never would have before. So I was wary and on alert.

Bubba stepped onto the dais, sat on the divan, and began to speak. That night he gave a talk called "The Saturday Night Massacre," which would change the lives of all his students. For the first time, Bubba declared to his students what he expected of them in their relationships and emphasized how life in a real spiritual community—his spiritual community—would be radically different from life in the conventional world. He criticized the world as a cult of Narcissus. He said it was the responsibility of his students to undo the cult when it appeared in their community. The various types of cult attachment included conventional marriage, which he called "the cult of pairs."

He criticized conventional marriage as having little to do with intimacy or real spiritual practice, mostly serving instead to reinforce one's identification as a separate self with two illusory selves mirroring each other.

I understood that I suffered from my attachments, and it made sense to me that if there was no separate self, then there could be true freedom, the freedom to love beyond the limits of self-interest. That truly would be selfless love. I'd experienced something like that at times in my life, like when I first met Donna, saw the fear in her eyes, and was moved to help her. This love seemed to come from a place prior to my conscious personality, perhaps, as Bubba's teaching stated, from someplace where we were already the same person, the same beingness. I could see that by loving all as one, impersonally, with no separation, we could love without holding back and that there would be no conflict coming from personal self-interest and attachment. But I wasn't sure how that played out in the world. If everyone was "the Divine" and ultimately without a separate self, then how did you choose your relationships? Did you just "love the one you're with"? I was confused.

It seemed impossible that people could live without acting out of self-interest and attachment, or stop seeking fulfillment through self-improvement. An egoic mind couldn't find its way beyond an egoic mind any more than a psychotic mind could find its way beyond a psychotic mind. It seemed to me that anyone who was truly serious about transcending the ego had to take on a teacher.

Bubba wasn't proposing a utopia, where everybody loved one another and nobody was ever unhappy. He was trying to create a community in which the enlightened, nonegoic state was the presumption, and each individual could have the best opportunity to discover that within himself or herself. Bubba's spiritual presence was so powerful and his freedom was so ecstatic that, maybe, with his help, we might be able to realize our own divine nature too.

After his talk, Bubba returned to his house with his entourage, where they partied throughout the night. The rest of us stayed in the dining room and partied together. But the only thing anyone really cared about was getting invited to the party at Bubba's house.

Donna and I spent the night in one of the cabins and awoke late the next day. By the middle of the afternoon, the party started up again in the dining room. Later that day, Bubba came over with some people from his party. He stood in the doorway, looking around and joking, asking the people who'd come over with him who they wanted to invite back to the party. A number of people were invited, and they seemed ready to leave. Then Bubba looked around and said, "Is that it?" He smiled when he saw Donna. "What do we have here?" he asked. Donna was invited back to his house, and I watched with a knot in my stomach as she left with him and the others.

The rest of us went on with our party, but all I could think about was Donna and what she was doing. Late that night, I went back to the cabin to go to sleep. Donna never returned.

Early the next morning, Bubba, his inner circle, and the rest of us all went to the bathhouse. I sat next to Donna in the large pool. But she was all over Bubba. I could tell they'd had sex, and that she didn't want to be with me. I sat around in the pool, intensely aware of how attached I was to Donna, even though I knew our relationship needed to change. Then Bubba started to talk. What he said was confounding and disorienting.

Bubba began by praising Donna, saying that she was "the Devi." In Hindu mythology, the devi is regarded as the manifestation of the cosmic female principle, the incarnation of the divine feminine in the world. Bubba was telling everyone that Donna was literally a goddess! He kept saying, over and over, that Donna was the Devi. He said that they'd been together for countless lifetimes and that she was destined to appear at this time—destined to be with him. This staggered not only me but also everyone there. Suddenly, from out of nowhere, Donna had arrived and was instantly recognized as a goddess! Not only that—she was now Bubba's main consort. She immediately moved in with Bubba and had no contact with me after that.

I had to go back to work the next day. I'd found a temporary job reviewing computerized tax forms. I didn't need to read, just compare characters and numbers. I wasn't doing well at it, and now I'd missed a day. I was afraid that missing another day would put my job in jeopardy.

Devastated doesn't begin to describe how I was feeling. I was in physical and emotional shock. As I drove home, I thought about how, only a few weeks ago, I was ready to leave Donna to study with this teacher. Now, she'd left me to be with him. We both knew our relationship hadn't been working and needed to change. But this had happened so fast. I was far more attached to Donna than I ever knew. Over the next few months, I realized I'd have to understand and accept the loss of her without ever having closure.

I had to reconsider why I'd joined Bubba's community in the first place. Bubba seemed to surround himself with people who could do him the most good: people who had money, who were good writers, who were beautiful and sexy. I seemed to be right back where I'd started, in a world that rewarded people who were more successful, more beautiful, or simply more valuable to someone else's self-interest. My revulsion toward these worldly games of status and privilege had led me to consider a spiritual alternative in the first place. I kept asking myself if Bubba was really doing all this for the "sake of his students" as he claimed or if it was just how he wanted to live and now he could play it out.

I thought about Emerson and people more extreme than Emerson, who seemed to have no empathy for others, without conscience, without self-inspection. Such people fascinated me. I instinctively recognized them. Their confidence and charisma seemed to come from being free of concerns about right and wrong, good and bad. It seemed the most powerful people I knew had these traits and the worst people had the most self-confidence. I wished I had their confidence and freedom from constant self-questioning and judgment. I wondered if this was a necessary requirement to be a strong leader. I wondered if Bubba was a sociopath, far more brilliant and powerful than Jacqui Schiff, yet still broken in some fundamental way and driven by a desperation and craving I couldn't see.

As with Jacqui, Bubba's arguments were unassailable and made me doubt and question myself. I wasn't sure what a true or healthy relationship was, and I felt profoundly alone. If Bubba's teachings were correct, I was only suffering my own attachments. When I examined my life, I knew it was true. It wasn't just my attachment to people but also to my ideas about what I should be doing and who I should be—my attachment to the hope of learning how to read and to my desire to be married and have a family. I was attached to everything I valued and desired, and I suffered all of it. And was it true that we keep coming back, lifetime after lifetime, as long as we have attachments to anything in this world?

I didn't even know what it would look like to be free of attachments. Did it mean being free of concern for others, as Bubba seemed to be? Donna wasn't going to survive without the support of others. I'd seen all kinds of handicapped people who needed others to live. How could they not need or be attached to other people? Maybe such people could never be free of attachments and therefore could never be happy. I knew I couldn't survive without help. How could I not be attached to the people who helped me compensate for my disabilities? I didn't see how I could be free of attachment to other people without being free of needs. And I didn't see how I could be free of needs.

I realized that the thoughts of suicide I'd had all my life were really about the desire to be free of my needs, so that I wouldn't suffer rejection at the hands of the people I depended on. Because of my needs, I inevitably became a burden to them, an object of pity. The more support I needed, the more they wanted to get away from me. I needed a deep and constant level of intimacy and communication, but that intensity made people withdraw. No matter how much they loved me, they'd often try to avoid me when they saw me coming. Even my mother, for as long as I can remember, had been trying to figure out a way to be free of me and my needs. I couldn't find self-respect when I needed others and they found me to be a burden. And I would rather be dead than be a burden to those I loved. This became so extremely painful that suicide seemed the only solution to my suffering.

That was when I realized I was very different from everyone else I knew. I was only alive because of my mother's unyielding insistence that I join the world. I'd resisted it with my whole body because the simplest input—a light, a touch, a sound—was overwhelmingly pain-ful. But because of my mother's constant connection to me, I was pulled into the world of others against my will. I'd left the safety of my small internal world, where I kept tight control on all sensory input. At that time my mother was the thread of my connection to this world, and I felt lost without it. This set my extreme, baseline need for connection; yet that connection could always be broken and was not reliable, which threw me into profound states of fear. I'd always felt stuck, and I'd vacillated between impossible options. I was unwill-ing to remain dependent on others my entire life, but independence, for me, required dealing drugs and living in a violent world where I'd have to resort to violence. And I had decided I would rather be dead than live that way.

For most of my life I'd felt betrayed that I had finally come into this world of relationships, where I had limited control over input, and along with that a disability that made it impossible for me to function in this world. It was as if I'd stayed here solely at the urging of other people, knowing that I couldn't participate in their world, and then they said, "Well, you're on your own now." They didn't believe, or refused to believe, that I lacked the capacity to function like everyone else. I couldn't integrate ordinary sensory input. I was so overwhelmed with sensory overload that just being alive was terrifying. I couldn't look into someone's eyes without being overwhelmed by their emotions and the relational demand. And the worst thing of it all was that I was only here because *they* insisted that I be here.

I could see now that it was impossible to base freedom from attachment on not having any needs. Everyone has needs. But my disabilities created needs that made me extremely dependent on other people—and at the same time those needs isolated me from those same people. My disabilities were profound and at the same time largely invisible, so that people often didn't believe they existed. When I'd tell people that I couldn't read or remember names, they wouldn't believe me. They'd say, "There must be something you can do about that." But there wasn't anything I could do, and nobody would acknowledge it. Nobody wanted to go there. The more support I needed, the more people wanted to get away from me. I needed a deep and constant level of intimacy and communication with someone in order to function, but that intensity made people withdraw.

To have self-respect I needed to be of value, but at the same time it seemed the only hope I had of ever having an equal relationship with someone was for that person to have disabilities and needs that were as bad as mine. Together we might bring enough value to each other to add up to one complete person. This was the chance I'd had with Donna, seemingly my only chance for self-respect. Of course, to psychologists and therapists we would appear to be two highly dysfunctional people in an unhealthy codependent relationship. That's what they always said.

My need for connection in order to function, and the way that my needs drove others away and isolated me, was so extreme and so painful that, at fourteen, suicide seemed the only solution to escape the cycle of suffering. I thought suicide would extinguish all my needs and the pain of not getting them met. Now, I was being presented with another alternative, another kind of suicide—an ego death.

According to Bubba's teaching, the ego was not an entity; it was not an objective thing. It was an activity. The primary activity of the ego was contraction. That contraction occurs the moment we identify with an illusory separate self, an "I." In the moment of experiencing that separate "I," we simultaneously realize a world of "others" out there. In the East they say, "Whenever there is an other, fear arises." It is true that there's an individual body and mind, but the contraction of consciousness into body-identification and fear creates an illusory "me," reinforcing the sense of separation. The Vedanta tradition refers to this as identification, differentiation, and desire.

Once we identify with an illusory self—the ego—fear arises, and a sense of separation distorts our perception of reality. Then the grasping for external objects, the attachment to external conditions and others, and the search to attain security for this apparently separate self become continual pursuits—even the point of life. This habitual grasping, attachment, and seeking reinforce the core contraction and the illusion of a separate self. And this cycle repeats itself in an endless loop, which is our suffering. Until we understand and awaken. But to the ego, this awakening is death.

I had once been willing to kill myself to be released of my needs and attachments. That took a kind of courage. Now, I saw it would be cowardly to commit suicide if I didn't at least try to live with my needs, whether they were met or not, and to surrender in the midst of suffering and attachment while I was alive. This would require greater courage.

As an infant and a small child I said no to experience. I chose to withdraw rather than suffer the overwhelming pain of stimuli I couldn't integrate or control. I chose contraction and denial of life and experience. Now, practicing the release of my conditioned patterns of fear and the sense of self they gave me was the radical opposite of that withdrawal.

As I came to terms with these insights and applied them in my life as best I could, I was also dealing with the aftermath of my sudden loss of Donna to the guru whose teachings formed the basis of my new spiritual life and practice. I wondered what Bubba would do when he discovered her dramatic mood swings, her desperate emotional needs and attachments, her terrifying psychotic rages. People had always judged Donna for her failings and weaknesses—she was a drug addict, she was manipulative, she was promiscuous. How would Bubba deal with her?

What I learned as the months passed was that Bubba did not judge Donna. He wasn't afraid of her. He seemed to be trying to get her to accept all aspects of herself—the same thing I'd been trying to do, but he took it to the absolute limit. He saw beyond her failings, her weaknesses, her brokenness. He appreciated and even glorified each broken piece of her, holding her in a state of wholeness and perfection, which he saw as her true nature. He held her as a goddess. I'd never seen anyone else do this before. Maybe this was the love of an awakened Heart. Maybe this love would put Donna back together.

If Bubba could do that, then I was happy for Donna and incredibly grateful to him. If Bubba could make Donna whole, then maybe he was for real.

24

Moving On

There was much more going on during this period than parties. A spiritual force was turned loose in our community, unlike anything any of us had ever experienced. The energy transmitted by Bubba triggered dramatic internal experiences and profound states of consciousness in many people. This spiritual transmission had its roots in the ancient Indian tradition of kundalini yoga. The source of the kundalini, a psychospiritual force, is the shakti, the primal life energy that animates all living beings. The kundalini is said to lie dormant at the base of the spine, like a sleeping serpent. One of the ways it can be awakened is by the initiatory touch of a spiritual master. It then rises up the spine, opening various energy centers in the body, culminating in the opening of the sahasrara chakra at the top of the head. When this chakra opens, a person experiences illumination, a merging with the Infinite, an awakening to the true self. Bubba's own gurus were adepts of this yoga and had awakened in him the powerful shakti that he now transmitted to his students.

When Bubba sat in formal meditation with everyone, his face contorted as he channeled this force. People sitting with him were often overwhelmed with yogic energy. Some shook or wailed uncontrollably as waves of shakti poured through them. Donna, extremely sensitive to this spiritual force, swooned and shook in ecstasy as the force of the shakti moved through her. She was the most extreme person I'd ever met. I'd seen her take drugs and act out wildly in the past. Now she was throwing herself into her relationship with Bubba as if it were a drug.

Meanwhile, I wasn't having any of these experiences. I suspected that those who seemed to be having them were putting it on or that maybe I just wasn't a spiritual type. But then one day I experienced the shakti. We'd all been sitting in a large meditation hall between the kitchen and the main house. Bubba had just left, and I began to feel a "buzz," as if I'd taken LSD. A powerful energy began to fill me. Colors got richer and brighter, and the room began to shimmer. Everything was suddenly alive. There was no future or past. There was only the present moment, in which I was part of everything. The peace of this was profound and primordial. It was a state of consciousness that existed prior to my human personality, long before my birth. It seemed to precede the first appearance of humanity, continuing up to this very moment, and would exist into an endless future. It was more real and true than anything I'd ever experienced. And this consciousness was my own nature and the source of my being.

In this state, I perceived my thoughts as passing illusions, not to be believed. I saw how my thoughts and fears, my desire to control my life and to survive, controlled me, possessed me, and created the very sense of me. And this was my dis-ease.

I was filled with profound appreciation and gratitude. This was the source of all the love and connectedness I'd ever felt in my life, including those moments in the hospital after my attempted suicide at fourteen, when I experienced an inner source that was awake and alive in me. I knew I was being sustained by a force that flowed through me now from an infinite source. I always had been. And I knew, for my life to ever work out, I had to trust completely in the reality of that source. This experience was a turning point. In Bubba's terms, I had "understood." This experience and the understandings it communicated were reinforced many times over in formal meditation with Bubba. What I felt in his presence was a magnification and a confirmation of my own Self, my true nature and being. The point was not to discover what was true about him but to realize what was true about me.

Except for Emerson, my family and old friends couldn't understand what I was committed to and were afraid for me. Even the few who did understand didn't believe Bubba had the answers. The choice I was making was impossible to explain to anyone who hadn't seen and felt what I had in his presence. I knew that following a false teacher would be more damaging than continuing on my own ego-based path. I also knew, at least intellectually, that Bubba's teaching was true, and what I'd experienced in meditation absolutely confirmed my deepest intuition about the nature of my own being. I realized it wasn't about following Bubba, or trusting anyone else, for that matter.

It was about trusting the thread of my own intuition and following my own path. Right now, I felt I needed a teacher; if that changed in the future, I'd move on.

As word got out about the extraordinary events taking place in Bubba's company, hundreds of people started showing up. The Free John community was not the only spiritual community trying to live out a radical experiment at that time. In Boulder, Colorado, Chogyam Trungpa, a Tibetan Rinpoche, was also forming a community around his lineage of Tibetan Buddhism. He was well known for his drunken parties and wild, unconventional behavior. In India, Bhagwan Shree Rajneesh had thousands of Western followers and would later bring his community to the United States. Bubba's teacher, Swami Muktananda, was opening Siddha Yoga ashrams here, and the Maharishi was spreading Transcendental Meditation far and wide, introducing meditation to mainstream America.

In San Francisco, the community of Bubba's ordinary students was beginning an experiment in cooperative living. A community organization was formed called the Free Community Order. We became spiritual renunciates. We all moved into large apartment buildings, where we shared a common kitchen and a common meditation hall. One three-bedroom apartment would house six or more students. There were several households like this.

Meanwhile, I continued to flounder from one job to another, always hoping just to collect as many paychecks as possible before I got fired. One time I got hired for a job, but when the phone rang after the interview, my new boss asked me to pick it up. He told me to be sure to take down the date and time. I didn't know the number of the month or the spelling. He told me to get out. I'd lost the job only minutes after being hired. At one point, I had a job sewing up corpses after autopsies. That didn't work out. I also ran an ad in the newspaper for doing appliance repairs. I'd show up at a house, often without any idea what to do. With my knack for fixing things, it sometimes worked out, but sometimes it didn't.

I began taking classes at San Francisco City College. As long as I was in school, I still had the Social Security support from my father.

Because I didn't have a high school diploma, there was no way I could actually get a degree, so I just took classes I was interested in for the sake of learning. I took classes in engineering and thermo-fluid dynamics. Calculus and physics were naturals for me; I did very well in them. But all my efforts and studies seemed like hard labor that never amounted to anything, and I didn't know if any of it would ever be any use.

Yet even with so much that I was unable to learn, I was still learning more than I knew. For the first time, I was living a non-goal-oriented life. I grew in my understanding of what I could and couldn't learn. This helped me identify and avoid the things I couldn't learn. Up to that point, I'd always been given things to learn that were supposed to be essential, but many of these things disrupted my ability to stay focused on what I could learn. I began to enjoy the experience of building momentum with my learning. I found that I learned more by pushing myself to my limits without violence to myself. I began to let kindness be the guide to my limits, always knowing that the further I could go now, the further I could go later on. I reminded myself often: I will do my very best in this moment, no more and no less, and let the future take care of itself.

My best chance to succeed was to do the best I could without attachment to results. When I failed, I would use that in my spiritual practice to remind me to go inside and rediscover what it is to be happy prior to my worldly circumstances. This gave me the strength to go on—not a Rambo kind of strength that attacks and destroys its enemies but a quiet kind of strength that allowed me to remain calm and clear in the midst of a crisis.

I committed myself to wasting no time. I spent no time with anything that didn't add to my learning or somehow build my chances for a career. I avoided anything that was detrimental to my health.

Staying on task when I had no idea how my life could ever work out was like being buried in the snow as a kid and not knowing how or if I could get out. I didn't spend time worrying if there would be enough air to breathe or enough room in the tunnel to dig my way out. I just made the best use of every nook and cranny, packing the snow around me as best I could in the moment, then putting my attention on the next handful of snow. If I did the best I could at each step, I'd get the best result. I might not survive, but living this way was my best chance. And when I was busy in this way, I wasn't suffering in those moments.

In addition to reminding myself to stay fully present in the moment and to let the future take care of itself, I also had the deeper understanding from Bubba's teaching that we are always already happy prior to our conditional circumstances. It became important for me to locate that feeling of prior happiness in order to stay present in the moment. Working with the issue of releasing my attachments had prepared me for finding this place of awareness and happiness.

25

Married, with Children

One of the primary responsibilities of Bubba's students was to communicate his teaching to others and to create forms of access for new people who were approaching. Those who were serious about getting involved with Bubba went through a series of screening interviews conducted by students who'd been around for a while. I was conducting some of these preliminary interviews one night when a beautiful young woman showed up. Her name was Cathy. I continued to run into her at community functions during the week; on the weekends, we'd meet at the sanctuary and take walks together.

Long story short, we fell in love and got married.

It was a relief to be in a relatively healthy relationship. Cathy and I were not dependent on each other, as Donna and I had been. We were both highly focused—I on school, and she on cooking for more than forty people. We both also had our meditation and other daily practices. Because of the structured life in the household, where meals were prepared and bills were paid, many of life's ordinary stresses were absent from our relationship. Many problems I'd previously thought to be psychological were actually practical. Just by living in a managed circumstance, the familiar relationship codependencies and emotional complications simply never arose.

I was constantly confronted by the paradox of Bubba and his teachings, which couldn't be understood by conventional standards, and I was always left with no certainty that he was who he said he was. Bubba's assertion that in reality there is no such thing as a separate individual self could easily be interpreted by the medical establishment as a form of mental illness. Yet this same realization has been spoken of by many spiritual teachers throughout history, particularly in the East. India is also full of stories of saints and sages who acted in completely bizarre and antisocial ways. Jesus went into a temple, overturned the tables of the moneychangers, and drove them and all their livestock out with a whip. St. Francis of Assisi talked to birds.

What Western psychology defines as "sanity" is based in a consensus reality that isn't universally shared by all cultures in all times. Many enlightened beings would be diagnosed insane by current psychological standards. Even the most basic principle of Eastern teaching—that the personal, individual self is an illusion—is incomprehensible and unacceptable to most Westerners.

I can't say I ever came to like Bubba, partly because there was no way to get to know him. He was not a conventional person with conventional goals, and it wasn't possible to form a conventional friendship with him. There never seemed to be anyone "there." I never saw him exhibit compassion or generosity toward any individual. The only thing he seemed to care about was making his teaching point.

* * *

Soon after Cathy and I were married, we moved out of San Francisco and over the Golden Gate Bridge to Marin County. We lived and worked with other students who were building a health-food store in Mill Valley. In May 1977, we had a baby, a beautiful, healthy boy. Fifteen months after that, my beautiful daughter was born. They were miracles. But now the greatest desire in my life had collided with my worst fear. I had a family. I knew in my body that this was a life changer. I felt I didn't deserve them, and the weight of responsibility was crushing. The world now had access to hurt me in ways it never had before, deeper than it had before, through my children. For the first time in my life, suicide was out of the question.

Shortly before my daughter was born, we'd moved to Sonoma County, where rent and living expenses were much cheaper. Although I had a family to support and needed to make something happen, I still didn't have a clue what it was going to be or how I was going to do it. Fortunately, I was soon to get a break. But it started with a loss.

I'd known from the age of seven that it was up to me to take care of myself. Nobody knew how to help someone who couldn't read. I'd always held on to the hope that someday I would learn to read. Then I could get a high school diploma. With a high school diploma, I could get a job. But time after time I'd failed. Now I was married with two small children, and I still couldn't read, I still had no GED, and I still had no job. Time seemed to have run out. Finally, I had to accept the fact that I would never learn to read and would never get a high school diploma. It was devastating. I mourned it like a death in the family, the death of who I'd hoped to be and the death of my hopes and dreams. I remembered as a kid staring at all the books on the shelves that filled our house, daydreaming about how I'd read them someday, so I could be as smart as everyone else. Now I accepted that I'd never be able to read any of the books the rest of my family had devoured and talked about enthusiastically. It hurt down to my soul.

Yet giving up on trying to learn how to read opened up possibilities I couldn't have imagined previously. I set out with a new vision, on fire with an intention born of necessity and desperation: my two young kids depended on me. Determined to find work or to at least get vocational training, I went to the California Department of Vocational Rehabilitation (CDVR) for help. I hoped there was some way to get around the problem of my lack of a diploma, that my inability to read could be treated as a disability. I met with a counselor who asked me what I liked to do. I told him I loved electronics, and though I couldn't follow written directions, I could read schematics. The CDVR normally provided help and training for people with physical disabilities so they could get work. If they used wheelchairs, the CDVR assisted them with access problems. The jobs they offered were generally low-level assembly-line work. My counselor had never dealt with someone who couldn't read before, but he recommended that I meet with the head of the electronics department at Santa Rosa Junior College (SRJC). If it seemed possible that I could get a job with a degree in digital electronics without being able to read, he'd see what he could do to get me financial support.

I met with Mr. Bacon, the head of the electronics department, who took my interest in electronics seriously. He knew earning a living in electronics required knowledge and skill but didn't necessarily require a lot of reading, though I'd have to find a way to learn the course work. With Mr. Bacon's support, I was able to persuade the SRJC to waive their requirement of a high school diploma, so I could work toward an Associate Science degree in digital electronics. That took care of the GED problem. Now I had to find a way to learn without reading. The solution was to have all the course material recorded onto audiotape. The CDVR agreed to pay to have the material recorded, as long as the SRJC would supply a document stating their opinion that such materials would enable me to graduate and find work. It was the biggest break of my life! I was finally going to get the help I needed.

I'd always suspected I might be smart and wondered if I might have done well in school if it weren't for reading and writing. Listening to the course material, I now excelled in school. Here, finally, was proof that I was school-smart, even if I couldn't read and write. The difference between believing I was smart and experiencing that I was smart was enormous. It had taken tremendous effort to change the policies of both the state rehab department and the junior college, but these changes opened the door for many individuals with disabilities who followed after me.

After completing the two-year program and getting my degree, I got my first job as a bench tech for an electronics company in San Carlos. On my first day, I showed up early, feeling both excited and anxious. After giving the receptionist my name, I sat down and tried to calm my nerves before meeting my new boss, José. José arrived a minute later and introduced himself. I guessed he was in his early thirties; he seemed very nice. As he led me to my bench at the far end of the factory, he explained that the company was a division of GTE that contracted exclusively for the U.S. military. I'd be working in the division that built microwave radios for land and satellite communications. We walked indoors for what seemed like six city blocks, through a series of buildings, and finally arrived at my workbench in the far corner of a massive building. The bench was impressive, filled with racks of expensive testing equipment. José explained that my job was tuning frequency modulating oscillators (FMOs) for microwave radio transceivers. I had over a million dollars of test equipment on my bench, and I had only limited lab experience with some of the most expensive equipment. Each FMO had to pass stress tests, which included cycling each one between freezing cold and burning hot temperatures. Each transistor was made of silicon and pure gold.

José was extremely gentle; the only time I saw any sign of sternness was when he told me that each transistor cost over seventy-five dollars. He said he'd started on this bench, that it was the toughest bench in the plant, and that I was starting here because I'd done so well with the technical questions in my interviews. He explained that new hires were all on probation for the first ninety days; after that, I'd be considered permanent and all my benefits would kick in. He said I'd have the full ninety days, but at this bench, he could tell by the first two weeks if a new tech was going to make the cut. I appreciated the confidence they had in me to put me on this bench. But I was concerned that this was becoming a setup to fail, and I badly needed this job.

Tuning the transistors was a highly intricate process; adjustments on any one parameter changed the readings on all the others. I had to adjust the frequency by moving the tuning conductor closer to the transistor deep inside the FMO and at the same time adjust the voltage and power to exacting parameters. I felt as if I needed three pairs of hands and three pairs of eyes to track and compensate for the slightest adjustment. I worked intensely that first day, but every transistor I tried to tune popped. Sometimes they popped without even touching the FMO. With every new attempt, I'd remember that my entire future and the security of my family was tied to whether or not I could adjust this transistor without it blowing up. Finally, late in the afternoon, with all my attention tightly focused on just the last few adjustments needed to get an FMO to the exact frequency, I got it. Then, to secure the adjustment, I laid a small amount of epoxy to the post of the power probe, just fractions of a centimeter from the transistor. I pulled my hand back, and it held. Just then, all my equipment gauges went to zero and the transistor blew! By the end of the day, I was sitting at my bench still struggling to get even one transistor not to blow. José told me, "Keep at it. It'll take practice."

Over the next two weeks I kept count of the blown transistors piling up next to my test equipment. All day I'd watch the pile grow. I remembered all the jobs I'd gotten fired from and was sure I was going to get fired again. As each transistor blew, I began to feel that old, horrifying darkness and sense of doom descend on me, with continual thoughts about the inevitability of my failure. As another transistor blew, I'd think, *This predicament is just who I am. It will follow me forever. It will always be like this.* But I'd also continually remind myself, *Don't believe your mind. Don't believe the story. All I can do is the best I can do, and let the future take care of itself.*

After two weeks I'd made much improvement, but I was still popping about 50 percent of the transistors. I'd add them up at the end of each day. At seventy-five dollars apiece, I was costing the company far more than they were paying me. I went into my two-week review trembling with dread and resignation, ready for the inevitable blow. I walked up to the chair by José's desk at the appointed time.

"Hi, José."

He was writing on some papers and didn't look up. "Hi, David, have a seat."

Right away I could tell José was being more formal than usual with me. Looking up at me with a polite smile, he said, "Okay, David, let's get to it."

I listened as he went down the evaluation list.

"Attendance: 100 percent. On time: 100 percent. Working as a team, you got a top score, which is very good. 'No delays on assembly line' isn't applicable to your position, but we all get measured on it. So, very good."

I kept thinking, *Yeah, but wait till he gets to the transistors.* I was seven years old again. I could almost hear the news in my head that I wasn't moving on to third grade.

Finally, he got to "consistency of work, very good." I felt some relief.

"Quality, very good." He looked up at me and asked, "Any questions?"

Was that it? He was done? He had given me all top ratings! I wanted to just get up and leave, but I had to ask, "What about all the transistors I've popped?"

"You're doing better than anyone else has on that bench," he said. "Other techs have popped more transistors than you and had fewer FMOs pass the stress tests with lower total productivity."

I couldn't believe it! I suddenly felt as if I had been crouching my whole life and now, for the first time, I was able to stand up straight and take a deep breath. A dark cloud that had always covered me lifted, and a blue sky, never visible before, appeared. As it appeared, I imagined horizons and possibilities I'd never allowed myself to imagine before. I had never experienced such relief and joy. For the first time in my life, I was a real person with a real job. I could take care of myself and support a family. I had no special considerations; I was just like everyone else. For the first time in my life, who I was was enough!

"Excuse me," I said.

I suddenly got up and turned away, afraid he would see my eyes tearing up or hear my voice crack. But I couldn't help it. Now, ringing in my head for the first time in my life, I heard, *I am enough! I am enough!*

26

Making a Difference

For the next few years, I couldn't be stopped at work. I moved to better jobs and worked as many hours as I could get. I discovered that I had an uncanny knack for troubleshooting. By 1981, I was twenty-seven years old and making a six-figure income. I owned two cars and a house in Marin County, California, and I knew very few people could do what I could do professionally. Within my first year out of school, I'd paid more in taxes than the government had paid for recording my books onto tape. Several years later, I was getting the top assignments in my field and being given all the hours I could work. I often slept for a few hours in the office, got up, and went straight back to work.

I was the go-to guy. On one of my first high-profile projects, the president of Fireman's Fund and American Express (back then they were the same company and shared the same data center) informed me that while his system was down they were losing five million dollars every twenty minutes on the insurance side alone. I knew this had to be true because he screamed it at me only inches from my face, and his neck was bright red. Some people might feel intimidated having a CEO of a Fortune 500 company yell in their face. But this was nothing compared to Chappy pinning me to a wall in front of an enraged Black Coalition, staring at me with blood-shot eyes, and saying, "I'm going to kill you, you little white piece of shit!" or to Yellow Shirt and Gold Chain trying to toss me down a tenth-floor stairwell. This CEO was a teddy bear by comparison. I sat down and calmly told him we could either talk about it then or I could work on it and we could talk later. He walked out and personally stood guard outside the switch-room door to make sure I wasn't disturbed by anyone. After two intense hours, I got the system back up and running.

I realized that what would be too stressful for most people was an enjoyable challenge to me. I was able to remain calm and function at my best in a crisis. I'd arrive at an office where everybody was freaking out and nobody knew what to do, and I'd just get to work diagnosing the problem and figuring out what the hell to do. I never began from a place of knowing what to do to fix the problem. I always started from a place of total ignorance and not knowing what to do. But I was used to being ignorant, confused, and not knowing, so it didn't bother me and I was able to remain perfectly calm. I developed my uncanny knack for solving problems by following my intuition. I was able to relate to and interact with a computer system as if it were a person. That's the best way I can say it. And I started hearing from my boss that I was leaving behind what he called "a wake of very impressed and happy customers."

One of my supervisors, a top-notch tech whose skills I respected, once insisted on going with me on a job to learn about a new piece of equipment I was working on. But he left in the middle. Afterward, I heard he had told his boss, "I can't watch David work; it's too nerve-racking. The way he works doesn't make sense to me. I don't know what he's doing, or why, or how he does it. But when he's done, everything always works."

When people from my past told me how much I'd changed and how I'd accomplished so much now that I had finally "buckled down," I'd think, *Screw you! I was working harder when I was failing.* From my point of view, it was the world that had changed and given me a chance. I just kept reminding myself to be completely present in the moment and to let the future take care of itself. It was only when I gave up the struggle to become more, to become better, and simply accepted the present moment and did my best, that the present worked out and the future took care of itself. Everyone else thought I'd done something different to earn it. But I knew I'd been given a gift.

* * *

In 1982, after seven years of marriage, Cathy and I began to move in different directions in our lives. We agreed to divorce, but we remained good friends. Shortly after that, I met my current wife, Maria. Right away I knew there was something special about her. Maria is beautiful, considerate, and very smart. She understood me and found my problems interesting, not problematic. She thought of me as her equal and seldom judged me. To her, everyone has strengths and weaknesses. I was newly separated, but I knew I wanted a healthy long-term relationship. We began living together in 1983 and married shortly thereafter.

At that time, Maria was working as a clerk in a natural-foods store. I knew she needed a career worthy of her intelligence and her extraordinary capabilities. I was making good money at the time, so I told her I'd support her in anything she wanted to do. One of my proudest accomplishments is supporting her through medical school, which included a residency at Stanford. For almost thirty years, she has been a miraculous source of unconditional love for me.

As time went on, Bubba's teaching seemed to move further away from his original path, which he called the Way of Radical Understanding. His insights into self-contraction and surrender into the prior freedom of our true nature and condition were replaced by a demand for unquestioning devotion and obedience to the guru.

Yet the average student had little or no contact with Bubba by this time. Exciting personal events with Bubba were replaced by lectures from self-righteous students and endless courses of study—neither of which were of any use to me. Increasingly, people were expected to devote their time and donate money to the community and the formal organization. People's "practice" seemed to be measured by how enthusiastic they were to do whatever they were told. What had started out as a radical experiment in living a spiritual life had calcified into a rigid and dogmatic organization that was becoming, it seemed to me, the letter without the spirit.

The end of my formal involvement with Bubba and the community came in 1987. Bubba himself had talked about how students can reach a point where they can no longer make proper use of their teacher. At the outset, I knew it wasn't about following Bubba; it was about trusting the thread of my own intuition and following my own path. It was time to move on. When I became Bubba's student, I did it with eyes open, choosing to enter into one of the most wonderful and terrible periods of my life, the adventure and ordeal of practicing a stringent spiritual life. I knew at the time that it was a rare opportunity to be around a truly extraordinary individual. From my first encounter with Bubba, the truth of his teaching and the confirmation of the nature of my own being through his spiritual transmission have never left me. But what I needed to find now was in myself. At the same time, I needed to make a life in the world.

With the assistance of computers reading to me, I was able to enjoy great success in the telecom business for over twenty-seven years. I started my own telecommunications consulting business, making well into six figures. At that time, the phone systems I worked on were room-sized mainframe computers. Gradually, the systems shifted from hardware-based computers to software-driven servers, and troubleshooting was no longer required because the "black boxes," as we called them, were just thrown out and replaced. My business began to suffer as Nortel, the maker of the equipment I specialized in and one of the largest telecommunication companies in the world, was pushed into bankruptcy. At the same time that the systems became software-based and required onscreen reading to be able to work with them, email became the primary form of communication. In the past, I'd taken work home, where I could do it in my own time and use the specialized software I had that scanned written information and read it to me. With Maria's help on reports and documentation, I could get by. But once email became the primary form of documentation and communication, my skills fell short. I was worried but at first still able to grow with the changes. It wasn't clear how serious this transition would be. Each step in the dissolution of my business took a bite out of me. By the end, I wasn't handling it well. It felt as if the walls were closing in around me, and I began to have panic attacks.

In 2001, I was hired by a major cell-phone company to be in charge of their landline phone systems. By this time, email had become the only allowable form of communication. Ironically, technology had made it possible for me to work, but now a new evolution in technology was ending my career. I'd done very well in the niche I'd found, but now I was in a different world. I shared the company of many people who were not disabled and also lost their livelihood at this time, but I couldn't help feeling that the past was coming back to haunt me. I realized how significant this shift in technology was, and I began to watch myself disintegrate.

Maria was understanding of what I was going through, but she hadn't seen my childhood struggles. She'd never seen me as the helpless, hopeless person I felt I was now becoming. Neither had my kids.

I had endured so much shame as a boy that I couldn't bear for them to see me as that person, much less for them to have that person be their husband or father. I really believed that person had vanished more than thirty years ago, never to return. But here he was once again, with no value, and no chance to rebuild or have a future. The things I held the deepest shame about, or felt the worst about, contained the densest core of the "me" that I thought I was.

The harder I struggled to avoid these painful truths, the harder it became to avoid them. It seemed it was my life's annihilation I was avoiding. Spiritual teachings point to the transcendent, but I was broken and stuck, trying to figure out how be productive and make a living. I saw no solution, and didn't know if there was one, or where an answer might come from.

This came to a head for me as a deep, unyielding depression, a monster of darkness I couldn't find a way out of. At the level of my mind, the content of this depression was the repetitive stories I'd told myself over the years to explain my life circumstances, leaving me with the conclusion that I had no value. I lost hope that repeating these stories could ever improve me, or that the brokenness which had defined my conditional identity could ever be fixed.

I sought counseling, hoping to gain some self-understanding and perhaps the perfect insight that would solve all my problems. But that insight never came. I saw that each insight was like trying to reach a goal by cutting the distance in half. I could keep having insights and cutting the distance to the goal by half forever but never reach the goal.

I began writing this book at this dark point in my life. I hoped that in the process I might discover a deeper meaning to my life, something true and fundamental about myself, and that I might find some answers to the questions that tortured me. I pinned my hopes on doing something. It seemed impossible for me to write a book. I couldn't read a book, much less write one. So, as I had done many times before, I took actions driven by necessity while trying not to get too attached to the result. As I struggled to tell my experiences as truthfully as possible, I realized that no matter how deeply I dug into my past or how perfect a job I did on the book, I could never capture who or what I truly am. The recognition that I couldn't be defined by my stories left me in a state of hopelessness that I would ever resolve the story of "me."

So I began to search for a spiritual solution to my dilemma. I listened constantly to spiritual teachings of a number of teachers, Byron Katie, Eckhart Tolle, and many others. The teacher who spoke most closly to me and my experience was Adyashanti.

Meanwhile, I continued working on the book for several years. And as I wrote, I realized that nothing from the past was my reality now. It was all in the past. The only thing that holds me to the past are the stories I still tell myself. When I began to write these stories, I discovered that I'd forgotten the events that caused me to create them in the first place. It was not the events or the people in the stories that I suffered from now. It was the stories themselves. As I wrote these stories and began to see how little they had to do with me now, I could let go of them. I chased down all the incidents in which I felt the "me" most hidden from my conscious awareness; the deeper I dug into the circumstances, motivations, and emotions, the more the "me" in these stories would dissipate into smoke.

In this way, the stories no longer had a hold on me.

When it came time to write about Donna, I found that my relationship to her served as a poignant archetype of this mistake. Even after I'd long put Donna behind me, the stories and lessons stayed with me and informed my thinking. These were the stories I'd told myself to make sense of things I didn't understand about our relationship, including what love is and is not. Why was Donna able to disregard me so utterly and easily after all we'd been for each other?

I concluded that her relationship to me had been based only on need and therefore must have had no substance, and so when she could get her needs met more effectively by someone else, she easily moved on without looking back. I wasn't sure what true relationship was, but I was sure it couldn't be based on need. The story for me was that I'd loved her, but we were very young and dysfunctional and incapable of a real or healthy relationship. Donna had great needs, depended on me in childish ways, and never could really love me. The biggest story I took away from our relationship was the story that my love didn't have any value. I can see that the theme of my life has been a question: *What is love? Does my love, or love itself, matter?* The question has played out over and over, demonstrated most dramatically in my relationship with Donna. After thirty years, I still didn't know if my love made a difference in Donna's life.

For more than twenty-five years, Donna had been living with Bubba and a small community of students on an island sanctuary in Fiji. Bubba had changed his name to Adi Da Samraj. His students referred to him as Adi Da or Bhagavan, but to me he was always Bubba. Over the years, I'd never been certain he was a genuinely awakened being. Bubba was an extraordinary person who defied all conventional expectations. I can say without any doubt that his teaching made a profound difference in my life and that his spiritual transmission confirmed my deepest intuition of my true self. I met many wonderful people and made many lifelong friends in his company. On November 27, 2008, Bubba died suddenly of a heart attack.

I immediately thought of Donna. What would she do now that he was gone? She'd devoted her entire adult life to him. What would her life be like without him?

I'd been enjoying reconnecting with my old friends from childhood as I sent them rough drafts of this book, hoping they could help with the accuracy of the events I was writing about. I hadn't had any communication with Donna for decades, and I had no expectation of getting her input. And then, out of the blue, I received a message from her.

At the time of Bubba's death, Emerson was in Australia on business. He took advantage of the opportunity to travel to the sanctuary in Fiji to pay his respects to Bubba and to share in the momentous occasion with his friends who were living there. When he returned home, he shared with me a conversation he'd had with Donna about our relationship.

Donna expressed to Emerson her understanding of our relationship, how it had been structured around the sorrow of our individual lives, and how my love and caring had helped her to find her own strength and capacity for relationship and devotion. She told Emerson how grateful she was to me for "saving her life." Most profoundly, she spoke of her ecstatic love and absolute, unwavering devotion to her guru and her gratitude for what he'd given her over the past thirty-five years.

I was struck by how the sorrows we experienced were in a way universal.

When Donna first left me to be with Bubba, I was extremely confused. I had an incomplete comprehension of who he was or what was going on around him. At the time, the only tangible measure I could rely on to make sense of him was to observe what effect he would have on Donna. Hearing her message through Emerson, it struck me how at peace she is, and it confirmed for me that she is the wonderful heart I knew so long ago. This was proof that I was right not to interfere, and a testament to Bubba's love for her.

When Donna and I were young, our individual disabilities were so extreme that neither one of us had a chance for a conventional life. Because of this, we were both forced to find a deeper meaning in life, pushed to consider the ultimate question of life itself. When I first met Donna, she was guarding a drinking fountain. Now she will be spending the rest of her life at Bubba's burial temple, performing a constant vigil and service to his continued presence in this world. This is something only a rare person can do, and Donna is that rare person. In the past, I'd hoped that Bubba could make Donna whole by putting all of her broken pieces back together. After hearing her message, I knew she was living from a profound place, and I believe she has awakened to a reality beyond our conventional perception of separate and separative existence. I understand that some people in crisis have encountered the Infinite and experienced the incomprehensible power of the Divine, and that such experiences can overwhelm and even shatter the ego. The conventional world tends to pathologize such experiences and to use them as evidence of insanity, further alienating the person having the experience, which accounts for a number of people who end up in mental institutions. Bubba didn't make Donna whole by putting all her broken pieces back together. He didn't believe there was any answer at the level of the individual personality or limited self. His teaching was to resort entirely to the prior, underlying condition of Awareness, where we all exist in an unconditional state of wholeness.

I knew Donna had spent her life confronting and inspecting the limited aspects of herself that could be said to describe who she was and what her life was. Bubba helped her break through that process to realize the condition of consciousness, or Awareness, that supports all life and is the ultimate truth of who we all are. I'm grateful for how the force of life itself drove me to confront and inspect all the limitations of my life and mind, breaking me down to find that this Awareness itself was all that was left. It's so amazing to me that two damaged kids continued to contemplate the ultimate issues of life, each coming to a point of complete frustration and despair in not being able to fulfill the story of "me." We were not all the things life and experience seemed to say about us: we were moved to realize the Heart, the pure awareness of being prior to birth and all limited form. That had been the source of our connection from the very start because it is the source of love itself.

The story that stuck with me all these years was that Donna and I had a relationship built on unhealthy dependencies and that my love had no value. When I joined Bubba's community, I was told our relationship was cultic and built on self-serving attachments. And the world had always told me I wasn't enough. After Donna left me and didn't even want to see me, I kept asking myself, *If I can't find anything of value that I can do in this world, and if the most selfless love I'm capable of has no value, then what am I doing here?*

But after receiving Donna's message, I saw that all my stories were just that—stories, fragments of reality that may be relatively true when seen out of context but that can only be rightly understood within a much larger picture. It's true that Donna and I were dysfunctional and childish, and in the world of the survival of the fittest, we had little chance to survive. After believing for thirty years that my love had not made a difference in Donna's life, I received her message that my love not only had made a difference but she felt that I had "saved" her life.

I don't need to know the larger picture to know that living from the Heart has value, even though it can't always be seen reflected back in the fabric of life. Whether or not we have what it takes to survive in this world isn't our measure. In fact, it's our brokenness and our awareness of our mortality that give us depth and gratitude in our loving. We all have value as the Heart that is our true nature. This Heart needs no justification to exist. It simply is. Donna said it best in her conversation with Emerson: "What does not perish is the Heart."

If I had not written this book, I might never have received the confirmation that I made a difference in Donna's life. Doing the most improbable thing in the world for me to do, writing a book, also turned out to be the perfect way to end Donna's and my story.

27

The Big Bang

As a kid, I learned to face down fear by trying to be stronger than my fear, trying to conquer it rather than letting it conquer me.

Later, I realized that by doing this I was still being controlled by fear in a more subtle way and creating a life based on fear. At eighteen, I realized the change I had to make was fundamental, to accept myself and do the best I could in each moment, instead of believing my worst fears about myself and my future.

As a middle-aged man, when my successful career crashed and my life fell apart, these insights from my youth weren't enough to pull me out of the darkness. Nothing from the past could help me avoid the truth about me. No prior insight or realization could do the trick. No amount of spiritual teaching, psychological insight, or contact with a guru were going to make any difference. This was a new moment. Everything in my life was dissolving. I had lost all hope. I saw and felt with stark clarity my utter lack of control over everything; how little power I had to initiate anything; how completely vulnerable and dependent I was on existence that wasn't listening to me, that didn't recognize or take me into account as an individual in the slightest. I saw how what I thought was my life wasn't mine at all; that the momentum in which my life was swept along had nothing to do with me.

I felt like all my life I'd been holding on desperately to a root in the side of a high cliff, terrified of letting go and falling. Finally, exhausted, I let go. And just as I feared, I was falling, but I was only falling. There was no bottom. All that was left was the endless darkness of a broken heart. Behind the darkness was a depth that was infinite. I felt as if I had dropped out of my mind and into a current I could not control, but in which I could flow. It struck me that when everything else was gone, all that was left was the Heart. All that I had been avoiding was exactly what I'd been looking for and cared about the most. Trusting in the Heart turned out not to be the leap of faith I had thought it would be; it was exhaustion. When everything is destroyed, all that is left is the Heart, broken, but still the Heart. No bottom, nothing to fear. I had no strength left in me, and no ground. Letting go was the beginning of freedom.

Around this time, I heard Adayshanti say something in a new way, as if he was speaking directly to me. He spoke of how we tend to identify with our minds instead of recognizing that we are awareness itself.

I realized that all identification with form was created by thoughts, and that identifying and believing the thoughts created my suffering. It was my mind attacking me. I wasn't the terrible or even wonderful things my thoughts told me I was. I was awareness itself.

✳ ✳ ✳

One night in 2009, I had a dream. In the dream, I was standing alone, feeling small and limited, feeling very much myself.

Suddenly, I was moving very fast through space. I was losing my sense of identification with my body. I was becoming less dense, lighter, and then transparent with a tail like a meteor, racing through space.

Leaving Earth, flying past all the planets in the solar system, I realized I wasn't just passing through space but also going back in time.

The planets and objects in space started to break up and became balls of gas. All matter was coming together to a single point. I thought it must be the source of the Big Bang. All matter, including the matter from my body, consolidated into a single point and disappeared, as if into another dimension. Then there was nothing but vast and deep emptiness. There was no time, no separation, just an infinite spacious Awareness.

Suddenly, out of the silence and emptiness there was an explosion.

Out of nothingness, matter appeared and expanded—the opposite of what had just happened. Gases and solid material began condensing and forming into galaxies and planets. I became aware that time was moving forward. As everything took its present form, I also took form as myself. But now the awareness and depth of the emptiness that I am stayed with me.

As my body formed, this ecstatic awareness remained. It flowed in waves through all my senses, then out into the space surrounding me and into the infinite. I was one with the infinite, riding waves of ecstatic energy. But suddenly, I had the thought that I was a limited form, separate and vulnerable to all this sensory stimulation. It was overwhelming. This limited form became fixed in space and began to collide with the waves of energy I had just been riding. As soon as I thought I was limited and identified as this form, I could see the logic of protecting myself. If I were just this small separate entity, then I'd have to control my experience and shut down my senses. The sensory stimulus was too much.

The Big Bang seemed to be the primal trauma, separating everything from its source. Everything that arose out of it, all limited forms, including myself, were the offspring of that original trauma—the trauma of separation from one another and from source. And yet it seemed that all form, in its essence, possessed an urge to return to its prior state of wholeness. As a limited form, separate from all others, I was left with only the craving for that oneness. I was now in exile. From this point of view, I couldn't help but make limited form into a kind of god and give it the power to define my reality and to reflect to me the meaning of who and what I am. Feeling dependent on my limited form to survive in a world made up of other limited forms, the resulting fear and suffering became intolerable, and I no longer wanted to exist.

Then I saw myself as a young boy, telling my mother I didn't want to be alive. I understood why I wanted to commit suicide. It wasn't death I wanted; it was freedom from the suffering and the isolation of my limited form. I had misinterpreted my true condition. I believed in the illusion of embodiment, of identification with form. I had traded my sense of wholeness in spacious awareness for what my body, my limited form, seemed to be telling me. All my senses told me that I was this body. Others with bodies acted as if I were separate from them. So I let the limitations of form define what I am and the world in which I lived. But it was all a case of mistaken identity.

But what or who am I that is aware of all this? It wasn't my body or my mind, because I was aware that I was observing both my body and my thoughts. This meant they were not "me." I was just the observing itself—awareness—not separate as an observer but resting as the "observingness" itself. As soon as I identified as "observingness," I was whole, and all suffering was released. Nothing born from the Big Bang could hurt me. I was no longer in conflict with reality, at war with existence. I was prior to form and limitation. I couldn't die because I'd never been born. I understood that life and death are not opposites. The opposite of death is birth, not life. Life is there before birth and after death. It's impersonal. The experiences resulting from the Big Bang did not define or limit my true nature, who I am in reality. To believe they did was to become lost in illusion. Experiences were to be fully lived and not avoided or controlled. They didn't limit or define who I truly was. This awareness needed no protection.

Then I awoke from the dream, but the dream stuck with me. In a way, the dream changed nothing, and yet it changed my relationship to everything. It marked the end of my spiritual search and the beginning of a true spiritual practice. Now I saw that saying yes to life, consenting to experience it fully, accepting it unconditionally as it appears, and myself as I am in any moment, and finding contentment in this, seemed the only sane choice, the only way out of the trap of my conditioned identity, the only hope of freedom, and the one thing I hadn't yet tried. Not grasping for security or struggling with things I can't control wasn't giving up the will to survive. It was giving up the need to escape, the need to control, and the need to know. If I could do this, it would no longer be me enduring and surviving life. Instead, life would be living me.

This was so profound a shift for me that I felt as though I had awakened to an unlimited freedom, and returned home to the

Awareness that is the truth of who I am.

Teachings that had once seemed to be just repetitive, heady philosophy came alive for me now. Over time there have been new depths to this Awareness. I sense an endless depth, where I fall deeper into emptiness, void of everything I cherish, where all that is left is the Heart. This Heart has always been with me, still and unchanged for as long as I can remember. It's so close to me that there's nothing closer, yet it's so vast and inclusive that it's infinite. So it was easy to miss it. The more I rested in this Awareness, the more intimate it became to me. I found that, in fact, I cannot be aware of anything that isn't contained within this vast Heart. There's nothing I can see, nothing I can feel, nothing I can know or experience, nothing I can be aware of that could exist outside of my Awareness. It's no different than in a dream, where things seem to be happening to me and there are other people in my dream, but in reality it's all happening within my own consciousness.

I learned to trust that if something happened outside of my awareness, then I wasn't meant to be aware of it yet. I could not and need not figure it out with my mind. With the realization that all experience is contained within the intimacy of this Awareness, I could now see how I'd objectified everything and everybody in my life. Even the activity of the mind, judging and categorizing, was within this Awareness. Yet I used this objectifying activity of the mind as a way to protect my sense of being a separate self. This was actually creating the illusory sense of being a separate individual.

Within the deep intimacy of Awareness, I could feel the pain I was causing with these separative thoughts. Every judgment aimed at the object would instead cause a division within me, and a loss of felt intimacy with Awareness itself, isolating me while having no direct effect on the object I was trying to neutralize or separate from.

All my life I'd been looking for relationships to resolve this sense of separation, when, in fact, I'd been creating it in myself. I related to all objects and all beings as other and separate, when in fact they are all me—arising within my own beingness just as intimately as "I" am arising within my own beingness. I'd been trying to resolve this separation through relationships, when the separation was actually in me.

When I looked deeply into who and what I am through the writing of this book, and when I lost the last vestige of hope that I could ever work everything out, then my will to struggle with the problem of my life collapsed and the solidity of myself finally broke. Oddly, this allowed the mind to wander more freely at first, untethered by my efforts to control it and without me perceiving it as a problem. In time, the untethered activity of the mind (which had previously dominated my awareness as the foreground of my subjectivity) and even the content of my identity gradually receded into the background of the awareness that was now emerging in me. I witnessed the thread of a force unfolding in me, with its own spaciousness and quietness, which imparted a growing ability to listen to life.

It was essential for me at first to identify with this awareness in order to dislodge from my intense identification with my mind. But as I began to feel the limitations of identifying with this awareness, this identification gradually, without my doing anything, began to fall away. I seemed to care less about "The Truth" or "enlightenment," whatever they are, and fell in love with truth, reflected in a thousand ever-changing manifestations.

The more I rest in the current of this awareness, the more I can see, feel, and experience life in its proper perspective, without being caught up and identified with the drama of personalities and events; without needing to judge, categorize, and figure everything out with my mind; and without making my peace dependent on knowledge I do not possess and outcomes I cannot control.

Although I'd never have chosen any of the difficulties life presented to me, in the end, from the larger perspective, they turned out to be instructive, even a gift, a form of grace. Not that I would choose suffering, or not act to remove the source of it from my life. But now, when suffering comes, I find it useful in a way I didn't before. It forces me to go deeper. In fact, I would never have come to this new place without it.

With this understanding, I can make peace with life by making friends with the present moment and all its conditions. In doing this,

I return to the awareness of the heart that is the truth of who I am, and I experience the peace of my own nature. The peace of awareness doesn't depend on the world giving me what I want on my terms or on me having ultimate knowledge about anything. The very needs for control, certainty, and getting my way keep me disconnected from the present moment, which is the only place I can experience who I am.

*　*　*

After the dream I no longer identified with my story in the way I had for most of my life. Until then I had been utterly identified with my limitations, and even my specialness, and all the ripples they caused in my life. Now, I felt released from the subjective weight and burden and the crushing self-consciousness of managing myself in the world as the person I had believed myself to be.

It was an unspeakable relief. It was as if the weight of the world had been lifted from my back, a weight I didn't even know I was carrying until it was removed. Gratitude for this freedom and peace permeates my life.

Epilogue

I began writing this story feeling a deep shame because my brother broke me, because life itself broke my will and made me feel weak. But I couldn't have been more wrong.

As it turns out, my true happiness is proportional to my yielding to the brokenness, not to my refusing to accept it or to my struggling to overcome it. In that snow tunnel in my childhood, I found a calm spaciousness when I gave up personal will. That spaciousness contains infinite potentiality and a quiet strength vastly more powerful than my personal will. It's what remains when I surrender to what is.

I've found that I can reside in that clear quiet place, profoundly aware and awake, with all my senses open, not holding back or shutting down. I can only find this beingness when I make friends with the present moment, no matter what the conditions are in this moment. For it is only in the present moment that the Awareness that is truly "me" ever exists. This meant nothing to me when the world was working for me – or as long as I hoped it could, or as long as I thought I had to do something, or had to be something I was not, or thought there was something missing from the present moment, or as long as I was ashamed.

After my dream and awakening, I was still moved to continue writing this book. Instead of being a story about me, though, it became a story about the failure and suffering that result from believing in the illusion of a limited and broken "me." It became a story about the dream of my human experience in my unawakened life. Key to the story were conditions labeled autism spectrum and dyslexia, from which my sense of identity and my life unfolded. After my dream and awakening, I saw that unfolding story with new clarity. I experienced autism spectrum as too much stimulus coming continuously from too many different sources.

From infancy, I had to shut out a significant range of stimuli and perceptions most people take for granted in order to survive. My highly sensitive nervous system often contracted in an automatic response, like flinching from a blow, shutting out painful or disturbing sensory awareness. In time, I became more self-aware and more conscious of the process by which stimuli overwhelmed me, and I became more able to dissociate to avoid it. As I matured, I learned to listen to my nervous system, and I gradually discovered, often under great stress, that I could consciously engage and to some degree manage some aspects of this process. I learned to fragment and to compartmentalize my awareness of stimuli, only allowing in what I was comfortable experiencing. What I could not tolerate, I left in an undefined fog. Gradually, I became able to handle more experience, more pressure and stress, more life. This is how I lived most of my life. Doing this, I was simply doing, to an exaggerated degree, what everyone does to live on a daily basis.

All humans operate within a certain spectrum, automatically filtering out unmanageable perceptions in order not to be overwhelmed by the continuous avalanche of stimuli that is life. For me, being on the autism spectrum meant being vulnerable to and overwhelmed by a range of stimuli most people can tolerate and manage. Because of this, autistic people stand out and seem abnormal. This was my experience. In the same way, all humans to some degree identify with and believe delusional and separative thoughts created by their minds, which isolate them from reality and the truth of who they are. This is true for everyone on the human spectrum, from what we call "normal" all the way to the extremes of what we call "schizophrenia."

I remember the schizophrenics at Jacqui Schiff's and how hard it was for them not to believe the ranting of their minds and the random things their minds seemed to be telling them. My thoughts weren't as delusional or overwhelming as those of the schizophrenics. Or were they? I had the constant ranting of stories in my mind that I believed to be true: *I will never have a family*, or *I'm not smart enough to make it in the world.* The mind was a distraction, a filter that isolated me from the reality and the truth of who I am. As Awareness, I could use the mind as needed; but as the mind, I had no access to my true Self. I'd been identified with my mind when in fact it was Awareness that was always with me and never deserted me. It was the only thing in my life that had never deserted or failed me. It never judged me or separated from me. The source of my suffering was in the identification with my mind, and the negation of myself based in a story that wasn't true that emerged out the painful events of my childhood.

As a boy, when I looked into my brother's face as he tormented me, he seemed not to be looking at me, his brother, but at an object in his way, something denying him what he needed most. He saw me as something to get rid of so that his life would work again. He was at war with the world, and I was the enemy. Looking in his eyes, I saw no empathy, no humanity, and it filled me with terror. In the depths of that terror was an infinite silence. I had sought safety in the world through empathy, but my pleading and pain inspired no empathy in him. The world offered only silence. So I split from myself in order to save myself. I made a sacred promise to my frightened self to stand in opposition to the world to fix it. To be safe, I would have to force empathy from an indifferent world, but to do this, I had to become a warrior. And so I went to war against the world to save a boy the world had abandoned—although in doing so, I abandoned myself. I went to war against a world where everyone seemed always to be pretending and hiding from the truth—denying or rationalizing as necessary the cruelty, suffering, and death all around. And in this way, I lost my true self and became like the world I was at war against.

In response to my childlike promise, my cries, and my war, the world offered only an infinitely deep silence. To be free, I had to admit that I couldn't save the frightened little boy to whom I made that sacred promise. To be free, I had to break that sacred promise and let him go, unsaved, into the silence. Now I know that in that infinitely deep silence lies the truth of who I am.

I found that I couldn't fix the world and make it have empathy. I couldn't defeat the world and make it right according to my understanding. The world doesn't listen to me, doesn't surrender to me, and it never will. Out of fear, I had confused enmeshed empathy with a free heart and the universality of compassion. I had to give up my attachment to empathy and to the world being different than it is. To do that, I had to forgive my brother, who is also the world, for his inability to have empathy for me. Only then would I let the world be, and only then would I be happy and free.

A Buddhist admonition says, "Put down your butcher knife and become a Buddha in that moment." To find myself, to have peace in the world, I had to surrender, to accept the world as it is. And in doing this, I've discovered that I'm able to act most effectively in the world when I let the world be. I can only experience the intimacy and deep silence of my Self when I put down my butcher knife and become the world's compassionate witness. Then by doing very little, I'm able to do the most. Then I find the heart hiding behind the mask of a world I thought was the enemy.

But this only happened for me when I fell into a deep depression where everything seemed unimportant, meaningless, and empty, and the distractions and illusions of possibility in the rat race died. All I was left with was the infinite depth and sorrow of a broken heart. It seemed my life always ended up here, in a place that was darker than dark, where the only meaning was brokenheartedness. It was the worst feeling in the world. But when I accepted it, everything fell away, and all that was left was the heart, albeit a deeply broken one.

Somehow, seeing the heart as all there is—sometimes broken, sometimes ecstatic—was inspirational. The heart is the source of all that I am and do. Understanding this, I don't need to be or do anything that is not sourced from the heart. Because it is all the heart, I can allow all experience, regardless of the intensity. Good feelings or bad feelings, it doesn't matter. This relieves me of a burden I had been carrying all my life, of what I think I am or am supposed to be or do.

In the dream of my unawakened life, I took life personally, and identified with all the things I had or did or thought I was. But I wasn't my job. I wasn't the role of a parent. I wasn't this story and all of my past. I wasn't this body, damaged and limited. I wasn't who or what I thought I was. I am Awareness, in this moment, living as this body, in this world. And life is not personal. Nothing is personal.

For the first time, I am free to experience the intensity of it all, including my old autism spectrum overwhelm. It is no longer necessary to fragment experience into good or bad, happy or sad. Everything is just something to experience, part of life.

My acceptance of brokenheartedness morphed into a quiet acceptance of all consequences, even death. Living more from the heart, I began to relax my conditioned autism spectrum demands and controls on life. There was only one priority, one task: to look and to listen for the thread of the heart and to live from the heart as best I could.

In my all-too-human life, I finally have the family I'd always wanted. It came in the form of my wife, Maria, who loves me in ways I didn't think anyone ever could. Although she met me when I was doing well and had much to give, she stayed with me through times that were darker than dark, always finding some way to love me. I have two wonderful kids, who have great depth and are exceptionally smart. They have never withdrawn their hearts from me, whatever my momentary missteps or however my public loss of face because of my inability to read. They also saw strength in me when I did not.

My wife and I live just a few minutes' walk from one of the most beautiful beaches in the world. My life far surpasses even my most hopeful dreams. I live a very comfortable life, with the freedom to live however life moves me. I will be forever grateful that I'm not in charge of the future.

I'm thankful that the fourteen-year-old kid I once was didn't succeed in his suicide attempt. If he had, I wouldn't have been able to touch the lives of those I've loved since. It was my daughter who encouraged me to write this book. I remember how heartbreaking it was when she was a little girl, before she was able to read, and she wanted me to read her a bedtime story. We only looked at the pictures because I couldn't read the story. Frustrated, she would try to read it, but I was unable to help her. As an early reader in her childhood, she became one of my main readers. Now, years later, she helped me to organize my ideas for this book and to find ways, with the help of others, that I could write it. She's also one of the funniest people I know.

My son is a rare and wonderful human being. He's had his own challenges with learning disabilities, and those challenges have given him an uncommon depth of humanity. He's the kind of person who meets everyone face to face and stands up for others. He is open-hearted and emotionally present. He has inner and outer strength and genuine confidence.

My wife and children are the kind of people my father would have been deeply proud of.

I've heard it said that happiness can be defined as "I love you," and suffering can be defined as "Do you love me?" When my father died, I was desperate, wishing he could know how much I loved him.

I wasn't thinking about whether he loved me; I only wanted him to know how much I loved him. When I'm on my deathbed, I know I will care more about whether I have loved than whether I was loved.

Editors and agents have asked me, "Who is your audience? Who are you writing this book for?" I told them I didn't know; I just had to write this. But now I think maybe it's for those boys and girls in crisis who might be looking longingly at all the books on shelves. Maybe this is the book they're looking for, with some of the answers they hope to find on those shelves.

If I had young David in front of me now, I would tell him this: "The fact that you can't read is not a personal comment about you. It doesn't diminish you or define who you are. It's just what it is. Yes, it's painful, and it makes your life difficult. But you will only suffer by worrying about it, feeling bad about it, believing it says something fundamental about who you are, and by turning such beliefs into sad scenarios about your future. If you listen to others, you might believe you're defective, a misfit who can't read. That isn't true. You're made of the same stuff as everyone else.

"You are, in truth, your heart's natural feeling of communion with all that's arising. You are the awareness of this communion with your experience, not the content of your life. You don't need to be something you're not; you only need to be the awareness you are, in the moment you find yourself in. Be that. Not because that's what you want but because that's what is—and therefore what and who you truly are. You may try to control, manage, and shut off unwelcome experiences, believing it will bring you the best possible life. But I've found that we're here to experience all of it, good and bad, without judgment or resistance of any kind.

"It was often the world's apparent denial of the heart's communion that you suffered. This looked like truth to you in the confident faces of others, from sociopaths to some of the most powerful. What you didn't see was the desperation in their endless cravings, the suffering and hollowness of their lives and in their hearts, a suffering they couldn't escape through the turmoil they caused or the temporary riches or power they accumulated.

"As you know, there's only one thing guaranteed in this life: you will not survive. If you insist on trying to be safe, on surviving by diminishing yourself and your world instead of trusting the power of the Source of who you are, then you'll suffer. If you think about it, what little you may have been able to control in your past is a tiny fraction of what has happened. So just be the awareness you are in each moment, let the heart's kindness be your guide, and do the best you can without attachment to results. Leave the future to what is greater than you. Let this free you to finally rest in truth, in the peace and happiness of your true nature. The rest is none of your business."